SQUIRE'S LEGACY

THE LIFE AND STRUGGLES OF CLIFFORD EARL WHITE, THE JUSTICE OF THE PEACE, CLEAR FORK DISTRICT, RALEIGH COUNTY, WV. 1948-1966

James Edward White and
Eleanor Triplett White

Writer's Showcase
San Jose New York Lincoln Shanghai

Squire's Legacy
The life and struggles of Clifford Earl White, The Justice of the Peace, Clear
Fork District, Raleigh County, WV. 1948–1966

Writer's Showcase
an imprint of iUniverse.com, Inc.

For information address:
iUniverse.com, Inc.
5220 S 16th, Ste. 200
Lincoln, NE 68512
www.iuniverse.com

ISBN: 0-595-16534-6

Printed in the United States of America

SQUIRE'S LEGACY

Dedication

For Ethel Odessa Smith White, (1942).
Loving wife and mother.

AUTHORS' NOTE

The happenings in this story are real and all family members are real people with real names, but the authors have taken some liberty in the telling of the story as it relates to persons outside the family by using pseudonyms for some and creating composites for others. Neighbors, for instance, may sometimes represent themselves solely or may sometimes represent a composite of two or more persons. The use of pseudonyms and composite characters is solely for the purpose of making it easier for the reader to follow sequentially the life of the man about whom the story is written and is in no way intended to distort the facts of the story itself. The authors' intent is simply to keep the story moving without otherwise naming all those who directly or indirectly helped to make the happenings within the story possible—folks like numerous unmentioned family members, neighbors, company doctors and ministers from the Clear Fork District. It is to be understood that this story is based on the authors' perceptions of the life and times of Clifford Earl White.

James Edward White
Eleanor Triplett White
—June, 2000

ACKNOWLEDGEMENTS

While this book is based almost solely on the memories of James Edward White, it would not have been complete without additional information given the authors by Jacqueline and David Akers, Cora White Morris, Richard White, Ruby Mills, Billy Legg, Robert Toney, and Patsy Kinder. For their contributions we express our utmost appreciation.

For the inspiration and encouragement to write this book, we are especially indebted to Vera Thompson Treadway and Rosalee Stover Peck, who are also from the Clear Fork District and have themselves written books about the area. Vera, a retired educator, provided much assistance with the technical nuts and bolts and also did some editing and proofreading during various stages of the writing. Rosalee, an instructor at Concord College, edited the first version of the book and gave us the push we needed to move forward from there. Further appreciation is extended to Kay Jones Cantley for her assistance with proofreading, and to Jane McGoldrick for consultative services. To the many others who read a page, a chapter or the entire work at some stage of development, your comments, suggestions and words of encouragement were truly valued and appreciated.

PREFACE

Throughout my adult years, I have been drawn to tell the story of my father's life, particularly of his years of constant struggle after a coal mining accident left him permanently disabled and his family subsequently severely impoverished. I am often reminded of how during this bleak period he so courageously fought to restore his life and the life of his family to a state of normalcy.

Because I was born at the time of my father's sudden misfortune, I lived with him in a somewhat parallel existence, gradually becoming his legs, his entertainer, listener, "go-fer" and caregiver. He was my mentor. When I think of how often I attribute my successes in life to my father's earlier influence, I realize that this story will not only be a tribute to him and to my dear mother who was his lifeline throughout, but an inspirational read for others as well.

As a child, I was an astute observer of the human emotions that were played out each day in my family. I was like a sponge, absorbing through my senses all that happened around me. Therefore, this story is told through my perceptions of what I was able to personally observe and from what I recall being told to me as I was growing up.

The chosen style for writing this story is for the purpose of bringing it to life, to stimulate feelings and emotions indicative of the feelings and emotions that were experienced by those in the story themselves.

—James Edward White
June, 2000

June 4, 1933—Ameagle, West Virginia

*I*T would be after midnight before he returned home because he was working overtime or "doubling back" as the coal miners called it. Overtime was a coveted opportunity given only to the hardest of workers, and my dad, Clifford Earl White, at thirty years of age was one of those workers. He had proved himself, not missing a day of work since taking a job as a motorman with Peabody Coal Company three years ago, in the year 1930, at a time the Great Depression played havoc in the coal fields and many men struggled to find work.

Though doubling back meant working long hours, sometimes from dawn 'til midnight, Dad relished the opportunity. It meant that he could now provide more than the bare necessities for his wife Ethel and three small children, Lee, Jacqueline and Billy. Another was on the way.

With little more than an hour of work to go, he looked forward to some much-needed rest and to being with his family. Standing to the side of his motor car, he shined his carbide lantern in all directions as he checked carefully to make sure that the earlier slate fall had been sufficiently cleared. He was especially concerned that there were enough support timbers in place to make the area safe again for workers on the next shift. He had just lifted his leg to re-enter the motor car when suddenly, without warning, a timber shifted and a small piece of slate—a piece so small he could easily have picked it up with his hands—fell directly onto his back. He fell forward to the ground and lay flat. Other pieces of slate began to fall on him, one on top of the other. Unable to move, he called for help.

1

The Early Years–1922–1929

My parents were married in Charleston, West Virginia, in June of 1922 when Mom was fourteen and Dad, eighteen. Though Dad's mom, Rosabelle, was against her son marrying one so young, she did not withhold her love and support from the young couple. After all, Dad was one of the sons most like his mom: he enjoyed reading and singing; he had perfect penmanship and spoke nearly correct grammar as she had instructed him to do. Rosabelle valued education and religion above all else and had great aspirations for her children in both areas, but the difficult economic times her family experienced during the child-rearing years at the earlier part of the century prevented many of her aspirations from becoming a reality. Nevertheless, Dad was greatly influenced by her teachings.

When Mom was nearing the age of six her father died of "blocked bowels," leaving her family in dire circumstances. Her mother Evaline was forced to find work wherever she could and thus found it necessary to leave her children without proper care. Subsequently, from a very young age, Mom was compelled to live with her older sister Orphie, and Orphie's husband Johnny. She attended grammar school alongside Dad and his sister Cora, who was the same age as Mom. "Ethel was a very good student," Cora said. "A smart cookie." Though Mom did not choose to complete her education and was never as keen as Dad with her grammar, she, nevertheless, had her strengths, the biggest one being her ability to relate well with people of all ages. This talent made her appear older than her years, which is why Dad said he always thought of her as being older than she was. She acted like she was older, he said.

*　　　　　　*　　　　　　*

After a short honeymoon in the city of Charleston, they moved in with Orphie and Johnny who lived in Belle, a suburb of Charleston. During this time, Dad worked extra hard at his job to put a little savings in his pocket and soon announced to Mom that he thought they were ready to "go it on their own." Thus they began their entry into the coal fields of southern West Virginia where Dad planned to work as a coal miner. Coal mining was familiar to Dad; he had begun working in the mines alongside his dad Opie and his younger brother Coy as a mere thirteen-year-old. "I'm an experienced coal-miner," he was able to say, by the time he was sixteen.

They were a striking couple as they boarded the passenger train in Charleston—Dad, in his three-piece pin-striped charcoal suit and matching hat, and Mom, in her flapper-style dress, silk stockings and high heel shoes. With radiant faces they held hands and looked from the windows of the train to the great outdoors on this sunny, yet crisp fall day in the autumn of 1922 as they headed to their chosen destination, a small mining community in Raleigh County called Marfork. The sky, teal blue and dotted with white cottony clouds, spread before them as it showcased the fiery autumn foliage of the rugged mountains and flowing valleys beneath its spreading canopy. "The leaves have pretty near peaked," Dad said to Mom. "Better enjoy them while we can."

*　　　　　　*　　　　　　*

Enthusiastic over what he considered to be his good fortune, Dad emerged from the mine office at Marfork and announced to Mom that he had gotten a job as a motor man on the day shift. They would have a company house in which to live and a line of credit (in the form of "scrip") which they could use at the company store to help them get started. He took Mom's hand, and with eager hearts they headed out to the boarding house for their first night's stay.

Early the next morning they went directly to the company store where they happily selected a few furnishings, namely a bed, table and chairs, and a stove. Then, with assistance from Charlie B., one of the locals whose horse-drawn wagon was used regularly to carry people's belongings from one place to another, they moved into the four-room company house they both wished was located a greater distance from the mine. The house was covered with coal dust and cinders, a fall-out from the coal trains that traversed the area several times a day. Bare spots in the yard, also covered with coal dust and cinders, appeared here and there from among the clumps of tall grass as a reminder that the yard needed care. Disappointed, but not discouraged, they looked to the clean and inviting surrounding areas that lay beyond the coal camp— the hillsides, the creek, and the narrow valleys where it seemed all available land was planted in gardens—and they felt better. They were used to coal camps, where all the houses looked alike and all the people who lived in them shared a common interest. Men worked in the mines and women worked at home.

*　　　　　*　　　　　*

"Ethel, I believe I'll be able to do some good squirrel hunting around here," Dad said as he scanned the gradual slope of the hillside across the creek from where they lived. "Maybe some grouse, too."

"Clifford, I've never cleaned and cooked a squirrel in my life."

"Nothing to it, Ethel. I'll show you how. I'll prepare it. All you'll need to do is dust the pieces in flour, fry them in lard and make some gravy from the drippings. That's the way Mom always did it."

"Oh, Clifford, I've got so much to learn." She pressed her head into his shoulder as she hugged him around the middle. He put his arms around her.

"You'll do fine, Ethel," he said. "The other women around here will help you, too."

*　　　　　　　　*　　　　　　　　*

Far from the bustling city of Charleston and its rapidly growing chemical industry, they were isolated now in a small coal mining community nestled tightly within a narrow valley between steep, but beautifully forested mountains, laden with a variety of colorful deciduous trees. They would travel by foot and receive their goods and services directly from the company store to which they were already indebted.

Marfork's one narrow, unpaved road—often filled with potholes and difficult to ford if the creek was swollen from heavy rains—was used more often by horses and wagons than by cars. Cars they would seldom see anyway: the only persons likely to have cars would be the coal operators and the company doctor.

Though they would sometimes feel lonely and miss the loved ones they had left behind, their days and nights were filled with new experiences and happy times as they settled into the beginnings of their life together on their own. In four months time they were able to lay claim to a few belongings, had a circle of friends, and the start of a family as on February 6, 1923, their first child Lee was born. The birth was extremely painful and difficult for Mom. Dr. Wright, the company doctor who delivered the baby at home, said she was too young to be having a baby.

Fortunately, Mom had the help of her neighbors: Beatrice, with the big brown, puppy-dog eyes, who lived on the left; and Thelma, with the narrow blue, you-can-depend-on-me eyes, who lived on the right.

*　　　　　　　　*　　　　　　　　*

As proud as a barnyard rooster, Dad cuddled close to his wife as she lay in bed with Lee snuggled close to her bosom. He gazed in wonder as he stroked his son's head saying, "Ethel, Lee's a beautiful child. He has your eyes."

Mom, looking up with a smile, said, "Now, Clifford, you know he's a handsome devil just like you. Just look at all these pretty dark curls." Blushing, she playfully ran her slender fingers through Lee's tiny ringlets.

"I want one of our children to have *your* hair," Dad said softly.

"Clifford, you've been in love with my hair since grade school! You got into more trouble over my hair!"

"I couldn't help it. You shook your head in that prissy way you have, and your curls would shake and bounce around. I believe you just did that to tease me."

The comment brought a giggle from Mom. "I'm sure I did," she said, looking up at him with reddened face and wide glistening eyes. "You were always looking my way with your eyes moving back and forth, back and forth, like you were in a daze, losing your place in your lessons, getting your knuckles rapped."

"Ah, but it was worth it," he said, stroking her long silky hair. "You'd turn around and give me that sweet look of sympathy and my heart would melt."

"Clifford, with all your shenanigans, it's a wonder you learned anything." She flushed at the memory of their earliest encounters when they attended the makeshift school above Evans General Store in Blakely.

Relishing their sweet love for one another and for their firstborn child, they lay lost in time until mother nature intervened with Lee's fretful squirms and fussy cries and ushered them back to the present. "Oh, sweet baby, you're hungry, aren't you," Mom said with puckered lips as she prepared to nurse and Dad looked on in idolization of his child bride who was not yet sixteen.

He wasn't sure he had done right by bringing Mom to Marfork, away from her family. He knew how much she missed her sister Orphie, with whom she had lived for several years. Yet, they were happy. And, they had good neighbors. "We're always here for you, just a holler away," was the way Beatrice had put it.

*   *   *

On one balmy Sunday afternoon in late May when the sky was powder blue and the air was surprisingly fresh, Mom hauled a straight-backed chair from the kitchen to the front porch where she said she planned to sit for a while and listen to the birds. She held a fidgety Lee in her lap as she bounced him back and forth in a rocking motion and sang *"Bye-oh-Baby-Bye-oh"* again and again into his ear. Lulled by the singing and the steady jerking motion of the chair, he soon fell fast asleep.

Joining them, Dad eased himself down onto the floor nearby. He braced himself against the porch railings with one knee up and one leg stretched before him and slowly rolled a cigarette. He had taken up smoking at age fourteen while living at the boarding houses with his dad and brother Coy. There, where men of all ages mingled in the after hours of work, most either smoked, dipped, or chewed to pass the time and dull the senses. Missing the intimacies of their immediate families, they had relied on each other for comfort and congeniality. Tobacco served a need.

Mom disliked the smoking, but Dad said that after six years of indulging he just could not break the habit. It relaxed him, he said. Helped him to unwind. Taking long even drags, he held the smoke briefly in his lungs before exhaling slowly through widespread nostrils. With each successive puff his body grew less tense, and before long he began to feel as content as the fluffy white nesting-hen he had spied sitting atop her eggs in the corner of the chicken coop.

How long they sat this way, enjoying the peace and serenity of their surroundings, they did not know. Time stood still on Sunday afternoons in the coal camps. Mom had stopped rocking Lee and was simply enjoying the motherly warmth of holding him in her arms as she gazed upon the redbud and dogwood trees highlighting the hillside beyond the creek. First to speak, she said, "I see Beatrice and Bud coming our way. They'll be here directly." She smiled in anticipation, as company enhanced Sunday afternoons.

With a happy face, Dad stubbed out his cigarette with the sole of his shoe and rose to greet his neighbors. Bud, whose slender frame bent slightly from the weight of nine-month-old Gerald astride his hip, reached to shake Dad's hand while Beatrice went directly to Mom. "Here, Ethel," she said, handing over a bundle of baby clothes, "take these for Lee. Gerald's already outgrowed them, and I ain't plannin' on havin' another one any time soon."

"Oh lordy, Beatrice," Mom said, her face brightening at the sight of the clothing. "You don't know how much I need these. Lee's outgrowed everything he has."

Dad went to the kitchen to get chairs for his guests. Beatrice obliged; Gerald climbed onto her lap, but small and wiry Bud declined a chair saying he'd just sit on the floor—like Dad. Actually he hunkered. "I've got so used to hunkering in the mine I can't sit any other way," he said in his jovial way of speaking.

"I know just what you mean, Bud," Dad said with a smile of understanding. "We grow old fast in these mines, don't we. Look like old men, all bent over with aches and pains. Afraid to stand up. Afraid we might hit our heads on something. Even out in broad daylight!" Both men laughed at the true-to-life imagery.

"Cigarette, Bud?" Dad asked.

"Nah, I'm a chew person, Cliff." Bud pulled a package of Brown Mule from his shirt pocket and slowly took off the wrapping, savoring the moment of relaxation. Using his pocketknife, he cut off a plug of the tobacco, stuffed it inside his cheek and moved it around a bit to soften it up. The rest of the Brown Mule he held loosely between his fingers, using it to gesture with as he talked.

Thelma, sitting on her porch, looked over at the small gathering and promptly called out to her husband Clint, who was stacking wood at the woodshed, "Clint, get Robert from out of that mud. He's already a mess. Let's go for a walk. Let's go visit next door."

Clint's mop of unruly reddish-brown hair shown like copper as he lifted Robert from his place in the yard and took him to Thelma, who hoisted him onto her lap. "Would you like to go visit Lee and Gerald?" she asked as she bounced him on her knee. "I bet they'd like to see *you*." Robert was a few months older than Gerald and Lee. He already walked and could say a few words—which he did not often choose to do. "He'd rather *do* than *say*," was Thelma's explanation.

Robert wanted to visit. He tugged and pulled and grunted all the while Thelma "spiffed" him up. Taking his hand she started down the steps of the porch, then turned back, calling to her husband, "Clint, get a little piece of that fatback on your way out. We'll take some to Cliff and Ethel." A common practice was to take a little something when you visited. A reason to be there, I guess.

Crossing the yard took only a few steps. "Hey, let's bust up this little party," was Clint's way of greeting.

"Hey, come on up and join us," was Dad's way of greeting.

Thelma pulled up a chair, hauled Robert onto her lap and handed over the wrapped meat. "Ethel," she said, "put this piece of fatback in your pinto beans. It'll give them a nice flavor." Mom thanked Thelma for the fatback, promising to use it the very next day. Robert wriggled off Thelma's lap and climbed down the steps into the yard. Clint kept an eye on him.

The three women sat on the porch and talked baby talk while the men wandered aimlessly about the yard and talked about problems at the coal mines, stopping occasionally to give emphasis to some matter. Eventually, they ended up at the fence where they alternately leaned their elbows on a fence post or leaned backward against it with bent knee and foot braced. Clint dipped, Bud chewed and Dad smoked.

*   *   *

Beatrice and Thelma, who already had a good start at being house-wives, were more than eager to teach Mom the rudiments of cooking and baking, secrets of mending and how to care for her newborn baby. They each had a copy of the latest issue of the *Rumford Complete Cook Book*, the same cookbook their mothers had used.

Quick learner that she was, Mom soon became a capable home-maker, too. Cooking became her favorite pastime. She was ever ready to please her husband's palate—so much so that if something she cooked did not please her she was not above tossing it and beginning again from scratch. She could not bring herself to serve something not cooked exactly right.

On one occasion, soon after Thelma had given her some hints on baking in the new iron skillet she had purchased at the company store, Mom baked some cornbread. Her face was all smiles as she took the golden brown bread from the oven, but she quickly dismayed when as she turned the bread onto a plate half of it stuck to the bottom of the pan leaving the other half to look scalped. Aghast, she was on her way out the door with the disastrous creation when Dad suddenly came upon her and teasingly exclaimed, "Ethel, what on earth happened to the cornbread?"

Mom smarted at the remark. "Nothing that can't be fixed!" she stated firmly as, pink-faced, she marched to the yard and flung the offensive bread to the chickens where it was disposed of forthwith.

Smothering a grin, Dad called from the doorway, "I didn't mean you should throw the bread away!"

"I'll bake some more," she hurled over her shoulder as she turned her back and walked rapidly in the direction of Thelma's to ask why the cornbread had stuck to the bottom of the pan.

When she returned, she said not a word but promptly baked more bread—this time, in a properly seasoned skillet—and when it was done she beamed with pride as the crusty brown bread fell smoothly from the pan. She served the perfectly baked bread with a smile.

"Ethel, this is *just* fine," Dad said without emotion, grateful as he was to at last have his meal.

"Clifford, you had better not be teasing me," she replied.

*   *   *

In the early morning hours, after the men had gone to work, the women frequently took turns at hosting. On one rainy spring day in 1924, when it was her time to host, Mom decided to bake bread pudding. Spicy bread pudding would make the kitchen smell good and feel cozy she thought. She banked up the cook stove with a little extra coal to make the oven nice and hot, then began to create her delicacy.

Beatrice had sent word that she and Gerald would not be coming over. Bud had worked the night shift, so they would be sleeping in.

Thelma and Robert came right on time. Robert wandered toward the pile of playthings Mom had placed in the middle of the kitchen floor for the boys' entertainment as Thelma helped herself to coffee from the speckled blue enamel coffeepot on the cook stove. She pulled a chair from under the table and gingerly curled herself into place. Thelma was fragile, thin as a rail, with a slight stoop, but had a huge appetite. "That little woman eats like a lumberjack," Dad often said.

Thelma watched closely as Mom brought her freshly made delight from the oven. "Ethel, you make the best bread pudding around," she stated proudly, sipping her coffee with both hands around the cup and elbows propped over the white enamel table trimmed in red. She watched Robert from the corner of her eye and waited for the bread pudding to cool.

"Play nice now," Thelma called to Robert as she saw him take a hefty swing in Lee's direction with a wooden spoon. Dodging the spoon, Lee covered his head with both hands and Robert readied to take aim again. "I said play nice, Robert. Do I need to take you home?" Thelma rose and gave him a threatening look.

Mom removed Lee from the line of fire and offered Robert a rubber toy as she attempted to pry the spoon from his tightly fisted hand. Robert gave her a *take-it-from-me-if-you-can* look. Mom gave him a *look* too—though Thelma didn't see it. Robert finally accepted the rubber toy and Mom put the spoon out of his reach and came back to the table. "Terrible twos," she said with a smile.

Thelma hardly noticed as she helped herself to a generous portion of bread pudding. "You had any more of that morning sickness?" she said, taking a gulping swallow of coffee.

"Nah, I think I'm finally over it," Mom said, continuing to eye Robert.

"I swan, you don't even look pregnant to me! When I was six months I looked like an elephant."

"Oh, Thelma, you're just saying that!" Mom was flattered that Thelma thought she still looked presentable. She'd heaved each morning for more than a month and was beginning to think that she looked as horrible as she felt. "Want more coffee?" she offered, not wishing to talk about it any more.

Thelma extended her cup with her left hand, as she slid the fingers of her right over the collapsible end of the table that had been raised to make a larger surface. "When you gonna get yourself a ironin' board?" she said. "You can't go on ironin' on this table. It's too low. You'll hurt your back liftin' them heavy irons. Them things must weigh five pounds each. That ain't good for a woman with child."

"They *are* plenty heavy," Mom said as she lifted one of the irons from its resting platform on the cook stove. "But I can't get a ironin' board right now. Clifford said he wants to finish payin' off at the company store before we buy anything else. You know how it is. Most of Clifford's paycheck is docked before he gets it. We've not seen more than a few dollars since we got here." She rose to keep Robert from hitting Lee again, and Thelma took another sip of coffee. "But, at least we'll have a place for the new baby," Mom said on her way back to the table.

"Bet you're hopin' it's a girl this time," Thelma stated flatly. "Every family ought to have at least one boy and one girl. I hope my next one's a girl."

"We're hopin' for a girl, too, but if not, well, I just hope he's as good as Lee is!" Mom looked in the direction of her son with a broad affectionate smile of a proud mother.

*   *   *

It was Election Day in November of 1924, and Dad, Bud and Clint were heading off to vote. "Ethel," Dad said to Mom as he left her standing on the porch with Lee holding onto her skirt, "I'm going down to make my scratch under the rooster, like Pop always does and what all poor people should be doing." He took a few steps and suddenly turned back, flashing a toothy grin. "Just think, Ethel," he said, "now that women can vote, if you were *old enough*, you could be going down to the poll with me and putting your scratch under the rooster, too. Help elect us a democratic president!"

"Well, you're going to see some changes for the better now that women *can* vote!" Mom retorted. "I just might vote for a Republican one of these days!"

The men walked away laughing. All would put their scratch under the rooster. They would vote a straight Democratic ticket, no exceptions. It was the party of the common man, Dad always said.

*   *   *

As Mom went into labor on April 14, 1925, Beatrice and Thelma came to her aid while Dad carried Lee next door to stay with Bud. "You're a big, big boy, a big two year old," Dad told Lee.

Bud reached for Lee and remarked in his teasing way, "Cliff, this here birthin' stuff is for the women. Now, if it gets to be too much for you, I'll be out here in the yard." Smiling in mock agreement, Dad raised his eyebrows and patted Bud on the shoulder before heading off to get the doctor.

The birth was again difficult for Mom, leaving her weak and spent and the company doctor saying she was a real trooper. The doctor lingered longer than the customary hour he would normally have stayed after delivering a baby. He kept checking and re-checking the baby boy, who had been given the name Lonnie.

When finally he made ready to leave, the doctor motioned Dad to follow. "The baby is weak, very weak, Mr. White," he said as soon as they were out of earshot. "If he has trouble before I get back to check on him, you send for me."

Nodding, Dad soberly shook the doctor's hand, thanked him for coming and ushered him to the door. Returning to his wife and seeing the anguish on her face, he said gently, "The baby will be all right. He's just not real strong right now." He spoke with assurance, but the concern for his newborn son's well being made him tremble inside.

During the immediate days that followed, Thelma and Beatrice took turns giving assistance to Mom, as she was barely able to care for her newborn baby and two-year-old son.

By the tenth day, after the customary nine days of bed rest, Mom was up and walking about. "Put on a pot of coffee," she directed as Beatrice and Thelma and their little ones descended upon her all at once. She hoped the scent of the perking coffee would make her feel stronger.

Thelma stoked up the fire in the cook stove and busied herself making the coffee while Beatrice settled the boys in the middle of the kitchen floor amidst the playthings.

The three women positioned themselves at the kitchen table and Beatrice was the first to share. "I heard that "Old Man" Bates beat up his wife again. For the life of me, I can't understand why the woman stays with him."

"I reckon she stays with him 'cause she's got nowhere else to go," Thelma said complacently.

"My heart aches for those poor children," Mom said. "I hear he beats on them a good bit too. They're too young to fend for themselves." She kept her eye on Robert who had begun to look menacingly from one to the other of his playmates.

Lee wisely moved away when he saw Robert raise a wooden spoon high into the air. A cry of pain from Gerald brought Beatrice to her feet just in time to prevent another lick to his head.

"I don't know what I'm going to do with that boy," Thelma declared. "He's been a holy terror since he broke two." She pulled him away from the others, upbraided him a bit, and then released him back to Beatrice's care.

As Beatrice sought to interest the children in play once more, a small, weak cry came from the bedroom—a cry barely heard over the sounds of the women's conversation and the children's play. Mom, ever alert to her infant son, hastened to see about him. Beatrice followed with Thelma close on her heels. "What's *wrong* with Lonnie, Ethel?" Beatrice asked, looking over Mom's shoulder at the tiny infant who whimpered quietly, struggling to let his needs be known.

"Poor little fellow," Thelma said. "He don't seem like he has the strength to cry."

"His color's bad, he don't look right, Ethel," Beatrice added.

At Beatrice and Thelma's queries, Mom's underlying worries surfaced. Taking Lonnie into her arms, she turned to the anxious women. "The doctor said he'd be back to check on him," she said, "to tell me what to do for him. Oh lordy, I hope he's going to be all right. I told Clifford last night, he don't seem right. He's too quiet."

Distraught, she took Lonnie to her breast and fed him the little amount he could hold. Then, scooting her straight-backed chair closer to the wall, she rocked him back and forth until he again slept and she herself was exhausted. Saying she could not stay up any longer, she plopped onto the bed and placed Lonnie close beside her.

The next day, Dad dropped by the doctor's office on his way to work. "Doc," he said, "maybe you had better make that visit. The baby's no better, and my wife is really worried."

Mom's eyes anxiously followed the doctor's every move as on that same day he examined Lonnie. The doctor rose and began to fumble with his stethoscope as he gazed out the window for what seemed *too long*. A long sigh escaped him, and he swallowed hard before turning to face her. "Mrs. White," he said, "you're doing fine. You'll be much stronger in a few days. As for the baby, I'm afraid I have bad news." He seated himself in a chair beside her and leaned closer, pausing briefly, so as to carefully choose his words.

"Your baby has a very weak heart," he said. Compassion filled his face as he looked into her scared eyes.

"A…weak…heart?" She shivered as she tried to comprehend.

"It's a birth defect. It won't get any better."

"It won't get any better?" The tremor in her voice confirmed her deeper fears, and she suddenly felt cold and heavy, unable to move, as if bolted to the floor.

"No, it won't get any better," the doctor said gently. "I wish I could say otherwise, but there is nothing I can do. He won't live long, dear. He'll probably die before the year is out." He stopped to put his hand on her trembling shoulders. "I'm so sorry to have to tell you this. I wish I could say it wasn't so."

After the doctor left, feelings of grief overwhelmed her. She carried her weak and helpless baby with her throughout the day from room to room as she wept uncontrollably and talked to him in the language only a mother has for her progeny.

Anxiously, she awaited her husband's return from work. As soon as she spotted him from among the men, who lumbered up the lane from the mine, she rushed to his side. Her face pale, her eyes red and swollen, she was sobbing hysterically as she pulled him toward the house and the sleeping baby. "Clifford, the doctor can't do anything for him," she said, her voice breaking. "He's going to die! His heart! He's got a weak heart, a birth defect. Oh, Clifford, what are we going to do? He's going to die!"

She looked to her husband for comfort as she sat on the edge of the bed, her hands squeezed tightly together, her face a study in panic, but Dad, momentarily stunned, could only stare vacantly into the distance. Though he knew Lonnie was weak, he had not expected to hear that he would die. He searched for words with which to comfort his wife, but none came. He wished he could take Lonnie to his mom, Rosabelle. She would know what to do. She knew all about babies. But, he had no way to take him there. He had to work, to provide for his family. It bore down upon him hard as he struggled to pull himself together. Finally, after swallowing the walnut sized lump in his throat, he finally managed to say, "I'll write to Mom. She'll help us all she can."

*   *   *

Rosabelle would not be able to come. Her own tremendous responsibilities forbade it. "*Son, give your son all the love in your heart. I'll pray for him, and I'll ask the pastor and all the people at church to pray for him,*" she wrote. But all the love and prayers they could bestow upon Lonnie did not change his condition. They did everything the doctor *and* Rosabelle advised; yet he grew weaker and weaker until they knew he had little time left. He died in the arms of his mother, just before reaching seven months.

"Ethel, you have to let me have him," Beatrice begged. "He's passed on, honey. We have to get him ready for burial."

"No, no," Mom sobbed, clutching Lonnie tightly to her bosom.

"Clifford, you're going to have to help us," Thelma implored.

"Ethel, you must give him to me," Dad said, his voice breaking as he slowly unfastened Lonnie from his mother's grasp and then turned him over to Thelma and Beatrice. A loud sob rose from his throat as he returned to his wife. In the privacy of their bedroom they both collapsed sadly onto the bed and wept as if their hearts were broken.

On a cool, overcast and windless October day they laid Lonnie in the tiny coffin Bud had made and carried him in a small procession of their closest neighbors to an obscure cemetery on a hillside on the outskirts of Marfork.

*　　　　　*　　　　　*

As seasons came and went, Lee helped to fill the void that Lonnie had left. Gleefully, he accepted the bountiful hugs and kisses his mother bestowed upon him many times a day. He had witnessed the coming and going of a baby in the family and had sometimes questioned where the baby had gone, but heaven was a concept beyond his understanding.

During this time Beatrice and Thelma each had another child of their own and Mom was there for them, but she still cried often over the loss of her infant son.

*　　　　　*　　　　　*

A year had passed when on a warm sunny day in late spring Mom had taken Lee, who was now nearing four, up the hillside to the cemetery where they had pulled weeds from among the violets they had planted a month before on Lonnie's grave. On their return, Mom stopped to show Lee flowering trees and shrubs along the way: mountain laurel, redbud and dogwood trees, golden forsythia, the dainty white flowers of the blackberry bushes, and the tiny leaves that had begun to break forth from the no longer dormant deciduous trees. "No time is prettier than spring," Mom said to Lee as she helped him pick a bouquet of flowers, which she would use to adorn the kitchen table.

As they neared home, Beatrice spied them from her kitchen window and ran to her porch. "Wait up a minute," she called, as she rushed across her back yard to the fence. "Ethel, have you heard the news?"

Mom tightened her hold on Lee's hand, puzzled by the concern she detected in Beatrice's voice. "What news?" she asked.

"About the mine layin' off workers. They might close down the mine!"

"Close down the mine!"

"That's what I've been hearin', Ethel."

"Oh, no, they can't do that. Beatrice, where did you hear this?" Mom reached for the gatepost on which to steady herself.

"Thelma told me, just today. She says Clint is readying to take off. Says he's not waitin' around. He's off lookin' for work someplace else right now."

"Oh, lordy, what will we do? Beatrice, are you sure?"

"I'm sure, Ethel. Bud's on the early shift today. I'm askin' him as soon as he gets in. You'd better ask Clifford, too, Ethel. We may all have to leave." Beatrice's eyebrows rose above her large widened eyes like exclamation points. She paused momentarily for her words to take hold, then hastened to return to the dinner she said might burn if she didn't get to it.

"Oh, dear, Lee. Oh, dear," Mom said indirectly to Lee as she guided him into the house, where, to keep her mind settled she nervously began to prepare dinner.

As the time grew closer for Dad's arrival, she went to the porch and watched for him among the shadowy men as they ambled home from the mine. As he neared the backyard gate, she placed Lee astride her hip and rushed to meet him. With a beseeching look, she asked, "Oh, Clifford, is it true? Is it true that the mine might close?"

Sighing heavily, Dad walked with her up the sidewalk and into the house before speaking. "Yes, it's true, Ethel," he said as he hung his work clothes on the hook behind the cookstove in the kitchen. He said nothing more for the moment and prepared for his bath.

"Why didn't you tell me, Clifford?"

"I didn't want to worry you just yet, Ethel. I figured you had enough on your mind. It's been the talk for awhile, but nothing has happened 'til today." He spoke his words as carefully and as gently as he could. "The first layoffs were today. It's just a matter of time before we'll have to go somewhere else."

"Oh, Clifford, we can't leave Lonnie." Mom still held Lee on her hip, giving her lithe frame a distorted shape.

"We have no choice Ethel. With a new baby coming, you're going to need a doctor's care and I can't be without work."

Releasing Lee to stand on his own, Mom dropped suddenly onto a chair. With her shoulders slumped forward and her hands clasped helplessly on her lap, she looked forlornly out the window toward the hillside. Tears fell silently down her cheeks.

Dad pulled a chair alongside her. "I'm sorry it had to be this way, Ethel," he said gently, "but we have to go on. I hear there's work over in Logan County. My cousin Joe lives at Crites. He'll put us up 'til I find work." He placed his arm around her collapsed frame and stroked her back. "You won't be able to travel after you're farther along."

*   *   *

They made one last visit to the cemetery, then returned home to make preparations for leaving. After selling or giving away what they could not take with them, they bid farewell to friends and neighbors who were doing the same. Just about everyone in the camp was leaving to go somewhere else to find work, but *they* were the only ones going to Crites.

Taking Lee's hands between them they started to the train station. Their lives were disrupted, their family broken and fragmented. They were, as the crow flies, not far from kin, but they may as well have been thousands of miles away—and now they would be farther yet. Questions filled their thoughts. *What would Joe and Rose be like? Would they ever see Beatrice and Bud and Thelma and Clint and their children again? When would they be able to come back to visit Lonnie?*

A shrill whistle signaled the arrival of the approaching C & O passenger train. They moved toward the railway platform and waited as the steaming train screeched to a stop. Handing their tickets to the conductor, they took one last look around before boarding the train. Mom made her way to a window seat where she stared longingly at the hillside beyond. As the churning train pulled away, she discreetly wiped away the tears that dropped uncontrollably from her eyes. She took Lee's hand and held it tightly, but did not speak for fear of dislodging the huge lump in her throat.

Following the line of the Coal River, the train chugged rhythmically through the valley as dark fluffy clouds of smoke puffed from its smokestack covering the tiny community of Marfork and other small towns and villages along the way with a spray of coal dust. Lee gazed with delight as Dad pointed to scenery along the way. As the train suddenly entered a tunnel, Lee gasped. Mom put her arm around him as Dad whispered in his ear, "It's only a tunnel. It will be light again soon."

*   *   *

Joe met them at the train station at Crites, helped them with their belongings, then escorted them to *his* house, where upon arrival they were greeted warmly with hugs and kisses from Joe's wife Rose. "Put your things in the bedroom here," she said kindly. "You'll stay with us 'til you find work and a place of your own."

Rose, at fifty, was well preserved and pleasant to look upon. Her stylish haircut, bobbed like Mom's, and her erect carriage and neatly groomed appearance set her apart from the typical miner's wives of the area who often referred to her as "stuck up." Rose was far from "stuck up." She was active in the community, always ready to lend a helping hand, but was not one for small talk or indiscriminate socializing. She had known better times.

She matched up well with Joe who was also caring and loving and looked an awful lot like the men on Dad's side of the family with medium build, light complexion, blue eyes and receding hair.

Joe and Rose knew how to make their guests feel at home by serving them a nice hot meal enhanced with plenty of in-season summer vegetables: tomatoes, squash, green beans and new potatoes.

"Did you grow these yourself, Joe?" Dad wanted to know.

"Nah, Cliff, feller just on the outskirts of town here has a garden big enough for the whole camp. Sells and delivers."

"But these are my own tomatoes," Rose said proudly. "Everybody around has a tomato plant or two."

After supper they went into the living room where Joe lit his pipe and Dad rolled a cigarette. Rose doted over Lee and shared pictures of her own now-grown children. As the evening wore on, the two families exchanged many stories, some happy, some sad, bringing both laughter and tears—both good antidotes for their weary souls. When Rose heard about Lonnie, she became distraught and put her arms around them both, saying, "Oh, you poor, poor dears." To have someone in the family help grieve over Lonnie was a comfort.

The mantle clock chimed ten times and Joe said: "Well, folks, it's past my bedtime; we'd best be turning in. Clifford, you'll want to go down to the mine early in the morning. I talked with Big Chew yesterday. He thinks he can get you on down at the Number Two mine. They're hiring right now. It's union, so you'll get a day's wages for a day's work with no shenanigans going on."

"Sounds good to me," Dad said with a tired smile.

Rose bedded everyone down as comfortably as she could. Mom said she liked the quilt. Rose was modest, claiming it had been made by a relative years ago. "With no more kids of our own around here we can rightfully call this room a guest room now," she said. Smiling brightly, her brown eyes twinkled as she glanced in the direction of four-year-old Lee who already slept soundly on a pallet on the floor.

As daylight approached, Rose hustled about the kitchen as she built a fire in the cookstove. She soon had the coffee perking and fresh eggs set out to go with the biscuits she had ready for baking.

Being summer, Dad went to the back porch to shave while Mom took care of her personal needs in the bedroom. Rose brought her hot water for the enamel basin. "For a nice warm sponge bath," she said. Mom hoped they would not have to stay long, but she truly enjoyed the luxury of being pampered. It had been so long since she had been a guest.

After breakfast, Joe announced he would be heading out to mine Number One where, as a fire-boss, he needed to meet with the mine "super" to point out some potential problems.

Dad set off in the direction of mine Number Two, where, along the way, he took in the sights: rows of houses lined up near the tipple on the road leading toward the mine, streets not well kept, and a gray and dingy looking company store. Not exactly what he had hoped for, but he figured it to be temporary anyway.

*   *   *

Big Chew, so called because he always had a sizable wad of Mailpouch in his already oversized jaws, greeted Dad at the mine's office and gave him a job on the spot. "You'll be working the second shift, Clifford," he said, as he shifted the wad of tobacco from the right jaw to the left and then spat a big blob dead center into a coal bucket in the corner of the room. Brown spots on the wall behind suggested that Big Chew was not always so accurate.

"You'll be working at the face of the mine, loading coal," Big Chew continued, while shifting the Mailpouch back to the other side of his mouth and swiping the tobacco drippings from the corners of his mouth with the back of his hand. "Shift starts at four, work 'til midnight. Start tomorrow. Go on over to the office and get yourself signed up for a house. I hear there's some doubles still available. Might get teamed up with an *I*-talian family. They fight a lot, but they don't speak English, so you'll get along."

"That won't bother me none," Dad said as he shook Big Chew's hand. "Right now I'm glad to have a job and a place to live. My wife's expecting a baby in a few months time."

*   *   *

Jacqueline Rose, named for cousin Rose, was born two weeks before schedule on October 15, 1927. It was another long and difficult birth for Mom. She looked lovingly at Rose, who had been with her throughout. "Oh, Rose, what would I have done without you?" she declared. "There was just no time to send for my mother or my sister Orphie."

"Now, just you shush," Rose said as she wrapped a blanket around baby Jacqueline and laid her close beside Mom. "How were you to know the baby would come early? It just happened. Don't you be thinking about such things. It'll just wear you down more. Now, I'll take Lee with me for a few days so you and Clifford can enjoy your little girl. If you need me, send Clifford. I'll come right over."

The next nine days of bed rest and recuperation was a pleasant experience for Mom as she was truly able to luxuriate. Rose brought Lee by each day and helped with the lesser chores. Dad had been changed to the dayshift, so he was home at night. The Italian neighbor Maria came frequently, too. She brought food and checked the fires, but stayed only a few minutes; she didn't speak English.

As soon as she was able, Mom walked with Lee and Jacqueline around the coal camp where she occasionally met up with another mother out doing the same, but she was never able to develop the rapport she'd had with Beatrice and Thelma. She missed them as much as she missed her family. Lee missed them too though he had taken a liking to Rose. She made over him a lot.

"If you don't watch out, I'm going to steal him, Ethel," Rose said on one occasion when Mom, Lee and Jacqueline were visiting.

"Oh, Rose, I couldn't do without Lee," Mom said, smiling at Lee as she took the blanket from around Jacqueline and seated herself on the living room sofa.

Lee beamed as he looked from one to the other of the two women, then, as if believing he must make a choice, quickly moved to his mother's side where he placed his hands lightly on his baby sister as she lay across her mother's lap.

Rose took Jacqueline from Mom and heaved her up onto her shoulder where she began to pat her back. "Well then, maybe I'll just take Jacqueline," she said, giving Lee a wink. Jacqueline burped loudly, delighting Rose and bringing a grin to Lee's face. He liked Rose.

A smile crossed Mom's face, too, as she looked up at her baby daughter. "I just can't believe it," she said. "When I was pregnant, all I could think about was havin' a girl. I just knew I'd be brushin' her hair and playin' with her curls. Jacqueline's not got a hair on her head!"

Rose crooked her head to get a better view of the hairless wonder. "Well," she said, "if you want hair to play with, I expect you'll just have to start making plans for another baby, this time one with hair!"

Mom pondered her plight, burst out laughing and then suddenly began to cry. Lee was immediately at her side, his little hands lightly tapping her shoulders. "What's wrong, Mother?" he said. He had called her Mother since a visitor had once asked him "Where's your mother?"

Hugging him tightly, she said, "I'm fine, Lee. I'm okay." Lee had seen her cry a lot since Lonnie's death. She determined then and there that she would work harder to conceal her feelings.

Rose looked on with compassion. "What is it, dear?" she asked.

Taking a deep breath, Mom straightened her shoulders, wiped away her tears and gave Rose a deliberate smile. "It's not that she has no hair, Rose, it's just that I'm so lonely for my family. I've not seen anyone for over a year."

"You're still so young, Ethel. It was hard for me, too, at first."

Mom was embarrassed. "If it wasn't for you and Joe," she began to say, but Rose interrupted as she put up her hand and looked out the window onto the porch, into the twilight. "It's the men, Ethel," she said. "The union meeting is over. Early, I'd say. What say we make some tea, crank up the Edison and have ourselves a little fun?"

Without waiting for a reply, Rose placed Jacqueline in the center of the bed in the guestroom and headed to the kitchen.

Taking Lee's hand, Mom followed. "What can I do to help?"

"Cups and saucers if you will. The flowered ones." Rose pointed toward the cupboard before turning to greet Joe and Dad as they stopped to hang their coats on pegs near the front doorway. "Meeting didn't last long," she said.

"Nah," Joe said, making his way into the living room. "Nothin' new tonight."

"We've got tea brewing," Rose told the men as she moved to the living room, placed a cylinder inside the Edison and cranked it up. Out poured some nice ragtime music and she began to dance. Mom's face brightened at the unexpected sight. "Come on, Ethel," Rose said, "Let's liven this place up a bit."

"That's a right good idea," Joe said, giving Mom a *"go on now"* look. He took a few short puffs from his pipe, then mockingly threw out his legs a few times too, before pulling up a kitchen chair. "I'm too old for this," he said as he eased himself down cross-legged onto the chair alongside Dad, who held Lee between his legs. "Why don't *you* give it a try, Cliff?"

"Nah," Dad said, "These old legs never had time to learn to dance."

"Why, you're just a youngin', Cliff," Joe urged. "Get on up there and dance with the women! Keep those legs limbered up. They'll grow stiff on you soon enough, workin' in the mines."

"I'd fall on my face for sure, Joe," Dad said with a fixed smile. "I'll just sit back here and enjoy the show."

While the women danced, the men indulged in their smoke, drank tea and looked on with delighted grins as their eyes followed the movement of the women. Lee, too, watched exuberantly as he shared a view of the "fun side" of the grown-up's world.

Before the first cup of tea was finished, a whimper came from the bedroom. "Uh-oh, party's over," Dad said as he released Lee to go to Jacqueline. Picking her up, he called out in haste, "Ethel, she's trying to eat her fists; I think she's hungry and I can't help her with that."

"Party pooper!" Mom said as she received Jacqueline into her arms and took a seat on the sofa where she began to feed her hairless darling.

A train's whistle pierced the air. Rose stopped the music and turned to watch as the train passed within view of the window. "You get right in the middle of a dance," she said, her voice rising, "and your music gets drowned out by a dadblasted old coal train!" Rose mockingly thumbed her nose at the train, then placed her hands on her hips and turned to her company as she laughed in amusement at herself. The house began to rumble and shake: the windows rattled. Rose threw up her hands in mock disgust and headed to the kitchen. "I'll fix more tea," she called over her shoulder.

After the train had passed and the little red caboose had moved out of sight, Mom spoke up. "And little good it does to mop the floor and dust the furniture," she said. "Every morning there's a new layer of cinders. Lee and Jacqueline have cinders in their hair. Well, Lee does, anyway," she said with a giggle as she looked down at her baby daughter and shifted her to the other breast. "We all do. You can't see the cinders in Clifford's hair though. He's just one big, huge cinder." Her face reddened in amusement as she reached for her husband and roughed his dark curls with her spare hand.

Amused, Joe said: "Ah, music and laughter are good for the soul. Truth is though, living in these coal camps can get your spirits down if you let it. Scrub your house down one day and its back to gray the next."

"Yep, either black or gray, not much in between," Dad said. "When I start out toward the mine, all I see is a bunch of black blobs coming towards me, like bogeymen coming from the shadows—and I'm one of those bogeymen!"

"Clifford, the big bogeyman! Remember the day you got caught in the rain, comin' in from work?" Mom said, holding back a laugh. "I thought we'd never get that rain," she said, turning to Rose. "I'd been prayin' for a good rain to clear the air so I could breathe something besides coal dust for a change. The rain finally came and I was standin' out on the porch, takin' in some good deep breaths of air, and up walked Clifford. He caught me off guard, and I screamed like he was the bogeyman. He had streaks down his face. Looked like a zebra!"

Dad's face lit up, so delighted he was to see his wife having fun. Rose, too, smiled as she poured more tea and proceeded to keep the conversation going. "Clifford," she said as she settled herself onto the sofa next to Mom, "how do you get on with the Italians next door? They're fun loving people, I know, but they pretty much stay to themselves, don't they?"

Standing, Dad mimicked, "Oh, we get on just fine. Old Silvanny nods at me and I nod back at him. He tips his hat. I tip my hat."

"It's the same with Maria," Mom said with a giggle. "She comes out to sweep her cinders. I come out to sweep my cinders. She smiles at me. I smile at her. She goes inside. I go inside."

"About all we can do is ogle and coo over each other's babies," Dad said as he poured a little of his tea into a saucer. He preferred drinking coffee and tea from a saucer after it had cooled to the temperature he liked.

"I hope we don't have to stay here much longer," Mom said, her voice changing to a more serious tone. "We can't get to know anyone. Folks here are always movin' in or movin' out for various and sunder reasons. I seen one family move out in the middle of the night."

"Husband most likely killed in the mine," Joe said. "*Or,* didn't pay his rent. Some of these miners drink up their payday before they get home."

"And some are just not good workers," chimed in Rose. "The company won't keep them if they won't work!"

"That won't happen to Clifford," Mom said. "He's a *hard* worker. But he don't like it here neither."

"We can't seem to get ahead," Dad said, looking to Joe. "I figured getting union wages I wouldn't be owing so much at the company store, but heck, I'm as deep in debt as I've ever been."

Joe uncrossed his legs and leaned forward, resting his elbows on his knees as he drew deeply on his pipe. "It takes a while," he said slowly. "Wouldn't be so bad if they didn't charge an arm and a leg for everything. A feller might get ahead a little sooner."

"I'm waiting for the day!" Dad said with a twisted grin.

Rose consoled. "I know it's hard for you and Ethel, Cliff," she said. "Especially, with these two little babies." She reached for Jacqueline, placed her on her shoulder, and continued talking as she walked her back and forth around the room. "It does take a long time. I wish I'd never seen a coal camp. Joe and I left a beautiful farm over in Mercer County, close to where your Uncle Walter lives now. We would've been happy to stay there forever, but we couldn't make ends meet once the children started coming. My folks never understood. They always wanted us to come back home. My daddy never did forgive Joe for taking me off like that. He's dead now. God rest his soul. But, he left us the farm and we're planning to go back there when Joe quits the mines."

"Which won't be long if I can help it," Joe chimed in.

"Stay for dinner," Rose said cheerfully. "We're having leftovers, but there's plenty for everyone."

"How about it, Ethel?" Dad said, noticing Mom's smile as she sat with her hands folded neatly in her lap. Rose and Joe provided the only social life they had.

*   *   *

Social life at Crites showed little signs of improving as the year 1929 rolled to an end, but work had been steady and Dad was coming close to erasing his debts at the company store. Things were just beginning to look up when, as fate would have it, the fallout of the Great Depression soon came sweeping into the coal fields, leaving a tumultuous swath of financial chaos along the way. Coal miners, who for the most part had little concern for what was happening with the stock market or national events, suddenly began to see their source for making a living tumbling down around them.

At Crites, where Dad still worked in Mine Number Two, the coal company took immediate and drastic action when they announced to the workers, "We have no money to pay you. We're closing our doors. You'll have to leave."

The loss of money and jobs left the miners and their families traumatized. Without even the very basics, they were faced with destitution and forced to move, adding to the massive wave of migration and unemployment already evident in southern West Virginia.

Joe and Rose decided to return to the farm. "Cliff, you and Ethel and the kids are welcome to come with us," Joe generously offered. "Can't promise you a thing, though."

Dad said he appreciated the offer, but said he'd just stick it out in the mines. "Coal mining is all I know, Joe. Some of the men are heading back to Raleigh County, a place called Ameagle over on Coal River. A big seam of coal, I've heard. A big operation. Should be some work there. I reckon we'll go, too."

"Could be just what you and Ethel have been lookin' for," Joe said, as Rose nodded in the background.

2

1930–1933—Ameagle, West Virginia

Joe and Rose went to their farm, near Lashmeet, in Mercer County. Dad and Mom took a few belongings and boarded the train, along with other families, and went to Ameagle, in Raleigh County, a place named for the American Eagle seam of coal. Again, considering himself fortunate, Dad was immediately hired as a motor man for Peabody Coal Company and assigned a four-room house at New Camp, one of three existing coal camps owned by the coal company. The year was 1930.

New Camp, which had once been part of a prosperous West Virginia farm in a wide flowing valley, was located a mile or so from the mine and beside a clean, swiftly flowing stream that had many good fishing holes and swimming spots. Houses and streetlights lined both sides of the road that divided the camp. "You can see people take pride here," Mom said, as she looked about with happy eyes. She was delighted to see that the railroad was not yet extended into that area, which meant for the time being the camp was clean, free of fallout from the coal trains.

Their house, like all the others, was painted white and trimmed in green and came equipped with 20 amp electrical service, a kitchen, living room, two bedrooms, front and back porches, outdoor toilet, coal house, fence and a wooden walkway leading from the front gate up to the front porch. They were pleased to see that a former occupant had added a cellar up against the embankment of the highway at the rear of the yard.

Dad walked with Mom, Lee and Jacqueline all around the yard. "Yard's plenty big enough," he said. "Lots of room for a spring garden. And we'll get us a dog. Put the doghouse right here." He pointed to a corner near the gate.

At mention of a dog, Lee came running. "We're going to get a dog?" he asked, clapping and jumping about excitedly.

"Yep, Lee, a dog,. We're going to have us a dog!" Dad's grin was as big as Lee's. "And chickens too, and rabbits!" he said.

Dad watched with glee as Lee ran about the yard, looking over the fence, under the porches and out into the community. "That boy is going to like it here," he said.

Jacqueline, who now had hair though it was straight and fine—the kind that ribbons disappear from soon after they are tied in place—surprised everyone by suddenly releasing her deathlike grip on her mother's skirt and tearing off after her brother. Her sudden show of independence delighted Mom, who turned to Dad with a gleam in her eye, saying, "Oh, Clifford, it just seems so right to be here."

Dad smiled and nodded in agreement as he put his arm around her shoulder and said softly, "You'll have plenty of room for your flowers, too, Ethel."

"I know," Mom said, her voice suddenly enlivened. "I already see places to put the roses and I'll put daffodils along the walkway. Oh, Clifford, won't it be pretty?" She walked excitedly from one end of the yard to the other as she pointed to her chosen locations.

"We already have a full-grown pear tree, too" Dad said, looking to one corner of the yard, "and the hollyhock bush is real pretty."

"But this leggy snowball bush will have to go!" Mom said flipping her hand toward the ill-fated bush as she made her way quickly to the back of the house where she took Jacqueline's hand once more and then turned with a smile to greet the friendly face she saw peering across the fence.

*   *   *

"You'll like it here," said next door neighbor, Mrs. Coots, as she invited Mom for coffee. Mrs. Coots, several years Mom's senior, was short and plump with small, twinkling blue eyes that beamed brightly from her round and glowing face. Her premature light gray hair was pulled tightly into a knot at the nape of her neck. A few loose strands hung randomly about her face and these she removed from time to time with the tips of her fingers or with a quick upward expulsion of air as she exhaled over her upper lip.

"This here's Herman, my middle one, a bit on the shy side," she said while squeezing her six-year-old son up under her arm and rubbing her pudgy hand over his rumpled hair. Turning to Lee, she asked, "What's *your* name?" Lee responded with a Cheshire grin, exposing his missing teeth, and waited for Mom to speak for him. Mrs. Coots soon shooed both boys away to play, then trotted off in the direction of her house with Mom and Jacqueline following close behind, like ducklings behind the mother duck.

Words trailed over her shoulder as Mrs. Coots continued on in a cheerful voice as she gave Mom the lowdown on Ameagle "We all live alike here, ain't no one person any different than the next," she said. "We all walk to the post office, get our groceries and everthing else at the company store. Fact is, everthing happens at the company store." She headed up the wooden walkway to her back porch where she stopped to rub her hand over some chipped paint. "Company'll send someone around to paint the houses come July. Do it ever year," she announced proudly and walked on into her house motioning the line behind her to follow.

"Sit down, make yourself at home. Everbody else does around here." Mrs. Coots pointed in the direction of a chair at the kitchen table. "Just bring your coffee on over any time you feel like it."

She stopped to introduce Jacqueline to her own two-year-old daughter Mildred. "Here, little girlies," she said, "take these toys and set yourselves down here in the floor and play."

Moving to the cookstove, Mrs. Coots poured coffee and continued her conversation. "I'm just a homebody. You'll always find me right here," she said, handing over the coffee and stepping back to contemplate what she would say next as her hands slid over her abdomen and out onto her hips where they remained as she looked about her.

Mrs. Coots wore a pink pinstriped maternity dress that struck just below the knees where it was slightly higher in the front than in the back. "Made by my own hands," she touted as she noticed Mom's look of admiration. "I make most all our clothes, now that I got me a sewing machine!"

"It's real pretty," Mom said, her eyes still roaming, as she took in the pretty pink and blue flowered curtains on the kitchen windows and the not-so-worn lattice backed chairs that fit snugly around the long kitchen table that had been recently covered with a brand new matching oilcloth.

Mrs. Coots recognized the feeling. "You'll be gettin you some of these pretty things soon, too, Ethel," she said with a light chuckle. "Just keep Clifford workin'! My man's been workin' here almost two years now, knock on wood." She stopped to knock on the nearest wooden chair. "Lots of folks out of work now. Poor things. Times is bad. But I don't think this mine'll go under. They're a big operation."

"Oh, lordy, I hope not," Mom said. "If you could've only seen what was happening at Crites where we come from. It was bad. Real bad. We were lucky. We got out with a group of folks comin' over this way. But a lot of people there didn't have a place to go to. Some of them poor people didn't even speak English."

"Oh, honey, I know. I hear tales ever day. It's a sight. We got to count our blessin's. Lord only knows what will happen to them poor souls."

"I can't stop thinkin' about them," Mom said. "If we hadn't of had a way to get over here, Lord knows where we'd be, right there beggin' for food I guess. Even so, we didn't bring anything much with us. We pretty much have to start all over."

"Well, you're here," Mrs. Coots said with resolve, still standing with her arms across her abdomen. "Got you a nice house and good neighbors! Life'll be good to you here. Mark my word!"

As if to make her point, Mrs. Coots moved toward her bedroom motioning Mom to follow. "I just got this chenille spread day before yesterday. Just got them in at the company store." She ran her hand over the center of the white, softly fringed spread where the outline of a large yellow and pink flower flowed from the center giving the room a focal point.

"That's real pretty, Mrs. Coots," Mom said as she openly admired the spread. "I hope how soon I can get me one. I'll just keep Clifford workin'!" She giggled as if the two now had a secret as she went back to her seat at the kitchen table where she continued to look about, unable to hide her curiosity. Shiny new linoleum graced the kitchen floor and dainty white doilies adorned the arms and backs of the dark green mohair sofa and matching chair in the living room. Everything was clean and smelled so good. *Was it the scent of Old English furniture polish?*

Interrupting Mom's thoughts, Mrs. Coots began to speak again, "There's three camps here," she said, continuing to pace alternately between the open door and the kitchen window as she kept a watchful eye on the children at play. "New Camp, Ameagle and Colored Town. Grade school's up at Long Branch, high school's down at Colcord, just opened up two years ago and the church is at Ameagle. The coloreds have their own school, church and barbershop. Everthing else is at the company store or right next to it. There's a doctor's office, post office, theater, pool hall, saloon, barbershop, boardin' house, soda fountain. Just about everthing you'll need. Ain't got no money? You can "cut scrip" at the office up until four o'clock."

Scanning Mom from head to toe, Mrs. Coots asked with a knowing smile, "When's *your* baby due, Hon? Mine's due in October."

"The doctor at Crites said December. We're hopin' it's another girl."

"I'd sure like me another girl too. Them boys are a handful," Mrs. Coots said as she took the coffeepot from the cookstove and poured another round of coffee before she headed to the icebox on the back porch. Returning, she carried a jug of milk and a bowl of butter. "Ethel, this here's good fresh cow milk," she said. "Here, try some in your coffee. Feller named Elmer Johnson, lives just up the river, up Fulton Holler, brings it around two times a week. May as well buy from him. It's too hard tryin' to keep a cow of your own. He talks funny, whispers mostly, but he's a fine feller. Clean and fair. Can't get any butter better'n his. Here, try a taste." Mrs. Coots leaned over the table, buttered a biscuit left over from breakfast, spread it with a dab of homemade strawberry jam, handed it over with a proud look and stood back waiting for Mom's response.

"MMmmm! This *is* delicious, Mrs. Coots!" Mom smiled happily as she bit into the biscuit and poured milk into her coffee. She liked her coffee black except on special occasions. This was a special occasion.

"You've got a real nice place here, Mrs. Coots," Mom said as she took another bite from her biscuit and continued to look about with excited eyes.

"Nothin' fancy," Mrs. Coots said modestly. "But what I have I'm willing to share. I know you'll do the same by me. That's what neighbors are for." She got up and headed for the stove again. Mom saw right away that Mrs. Coots was not one to sit for long spells. Not like Thelma and Beatrice. But, she liked this woman who was a mixture of sister, friend and mother rolled into one. Right now she needed all three.

"Looks like Jacqueline's taken a likin' to your Mildred. I can't believe they're both the same age," Mom stated matter-of-factly as she observed the girls mostly staring at each other and playing independent of one another, yet they *were* playing with the rubber dolls, pots, spoons and other bric-a-brac Mrs. Coots had given them to play with.

Pleased to see that Jacqueline was relaxed and comfortable with someone other than herself, Mom allowed her thoughts to switch suddenly to her new one on the way. "What's the doctor like?" she asked.

"Oh, you'll like Doc Williams," Mrs. Coots answered as she leaned against the door frame of her bedroom. "He delivered Mildred, right here in this house. A real good doctor. He'll take good care of you."

A commotion outdoors drew the women's attention to the back porch where Herman and Lee stood gulping water. As they passed the white enamel dipper back and forth between them, drops of perspiration rolled from the tops of their wet heads and down over their dusty cheeks. "What have you two been up to?" a grinning Mrs. Coots quizzed from the doorway.

"Nothin', just runnin' and playin'," Herman said in his lackadaisical way as he hung the dipper back on the wall and then hurried down the stairs and back into the alley. Lee was fast on his heels.

"I can tell they're gonna be big buddies," Mom said approvingly as she repositioned herself at the kitchen table.

"Guess they'll have Mrs. Rutledge in school this fall—wife of the mine foreman," Mrs. Coots said as she turned from the doorway. "She's a *good* teacher, and your kid's gonna learn from her."

*   *   *

Mom liked the warm and friendly atmosphere of the Coots dwelling, but she didn't want to wear out her welcome on her first visit. "I sure do thank you for your hospitality, Mrs. Coots, but I'd better get on back. Clifford will think I've left for good!" Jacqueline was already tugging at her skirt.

Mrs. Coots escorted Mom and Jacqueline to the fence gate and waved them goodbye. "I'll be right here if you need me," she called after them.

"And I'll try to do the same for you." Mom said, turning back to look once again at this total stranger with whom she had just shared her life story and with whom she felt right at home.

          *   *   *

Unlike Crites, the social life at New Camp proved to be pleasant. As new families moved in, friendships were forged. Strangers soon became close; friends and neighbors became like family; children found new playmates. With weddings, newborns, church activities, birthdays and holiday happenings, the coal camp was lively and festive. Life was difficult: money was hard to come by, yet happy times were plentiful.

In October, Mrs. Coots gave birth to a boy, Joe Bob. Mom gave her the helping hand she needed. When Billy—named for his paternal great grandfather—was born in the early hours of December 13, 1930, Mrs. Coots came to the rescue. "Now Ethel," she said, "There's no need for you to worry about buyin' clothes for Billy. I've got all these clothes that was give to me. They'll be yours for Billy just as soon as Joe Bob outgrows them. That's the way it is here. We look after each other."

Mom was grateful for the hand-me-downs. She had no extra money for baby clothes anyway. She and Dad were way over their heads in debt after buying beds and living room furniture on credit at the company store.

          *   *   *

Though Mrs. Coots was a busy woman with much to do, she still took time to see that Mom had some of what she called the "niceties" for her home. "I want you to have these doilies, Ethel," she said to Mom one day. "Put sugar starch in them if you want to keep them standin' up. Crocheted them myself. They'll look real nice against that pretty new blue mohair sofa."

Mom took the doilies and placed them on the back of the sofa, then stood back to admire them with a look of delightful pride. "Mrs. Coots, you've got to show me how to crochet like this," she said.

"Not a problem," Mrs. Coots said, happy to oblige. "And, I'll show you how to sew on my machine, too. Matter of fact, Ethel, there's a family movin' out down the way. Husband's been killed. Poor thing. She's havin' to sell everthing she's got. Goin' back to live with her Momma. You can get you a nice sewin' machine. She just bought it brand new not more'n a month ago. She'll have to sell everthing she has. She's got to clear out of here by the weekend."

Mom suddenly recalled the family at Crites she had seen move in the middle of the night. Same situation. Husband killed in the mine. Terrible tragedy. It seemed so awful, so cold and so unkind. But she went with Mrs. Coots to see about getting the sewing machine just the same.

"We can't afford it right now, Ethel," Dad said when Mom approached him about buying the machine. "We can't be frivolous with our money. Not now. Every penny I make is already accounted for."

Mom looked a bit dejected, but Mrs. Coots understood just what Dad was saying. "There'll be other opportunities, Ethel," she said, recalling how long she had waited before getting a sewing machine. "Besides, my machine just sits there a lot. You can use it anytime you want. Make you some pretty clothes. I just made this dress." She patted the flowered calico print that still hung shorter in the front than the back even though she was no longer pregnant.

Mrs. Coots walked to the kitchen window and peered out. "Lookathere, would ya Ethel," she announced with pride. "We've got us a regular match up here. There's Lee and Herman, Jacqueline and Mildred, and Billy and Joe Bob. All playin' and havin' a good time. Now ain't we lucky!"

Mom said she thought they should celebrate. "You go put on some coffee, Mrs. Coots. I'll bring over some gingerbread." Mom was elated that she now had time for herself, and she filled her moments with as much pleasure and happiness as she dared.

*　　　*　　　*

June 4th of 1933 was a glorious day, a good day to be out and about. Mountain laurel peeped from across the creek where the trees hovering above it sculpted the hillside with brilliant, contrasting shades of green. Mom's roses were blooming and the hollyhock bush was loaded to bear.

Mom was in the yard gathering green onions, leaf lettuce and radishes from her spring garden when she heard Mrs. Coots call from over the fence. "Ethel, you're expectin' again, ain't you? I bet you're hopin' it's a girl, too!" She took a clothespin from between her teeth and pinched it over the middle of the billowy white sheet she had just hung over the clothesline. After adjusting the forked sapling she used to support the clothesline, she spread her arms wide and gave the sheet an extra fluff before coming to the fence to chat.

"Mrs. Coots, you see all and know all, don't you?" Mom chuckled while giving over some of her pickings to a grateful Mrs. Coots. *What could she say?* It was all she thought about, having a little girl. It wouldn't matter, of course, but she really longed for another baby girl. Her own live doll you might say. Someone she could dress in pretty frocks, someone with long trusses that could be brushed and curled and set with pretty ribbons.

*　　　*　　　*

During carefree moments, fancy prevailed in Mom's imagination, but reality ruled her life. Living everyday with the inconveniences of coal camp life, she bore her burden along with her friends and neighbors and seldom complained.

Besides, living conditions at New Camp were hardly intolerable. In fact, she considered them a pleasure when compared to Marfork and

Crites. There, she had welcomed a good rain to freshen the air. Here, she welcomed the rain to assist with the chores. Mrs. Coots often reminded her, "A good soaking rain is an angel's blessing. It keeps the rain-barrels filled, waters the gardens and settles the dust!"

Rain or shine, folks in the community were out and about during the daylight hours tending to their water needs. With no indoor plumbing, water was toted from one of the outdoor pumps located throughout the community.

Nine-year-old Lee had the water duty most of the time. He could barely carry the buckets half-full, but he didn't mind the task; for in doing so, he found opportunity to meet up with his buddies, who would themselves be carrying water. It was a good time to set the buckets down to give his hands a rest or shift the bucket from left to right to give his arms a rest.

*   *   *

"Hey Lee, wait up a minute." It was Herman, coming on the run.

"Can't play now," Lee said. "Gotta carry two more buckets. Today's wash day."

"Go to the creek. It's faster. Come on, I'll help you."

"Her-man!" called Mrs. Coots. "Get in here."

"Ha, you got to carry your own water!" Lee laughed.

"Nuh-uh," Herman said. "I carried my part. It's Mildred's turn." But, Mrs. Coots thought differently. "Mildred's not strong enough to carry these heavy buckets," she told Herman as she handed him a bucket and ordered him to the creek.

"Come on, Lee. Let's get this done!" Herman said, as he rushed toward the creek.

Washday was an all-day job as it involved carrying and heating water, scrubbing, wringing, rinsing, bleaching, starching, hanging, folding and finally making preparations for ironing, which, though set aside for another day, required a whole new set of tasks with dampening, rolling, heating, ironing, folding and hanging.

Because water had to be carried several times a day, folks found ways to preserve it—which often meant reusing it. The sudsy water from washing clothes was perfect for scrubbing the porches and outdoor toilets. And dishwater and bath water might just as well water the flowers.

In the warm summer months, Mom often sent Lee and Jacqueline to bathe in the creek. Along with their playmates, they skipped rocks, splashed, looked for crawdads and lounged the time away. Kids especially liked the "chute" which was a large solid rock formation that had a smooth and slippery carved-out area in the center. Sliding down the chute and ending up in a little dip, commonly called the "bathtub," was a lot of fun!

"Your Mom and I used to slip off to the creek to bathe, too," Dad once confessed. Weather permitting, this was a special outing for them on the days he worked day shift. He said it was a heck of a lot better than the little NUMBER THREE metal washtub the family used for bathing.

"Clifford had to scrunch up in that tub," Mom later recalled. "His knees were higher than the sides of the tub. I poured water over his head and shoulders so he could wash his arms and face and then I'd wash his back. By this time the water would already be black with coaldust."

"Bathing in the creek was a heck of a lot more gratifying!" Dad said. "It also made for one less chore."

Daily living in the coal camps called for many outdoor chores. Water chores, garden chores, kindling chores, and more. Dad said Lee and Herman knew best how to handle chores. "They even turned slopping hogs into a social event," he said.

Like the Coots and many other families in the coal camp, my family had a hog. The smelly and dirty hogs were kept at collective pens located on a little rise a good distance from the houses. Two big, beautiful beechnut trees grew there. Dad said that when the beechnuts were in, the hogs had plenty of company. Lee and his buddies called it hog heaven!

Mom had plenty of responsibilities of her own, but she always took time to pamper her flowers. Warm spring rains spawned yellow daffodils that lined the sidewalk and the front fence. Soft velvety roses of all colors lined the sides of the house during the summer months before they yielded to asters, mums, dahlias, and marigolds when cobalt autumn skies arrived. She fertilized all her flowers with chicken manure, straight from the coop, or rather, as Lee said; "Whoever cleaned the chicken coop fertilized Mother's flowers!"

On this day, June 4th, with Dad working a second shift and no real need to hurry, Mom decided it a good time to pick some of her favorite white roses. Declaring they smelled "so good," she arranged them in a small bouquet and set off with them to visit her dear friend, Bessie Legg. She and Bessie shared many interests, most of which evolved around the Presbyterian Church where both were actively involved in a women's group called the *Willing Workers,* an organization created to give aid in the form of sewing, baking, or mending for the less fortunate in the community.

Bessie was happy to see Mom. "Ethel, I declare you have the prettiest roses around," she exclaimed. "I can't get mine to bloom like this."

"Have you tried chicken manure?" Mom said with a snicker.

"Ethel, is *that* your secret?" Bessie's blue eyes twinkled and her smooth, rosy cheeks dimpled as she smiled. She ran her hands over her freshly ironed apron and raised her eyebrows, which brought her spectacles down on her nose. She had just washed and set her strawberry blonde hair. Mom said she liked the style.

"It will never look like yours, Ethel."

"It's not supposed to. Each to his own!" Mom said. Her face radiated a light shade of pink as she watched Bessie, whose height matched Mom's, reach high into her cupboard for a can of *Vienna Sausages.* She knew that Bessie would use the sausages to make little sandwiches to which she added mustard and a sprinkling of onions. The sandwiches were a favorite of Mom's.

"Who would've thought Joe Cairns would pass so quickly?" Bessie stated simply as she arranged the sandwiches on a plate and placed them on the kitchen table that was covered with a pale pink tablecloth and graced with Mom's roses. Her blue eyes sparkled as she motioned Mom to sit.

Mom adored Bessie. Bessie had a way of making their visits special, like little girls having a tea party. "Tomorrow, we'll take something over to the Dowdy's, Ethel? They just moved in down at the end of the lane. And, Sue Owers just had a baby boy." Mom listened carefully. She would have news for her husband tonight.

*   *   *

As evening drew nigh, the kids, fed and bathed, gathered around the table model Philco radio to listen to their radio favorites, *Amos and Andy* and *George and Gracie*. Mom listened, too, as she sewed and mended. Lee had a hole in his overalls; Jacqueline had ripped the hem from her dress.

Jacqueline and Billy fell asleep; Lee helped tote them off to bed. "Be sure to bake some of that good gingerbread, Mother," he reminded, before he himself turned in.

"It will be in the bread drawer," Mom assured him as she made her way to the kitchen to bank up the stove with a little extra coal to get the oven hot enough for baking. She had long ago determined that as long as there was a hungry little hand reaching for something in the bread drawer, it would never be empty.

An hour later, with the baking done, she found herself glancing at the clock. Clifford would not arrive for yet another hour, which meant she had plenty of time for herself. She gathered water from the rain-barrel, bathed, applied her special scent and then brushed her hair the necessary fifty strokes. She said the brushing gave it the sheen Dad loved so much.

This was a special time for them, late evening. The kids were asleep and they could talk freely, share their thoughts and the happenings of the day, though Dad would only talk about insignificant happenings at the mines. He never wanted to worry Mom. She knew of the dangers and perils of the coal mines, the close calls, the unexpected explosions and the gas leaks, but they did not talk about these things. He had his job. She had hers. He was not stupid. He would not be careless.

They deliberately kept their conversations light: gossip from the neighborhood, funny things that had happened with the children, stories which would make them both laugh. "Working in the mines was stressful enough," Mom remembered. "Especially when Clifford worked two shifts in a row. He had enough on his mind."

*   *   *

Her thoughts turned to what she would tell him tonight as she took the tub from where it hung on the backside of the house and placed it near the cookstove where it would be nice and warm. She looked forward to greeting her husband and helping to soothe away some of his aches and pains. It was one of the small pleasures she could bring to his life.

Humming one of her favorite hymns, *The Old Rugged Cross,* she laid out a little snack. "Clifford always enjoyed having a small taste of something. He'd say, 'Ethel, what do you have in the drawer today?'"

Moving to the kitchen window she raised the shade and gazed at the dark, night sky. She looked for the sprinkling of stars as they peeped dimly through the flat, streaking clouds. Time was drawing nigh. Clifford would soon be home, and she looked forward to their few precious hours of intimacy before the sun rose and he would too soon be off again to the mines.

3

The Accident

The knock was soft, barely audible. She knew it wasn't Clifford, and she was immediately fearful. Her knees grew weak and her chest cavity sounded an alarm as she cautiously opened the door and looked into the faces of the familiar coal miners. The Stover brothers, Bobby and Carl, stood before her—two big, strong fellows whose funny antics had been fodder for some of Clifford's stories from the mines. She knew something was gravely wrong.

The brothers stood close, as if to give each other support. Bobby, the older of the two, moved forward and said quickly, "Ethel, there's been a slate fall. Cliff's been hurt."

"Bad," Carl added compassionately. "He can't move his legs."

"No, oh no," she gasped. Her eyes froze in terror as she stepped backward with her arms stretched before her as if to push the men back into the darkness whence they came. She backed tightly against the nearest wall where she sought desperately to fend off the terrible news they had brought. *It's only a dream. A nightmare. Please let it be a nightmare!*

She heard the voices of the brothers who remained within arm's length though their faces blurred before her. A sinking feeling of hopelessness and despair came over her and she slid helplessly to the floor. With her back against the wall and chin against her chest, she raised her hands to her face and began to sob. She could not make the nightmare go away.

The two brothers, kneeling beside her, gave her the time she needed to regain her composure before Bobby said, "We're sorry as the devil to bring you this news, Ethel."

"Sorry as can be," Carl said. "It happened so fast. He was giving help when it happened."

Carl looked on with compassion, but finally said, "Ethel, you'll have to go with us to the mine."

"I know, I know," she said through intermittent sobs as she slowly lifted her head and leaned backward. Holding her hands upward for the assistance she had minutes before refused, she rose slowly from the floor. With unbearable sadness overtaking her, she looked about the house as if to know it would never again be the same. She peered within the children's room and saw that they lay snuggled inside the covers of their beds, blessedly unaware of the heartache they would have to face come morning. Then, as if coming to her senses, she turned abruptly and fled to her room to shed her nightclothes while sputtering barely coherent directions over her shoulder to the men, who stood helplessly nearby. "Go next door. Mrs. Coots. Get Mrs. Coots. She'll know.... The kids. Get Mrs. Coots," she said. By the time they returned she was already on her way to the mine.

The men attempted to keep pace with her. They knew she was with child, and they worried that she might stumble in the darkness as she raced ahead of them in deliberate and hurried strides.

By the time they reached the mine, a crowd of men, women and children, alerted by the mine's shrill whistle, which still blew loudly, had already gathered. News traveled fast in the coal camps—especially bad news. Everyone had an urgent need to know whom the injured one was, as it could well be his or her own father, husband, son, or closest friend.

As she pummeled her way through the crowd, she heard bits and pieces of scattered conversation.

"A slate fall."

"Probably a broken back."

"Ambulance is taking too long. He might die before it gets here!"

"A good man. A hard, hard worker."

The crowd moved toward the hoist, or man-trip as some called it, which was a lift used to transport men up and down the hillside to and from the mine. It was located about halfway between the tipple, where coal is cleaned, sorted, processed and loaded, and the lamp house, a building where miners store lamps and other items not taken home each day. She headed for the hoist, knowing her husband would be there.

A flood of fear spilled over her as she looked about in all directions, struggling with all her might to keep her composure and to find the words she was looking for. "Wh…where is he?" she finally stammered.

Many of the onlookers recognized her at once and a sudden, eerie silence fell upon them as they slowly, one by one, lifted their eyes upward—toward the hoist.

She followed their eyes and looked far up the dimly lit mountainside into the darkness where she could see the man-trip begin its slow descent.

With dramatic finality, the whistle ceased blowing and the loud and clamorous machinery began to shut down. The monitor, which normally moved up and down the slope, shrieked to a halt. A deposit of coal fell with one final booming clash into the large coal bin at the top of the tipple, and the drone of a car returning to pick up another load of coal faded into the distance.

The only sound now coming from the shadowy hillside above was the clickety-clack, clickety-clack of the man-trip as it crept slowly down the steep incline toward the silent group of onlookers who had gathered to pay homage to the injured miner. *Clifford* was on his way down.

She stood motionless as she heard the dreaded words "He can't walk" come down the line and she knew that this was going to be bad. He might even die. She looked in horror as she saw heads begin to lower, symbolizing the profound sorrow the onlookers felt for their fellow worker, and she succumbed at last to the fears that by now overwhelmed her. Unable to "hold on" any longer, she sobbed uncontrollably.

A bystander reached out to console her and she graciously accepted the much-needed comfort though she knew and understood that the one consoling was also relieved that the injured was not one of her own. There were sordid consequences for families after such tragic accidents. Those gathered knew fully well what lay ahead for her and for her family. *Clifford won't be able to work. They'll have nowhere to live. How will she get money to live on? What will she do with the kids while she is with him? What if he dies? They have a baby on the way.*

Her thoughts were frantic. *Oh please, dear God, don't take him from us. We love him so.* She looked into the future and saw her children's furrowed brows, their worried eyes imploring her to explain what this all meant. And oh, how she wished that Clifford's injury could somehow blessedly be "fixed." *Please, dear God, please don't take him from us.*

She gripped the hands of the two brothers who had not left her side since bringing her the news, attempting to siphon from them the strength she needed to "hold on." She continued to pray silently, "*Oh, dear God, please let the doctors be able to "fix" him.*" She was so afraid.

The clacking sound of the man-trip became more pronounced as it neared the bottom. As the crowd broke away, she released the hands of the men and rushed forward toward the man trip and to her husband. Though dazed and in shock, she took a few deep breaths as she squared her shoulders and forced herself to stand taller. Clifford must **not** sense her fears.

She first caught sight of the whites of his eyes through the coal dust covering his face. As they made contact he blinked and looked away as if to convey that he had somehow allowed this terrible accident to happen. The doctor was with him, holding his head and listening to his heart. Blood oozed from his nose and from the bandages wound tightly around his torso.

She gently took his hand and put her face close to his, at once feeling the dampness of his tears as they mingled with her own. Touching him gently, she whispered, "I love you Clifford. You'll be all right. You will, I know you will."

She knew that he wanted to tell her something, to somehow explain, but no words came. She followed the movement of his eyes as he looked up and around, and she saw the tears well up. The expression on the faces of those in the crowd told him his situation was bad.

4

The Hospital

The hospital was in Charleston, more than fifty miles away, and the ride in the ambulance was long and harrowing. Strapped tightly to a board and filled with painkillers, Dad drifted in and out of awareness until his eyes glazed over and he fell into a state of unconsciousness. Dr. Williams hovered over him. Mom held onto his hand as her thoughts vacillated between a prayer of *"Oh, God, please help us"* and remorse and regret of *"Oh Clifford, if only you hadn't worked that extra shift."*

Upon arrival at the hospital he was whisked away immediately, and Mom was left to wait with Dr. Williams and the ambulance crew for final word on his condition. She looked to Dr. Williams for encouragement, pleading with him to tell her that her husband would not die, that he would be all right, but the doctor would give no such assurance. "Mrs. White," he said, "I truly wish I could be more encouraging. His injury is really bad. We'll just have to see what the doctors have to say."

Mom paced the hallways as the waiting and not knowing seemed an endless amount of time. Her eyes pleaded for some sort of comfort from every doctor who came from behind any door. Finally, in the wee hours of morning, a drained and anguished-looking doctor appeared. He motioned Mom, who had risen halfway from her chair in anticipation, to remain seated.

"Mrs. White," the doctor began, speaking slowly and compassionately, "your husband has experienced a serious trauma to his body. He has lost a tremendous amount of blood. He has many, many internal injuries. He has broken ribs and his lungs are crushed. His spinal cord has been severed completely. He has no feeling from his waist down. We see no signs of neurological activity, and he doesn't appear to have adequate circulation to his legs. His condition is very serious. We're doing all we can to keep him alive."

Mom rose to face the doctor who had delivered the news. The panic inside her exploded as she asked, "Does this mean he's going to die?" Her voice seemed not her own, and her eyes begged not to be answered in the affirmative.

"He's very, very weak," the doctor said. "He's had a tremendous shock to his system. Only time will tell."

Whirling, she looked at the doctor's face and at the faces of all those around her. She could see they all expected her husband to die, and she found herself suddenly beset with a strong determination to see them wrong. "He's **going** to live!" she said to those around her. "He's **not** going to die!"

*   *   *

Daylight came creeping through the windows and a new shift of hospital staff came aboard. Mom awoke and sat upright on the waiting-room sofa where as exhaustion had finally overtaken her she had slept fitfully during the past few hours. She was alone. Dr. Williams was gone. He had returned to Ameagle with the ambulance crew. She rose from the sofa and went immediately to inquire about her husband. "He's sleeping, Ma'am. Right now, we cannot tell you more," she was told.

She knew that she looked haggard, but she didn't care. Her immediate concern was for her husband, and she hovered as near to him as she was allowed. A short while later her sister Orphie arrived. Orphie pleaded, "Ethel, you must get something to eat and get yourself some rest."

"But he might die, Orphie, and I won't be with him. I've got to stay with him."

Orphie was persistent. "Let me take you home with me for just a bit. I promise I'll bring you right back."

"Where are the children?" Mom asked of her sister. "Oh, do they know yet?"

Orphie explained that the children were now in *her* care and implored Mom to go with her to see them.

Torn between leaving her husband, who hovered between life and death, and seeing her children, whom she knew were devastated, Mom remained fretful. "Oh, Orphie, what if he calls for me and I'm not here?"

"Ethel, I'll bring you right back," Orphie continued to plead. "I promise."

With reluctance, Mom left the hospital and went to her sister's home where upon arrival she was able to visit with her children. Lee, who was nine, better understood the seriousness of the situation. Jacqueline and Billy did not. They cried as Mom prepared to return to the hospital. Her eyes bright with tears, she forced herself to break away from them and get into the car, where during the ride back to the hospital, she unburdened her fears to Orphie and allowed herself to cry. Orphie comforted her sister as best she could, but she was preparing for the worst. Orphie was doubtful that Dad would live.

Mom stayed at the hospital day and night, taking reprieve only when necessary. From her vantagepoint she watched and listened as the doctors and nurses came and went. She questioned them about her husband's progress. They did not speak to her in encouraging ways, but she nevertheless resolved her position to be that he **would** live and that somehow the two of them would resume their lives together as before.

During the time she was allowed to be near him, she did her best to communicate to him that he was loved and needed. She was the first to notice improvement when during the early part of the third week his eyes became clearer; his skin regained some color and he was slightly more alert. "He's getting better, doctor," she persisted. "I can tell he's getting better."

The doctors acknowledged her astuteness, saying: "Yes, he is, Mrs. White, and truthfully we did not expect to see this kind of improvement. It is encouraging. For right now, he is showing progress. But we must tell you that it is most likely temporary. We are still greatly concerned about the inadequate circulation to his legs. There's an almost certainty that gangrene will eventually set in, and when it does, he will die."

The fear inside her burned. "What can be done?" she questioned. "Can't something be done? You can't just let him die! Isn't there something you can do?"

The doctors weren't sure. They would have to discuss it. After much consultation, they voiced their decision clearly to Dad, who had told them he wanted to know. "Mr. White, we're encouraged that you are seeing some improvement, and we would really like to see you live. Your family would like to see you live. But, we must tell you that we can't determine that there is adequate circulation to your legs. Without circulation, gangrene is sure to set in at some point. Unfortunately, once that happens there is nothing we can do.

Dad knew about gangrene. He had heard the war stories from his brother Corbitt, about men having legs and arms amputated due to gangrene. Tremendously alarmed, he asked, "Isn't there something that can be done to prevent that from happening?"

"There is only one thing we know to do to prevent that from happening and that is to remove your legs."

Using what movement he could, Dad shook his head no. But the doctors went on persuasively. "It's the only way we know of to give you your best chance for extending your life, Mr. White. And it will have to be done now. Immediately. It is not something we can take chances with."

Left to consider the option, Dad hardly slept. It upset him terribly to think of not having his legs. To him, it was like being only "half a man"—an intolerable idea.

"Ethel, I'd as soon die!" he said, after a night of thinking about it.

"Clifford, I've had nightmares thinking about it, too. But, I want you to live. If it's your only chance of living, then you've got to do it."

"Ethel, in my heart I do not believe that I will die. I'm going to get through this."

"But, what about the gangrene, Clifford? The doctor says nothing can be done once it sets in."

"It won't happen, Ethel. It won't."

"Clifford, how can you have so much faith?"

"I just do, Ethel. I really believe that I will walk again; I do. I can't let them cut off my legs. I won't do it." He was barely able to utter the words he felt so intensely, but he made sure he was understood explicitly.

They talked about it at great length, and in the end Mom stood by him as he informed the doctors that amputation would not be acceptable under any terms. His response to the doctors was an, "Absolutely not!"

And so he lay there struggling with what would be his fate. He was paralyzed from the waist down and barely able to move his head and fingers, yet he was determined that the doctors were wrong, that he would not die, and that he **would** walk again.

5

Discharged

Mom wanted the nightmare to end and be over. She wanted her life to be what it had been a month before, and the years before that. She knew that time was precious, and she pleaded, "Stay with us, Clifford. We need you. We have a little one on the way. You know I can't go on without you! We have so much to look forward to."

As her pleas increased, Dad's determination to live intensified. "Please do not be so alarmed, Ethel; I'm not going to die," he told her, barely mouthing the words as he drowsed back and forth in and out of an exhausted state.

During times when he was alert, he implored all those who visited not to worry because he would be all right.

Lee and Jacqueline came to see Dad. Jacqueline, whom Dad called "Sissie", never forgot her visit. Only five-years-old at the time, she remembered the room as seeming to be draped in white sheets. She could barely distinguish Dad's dark curly hair as it emerged from somewhere near the top of the bed. "Somehow," she recalled, "he managed to turn his head and look down at me. He was so white looking and his movements were so slow. Yet, he found enough strength to smile and say, 'Now Sissie, I'm going to be all right. Don't you worry, I'll be home soon.'"

On one of his mother's visits, he told her decidedly that he would soon be back on the farm to help her out.

"Oh, Clifford," she told him, "I'm praying hard for you. We all are. Mrs. Pickering is meeting with a prayer group right now. Preacher Baugh has prayed long and hard. God hears your prayers. He knows where you are, and he's with you this very minute. He holds you in his hands. He will see you through."

"I appreciate the prayers, Mom," Dad said. "Thank everyone who is praying for me. Tell them I won't disappoint them." Rosabelle smiled as his voice faded away. "I love you, son," she said before being ushered from the room.

During the next two weeks, Dad's condition remained much the same with no changes for the better or for the worse. Without amputation, the doctors were certain that it was just a matter of time and saw no reason to keep him longer. They discharged him to go home.

"Mrs. White, we cannot do anything more for him here," the doctor said. "We're going to release him to your care, allow you to take him home."

The abrupt decision to discharge Dad from the hospital left Mom perplexed. "Does this mean he's going to live?" she asked, her feelings somewhere between skepticism and hope.

"I wish we could be more encouraging," one doctor said. "But, we don't want to get your hopes up; there could be a deterioration of his condition at any time. You'll have to be prepared for that."

"He is very, very weak," another doctor told her. "Truthfully, we really don't expect any further improvement. I wish we could say otherwise."

"He'll be able to eat pretty much what he wants," the first doctor went on, but Mom was no longer listening. Somewhat dazed and with heavy heart, she imagined the worst. With her were Dad's brother Coy, who was on furlough from the Navy, and her sister Orphie. All were stunned.

Coy turned his pleas to the doctor. "Isn't there something else you can do for him? Some place else you can send him? He's got the will to live. He just needs a chance." Seeing the answer to his questions in the doctor's face, he sat down with Mom and Orphie. They all cried.

The doctor was compassionate. "I truly wish I could give you more hope. I know this is very hard for all of you."

For Mom, the news was unbearable. Away from Dad, she allowed her fear for their future to finally break loose. She turned to Coy, who loved his brother as dearly as she did, and implored, "What will I do, Coy? I have no one to help me with him. He will have no doctor. What am I going to do for food? We'll have no money. What if we have to move out of the house?"

It broke Coy up. He searched for the strength he needed in order to give his sister-in-law the support she was seeking. "Ethel," he said through tears and anguish, "I would gladly give a leg if it would help him walk again. The doctors don't give us much hope. We'll just have to put our trust in God to help us through this. Cliff is determined. He wants to live. We'll do all we can."

Orphie embraced her sister tenderly. "We'll all help, Ethel," she said. "We'll work out a plan of some sort. Someone will be there when you need them."

"But we live so far away."

"There's plenty enough of us that we can take turns, Ethel," Coy said. "We won't let you bear this burden alone."

Mom said she was grateful. She realized it was the best they could do for the moment.

Once more she pleaded with the doctors. "Isn't there somewhere else I could take him? You can't just send him home to die."

"Mrs. White, we're not sending him home to die," the doctor said. "We know of nothing else to do."

The doctors looked on in pity and continued to give directions to Mom on how to care for a paraplegic. He would be confined to bed. No crutches. No braces. No wheelchair. No hospital bed. She would need to bathe him, help him with urination and with his bowel movements. Turn him. Give him medication. Change his bandages.

"We suggest you keep him as comfortable as possible. Keep him very still at all times. Any unusual movement could bring on worse paralysis or gangrene, or even death," they told her.

"I don't know if I'll be able to do all these things," she said.

"Do you have someone who'll be able to stay with you, to help you out?"

"Her family will help," Orphie spoke up. "She'll have someone with her when she needs them."

"That is good to know," the doctor said. "This is going to be a tough job."

Mom went to give Dad the news. "Clifford, you're going home," she told him in a cheerful voice. "Coy is taking me home today, and we're going to get set up for you. You'll come in the ambulance, tomorrow. Coy's going to stay with us for a few days and then Orphie said she'd come. After that, Mom will come. In fact, the whole family has volunteered. You'll have lots of company! The kids are excited."

Dad smiled through tears of joy. "Ethel, I love you so much," he said. She hugged him gently and wiped away his tears. "I love you too, Clifford."

"Tell Sissie," he said, his voice choking, "that I'll be coming home."

6

Homecoming

M rs. Coots came to the gate as Mom and Coy arrived. She had been the good and loyal neighbor who had stayed in touch with the family, passing information on to others in the community.

"This here's Clifford's brother Coy," Mom said. "He's going to help me set up for Clifford. We're bringing him home tomorrow."

"Glad to meet you, Coy." Mrs. Coots said, extending her hand.

"Same here, Mrs. Coots," Coy said, tipping his hat as he shook her hand.

"You look a good bit like your brother."

"Lots of folks say that. Poor Cliff. He's got a tough row to hoe. I wish like the dickens that he could undo what's been done."

Mrs. Coots, suddenly at a loss for words, shook her head in agreement. She had been given to believe that Dad would live only a short while, and she was gravely concerned for the family. "Ethel, what will you do, honey?" she said. "How long did they give him to live?"

"Clifford's going to live, Mrs. Coots. He's **going** to live."

"Oh glory, Ethel, I pray with all my heart that he does."

"We're just going to need so much help."

"Now, honey, I've talked to everbody around here. There's plenty of folks around ready to give you a helpin' hand. Don't you hesitate to ask when you need somethin'—anything."

Coy excused himself to go into the house to begin preparations.

Tears flooded Mom's eyes again as she continued her talk with Mrs. Coots. "We're just so lucky to have neighbors like we have," she said. "My mom said she would help us, too. Lord knows how. She's got problems enough of her own."

"What about insurance, Ethel," Mrs. Coots went on. "Don't Clifford have some insurance?"

"Yes, but it's no good. He's been payin' four dollars a month for insurance since he started in the mines in 1921, but it's not worth the paper it's printed on. It don't provide a thing for paralysis. It won't pay a penny," Mom answered.

"That's disgusting." Mrs. Coots remarked. Her hands were on her hips! Her lips tightened. She was ready to do battle. "Well, what about the mine superintendent? Have you been to see him? Won't he do something to help? Ethel, you've got to have some help!"

"I've already been there, Mrs. Coots. May as well have been talking to the deaf. He told me he was real sorry for me and for my family. I think he was surprised Clifford was still alive. Said he'd think about the house. What on earth will I do if they make us leave the house?"

"You'd think they'd have some feelin'," Mrs. Coots said, stomping lightly. "Can't they see you're expectin'? What on earth do they expect you to do?"

Mom looked as though she might break into tears again any second. Mrs. Coots put her arms around her and patted her back.

"Well, don't you worry, honey, somethin' will work out for you. Folks here in the neighborhood will do what we can. Bessie and Mary Gillespie have already said they'll help with the meals, take turns for a few days. What about money? Have you saved any money? Clifford was gettin' all that overtime. I was hopin' you'd saved a little money."

"We saved some. Not much. Most of it's already gone," Mom said with resignation, disengaging herself from Mrs. Coots and turning toward the house. Money was a huge concern. No one she knew had any to spare.

Mrs. Coots did not expect Dad to live. She thought that sooner or later she would have new neighbors. That's the way it was in the coal camps. "There'll be plenty of men in line to get Clifford's job," she said. "They don't wait a minute once the word gets out. Feller down the lane got his hand all smashed up about two years ago. They was men there askin' about his job within a week. He went back to work before it healed. Had too. A injured miner ain't no use to the mine."

*   *   *

Once inside the house, feelings of pent-up sorrow overtook Mom as she looked about the bedroom she had once so happily shared with her husband. Now it would be only *his* room. Actually, it was to become the boys' room because she was moving Lee and Billy in also.

Coy wasn't sure it would work. "Ethel," he said, "this room's not big enough for two beds. Besides, them boys shouldn't be in here with Clifford what with all that he's going to have to be put through."

"We have to make it work, Coy. We'll need all the room we can spare for sleeping. The boys will understand. I've got to save the sofa in the front room for visitors. There'll be someone here a lot of the time."

"That's true," Coy conceded, as he helped dismantle the iron bedstead and reassemble it in the next room.

"See," Mom said. "There's space enough. Anyway, Clifford will like having the boys in the room with him. He's a people person. When he feels better, they'll be good company. Jacqueline can sleep with me for now. Its time she had a bed anyway. She's been sleeping on a pallet on the floor just about all her life."

Looking back into Dad's room, Coy said, "Yeah, it don't look too bad, Ethel. I guess it will work. There's more room in here than I thought. We'll need to move this wardrobe over a bit, though, out of the way here. And Cliff's going to have to have some place for his medications and medical supplies. Do you have anything?"

Hauling a double sized wooden food crate from the kitchen, Mom asked if it would do. "The drinking water can go back onto the porch," she said.

She brought the radio from the front room and placed it on the nightstand between the beds. "He'll want the radio," she said. "It will keep him company."

"Do you have anything for him to read?" Coy asked as he checked the open light bulb hanging from the ceiling in the middle of the room. "When he feels better, he'll want to read. He always has liked to read."

"I'll get Bessie to help me with that. She can get him some things through the church," Mom said.

Coy looked around. "I guess he'll have enough light from the windows during the day."

A light knock sounded at the open door. Mom rushed to greet her friend with open arms. "Oh, Bessie, it's been a nightmare. I don't know how I'm going to deal with all this."

Bessie set aside the dish of food she was carrying and took Mom's hands. "Ethel, I'm just so, so sorry," she said. "Mrs. Coots has told me everything. Who would ever have thought? You're bringing him home tomorrow, right?"

"We're getting ready for him now."

Bessie turned to Coy. "You would be Clifford's brother?"

Coy extended his hand. "Name's Coy."

"I'm Bessie Legg, a friend of the family. I've brought you both over a bite to eat. Not much, but it'll hold you over."

"That's mighty kind of you, Bessie," Coy said. "I could use a little something right about now."

"Bessie always appears right about the time you need her most," Mom said.

"Maybe there's something I can help you do while I'm here," Bessie offered.

"Thank you just the same, but we've just about got her licked," Coy said. "We'll be headin' back out shortly."

"Then I won't linger," Bessie said.

The women exchanged hugs, and Bessie turned to leave. As she passed through the open door, she turned back, saying, "Ethel, now I've already spoken with Reverend Pindar. He'll come by to see Clifford in a day or so. There'll be some help coming from the church. You can count on that. We've already gathered a good supply of canned food." Then Bessie left with a sad but reassuring smile.

*   *   *

Folks came from all over the neighborhood as they saw the ambulance pull up to the front of the house. Some wanted to speak to Dad, to say how sorry they felt about not being able to visit him at the hospital, and some just wanted to see what a paralyzed man looked like.

"Oh, Ethel, he looks so bad, honey. Are you sure he's going to be all right?" Mrs. Coots asked when out of hearing distance of Dad.

"The doctors didn't give us much hope, Mrs. Coots. It's going to be real rough; we know it. But Clifford is determined to live. He **will** live." Straightening her shoulders, she held Mrs. Coots's hands between her own as she implored, "Oh, Mrs. Coots, I love him so. Why did this have to happen to us?"

"Ethel, the Lord works in mysterious ways. Maybe we'll understand in due time."

"I'll talk with you every day, Mrs. Coots. I know I can come to you when I'm down and out. I can't let Clifford ever see me like this."

"Ethel, I'm here anytime you need me. Told you that when you first moved in here. Nothin's changed."

7

For Better or for Worse

Maybe it was because Dad had been in the hospital for so long, or maybe it was because Mom was with child and everyone expected that Dad would soon die, or maybe it was because someone in the coal company had a change of heart, Mom did not know, but somehow she was granted a waiver on the rent and was told that the family could remain in the house.

Ecstatic over the news, she hurried to tell Dad. "They're letting us keep the house, Clifford. And we don't have to pay rent. Not yet, anyway!"

"Oh, thank God. That's a blessing," Dad said weakly, mostly under his breath.

Pacing back and forth, with the stern look of a fierce warrior, Mom showed that she was prepared and ready to defend her domain. "We'll take this day by day, Clifford," she said. "Day by day!"

Dad gave her a faint smile. To know they now at least had the security of a place to live was one less worry for him as he lay helplessly confined to a bed on one side of a bedroom—his life shattered, no money, no job and unable to have sex with his beautiful wife. He was thirty years old.

During much of the day and part of the night, Mom was at his side tending to all his personal needs, careful to give him as much privacy as possible. For Dad it was agony. "Ethel, I wish with all my heart that you did not have to do this," he told her. But Mom answered him lightheartedly.

"Clifford, I married you for better or for worse and this is the worse, but it's certainly no time for you to go getting embarrassed. Besides, you don't have a thing I've not seen before."

She kept his room light and airy, the door open, the shades up, and the curtains pulled back during the day to ward off those times when he might feel claustrophobic, all cramped up as he was in one corner of the room. The walls were bare except for his hats and a calendar Mom had hung close to his bed. The only real color came from the fresh flowers Mom kept about, but Dad declared the room was a right smart better than the hospital. "Here I have Ethel's beautiful flowers, the boys to keep me company and a lovely wife to look upon each day." He said the cheerful atmosphere was healing.

Dr. Williams, who continued to check on Dad frequently, though not expected to since he was the company doctor and Dad was no longer affiliated with the coal mine, said he also thought home was a right smart better than the hospital. "You've got yourself a loving and good wife, Clifford. Now you behave yourself and make life easy for her. Having your boys in here with you will keep you good company, too. You'll not have time to get bored."

"I'm blessed, and I know it," Dad told the doctor weakly. "As soon as I can get these legs moving again, I'm going to take Ethel dancing."

"Listen to him. He never took me dancin' in his life," Mom retorted, though she blushed with delight at the thought.

"Well, there's always a first time, Ethel," Dad said, his voice attempting assurance. "I'll dance on the moon when I get these legs going again."

"I'd sure like to see that," Lee said, entering from the back porch, his nine-year-old arms laden with kindling wood for the cook stove. "Now, *Mother* can dance. I've seen her. But Dad, now, he just might be tellin' one."

Laughing, Mom rose to assist Lee with the wood by taking a few pieces at a time and placing them in the kindling box behind the kitchen stove. Then, giving him a hug and a pinch to the cheeks, she said to him: "What would I do without you, Lee? You've helped me so much."

Used to the hugs and praise, Lee just grinned.

"You've got a good boy, there," Dr. Williams said as he stooped to listen once more to Dad's heart. Rising, he said, "Sounds a wee bit stronger, Clifford. Must be all this talk about dancing." A wide grin spread across his broad and rosy face as he put his stethoscope into his bag and prepared to leave.

Mom sat at the edge of Dad's bed. "Clifford," she said, while pointing in the direction of the doctor, "you can bet I'm gonna hold you to your promise. Dr. Williams here is my witness. You can't move these legs now, but when you can, you **are** going to dance! He'll dance!" Her face shone pink as she rose to see the doctor out.

At the door, she spoke softly. "Dr. Williams, I don't have any money to pay you right now, but as soon as I'm able, I will take care of this bill. I don't know what I would have done without you. You've been so good to come here like you have."

Dr. Williams only shook his head. "Ethel," he said as he stepped out onto the porch, "don't you even think about paying me. It makes me feel good inside to be able to help you. I'm awfully sorry this has happened. I wish it could have turned out differently."

Mom looked at the doctor with strong admiration. "You know we don't want to take charity," she said. "But we have no choice right now. Someday I'll find a way to repay you."

Still shaking his head no, the doctor said, "Clifford's a good man, Ethel. Just take care of him as best you can. I'll be around every now and then. I've left you some bandages and cotton gauze, some antiseptics and some tape. You have a lot on you, honey. You'll need all the help you can get. Now take care of yourself, too. And, when your time comes, you send for me. Hear?"

Mom said she truly appreciated these and other acts of kindness from people in the community. She was now the sole provider for her family. "I know I can't do it alone," she said. "I need lots and lots of help."

*   *   *

The garden had dried up while the family had been away during Dad's stay in the hospital. But, with the help of family, friends and neighbors who shared from their own gardens Mom soon had much in the way of canned foods. With at least some provisions, she knew they would not starve.

As planned, family members came periodically to give help. Usually arriving one at a time, they quickly made themselves at home. The males slept on the mohair sofa in the living room and the females slept in the bedroom with Mom and Jacqueline.

Lee was given additional responsibilities. He helped with the laundry, carried water, slopped the hogs, fed the chickens, chopped wood, cleaned the chicken coop and helped in the kitchen. And, in between, he kept the kids out of the house. While there had to be times when he ached to get away from it all, Lee would simply say, "Mother, what do you need me to do?" His friends soon stopped inviting him to join in the fun. He was always too busy helping with the family chores.

Knowing that young children do not seem to understand the seriousness of such matters, Mom conveyed to them that things would be better soon. "Just run on with Lee and play," Mom would say to Jacqueline and Billy. Lee would take them to play in the alleys, in the yard, or at the creek. Under his watchful eyes, they were happy.

8

Watching

During those first months at home, Dad could only move his head from side to side, lift his arms, and move his fingers. Truly weak and utterly helpless, he could only *watch* what was going on around him.

He *watched* as his wife labored to run the household, care for the children, and tend to all of his needs. He *watched* as she grew larger each day as the baby grew inside her womb. He *watched* as the neighbors came to bring food or to "give Ethel a moment to rest." He *watched* as family members came and helped in whatever ways they could before they went on their way. He *watched* as Billy and "Sissie" cried and clamored for the attention they needed. He *watched* as his son Lee assumed many of *his* manly responsibilities. And, because he could do nothing but *watch*, his heart ached.

He realized that this had to be the lowest point in his life. Depression could easily have set in, but as he watched his wife and his son Lee assume the family responsibilities he knew that if they didn't give up then neither could he. In later years, he told everyone, "If it hadn't been for Ethel, I don't think I could have made it. She kept everything going. She never gave up hope."

Indeed, Mom did sense his thoughts of despair. She did what she could to keep his spirits up. She would climb onto his bed, stroke his hair, and lightly massage away his pain as she engaged him in conversation. She would say, "Clifford, what do you think we should name the baby?" getting him to focus on something positive and, at least for the moment, offer an escape from his helplessness. They concentrated mostly on names for a girl because that is what she wanted most of all. They settled on the name Mary for a girl but if it were a boy Edward sounded good.

Only a few visitors were allowed as Dad still required much care and was too weak to visit with anyone for very long. Mom always greeted visitors graciously though and thanked them for coming. Not letting her husband know how tired and weary she was, she welcomed the opportunity to sit and socialize for a few minutes.

*   *   *

Mrs. Coots was a frequent visitor. "I've brought you a pot of pole beans and new potatoes fresh from the garden," she said one hot summer day, stepping onto the back porch, then on into the kitchen.

"On a day like this! The heat will kill you." Mom said.

"When the gardens come in, you've got to work them, heat or no heat. Anyways, Herman and Lee did all the pickin'. All I did was the cookin'."

"Next year, we'll have us a garden again," Mom said as she took the pot of beans from Mrs. Coots and carried it to the door of Dad's bedroom. "Look, Clifford," she said. "Mrs. Coots has brought us some fresh pole beans, right from the garden."

Dad raised a hand and gave Mrs. Coots a weak wave. He liked her. Her presence cheered him, he said.

"See, Mrs. Coots, don't Clifford look better?" Mom said. "He even let me read to him a little today."

"She reads me love stories. Then she cries," Dad commented softly.

"Oh, goodness, Ethel." Mrs. Coots muffled a laugh as she looked in on Dad through the doorway. "Clifford, I'd say you look a right smart better. Maybe those love stories are doin' you some good."

"And helping me, too," Dad said with a smile.

Mrs. Coots did not linger. Smiling, she began to make her exit. "Hope you like the beans, Clifford. I'll be on my way now."

As she neared the kitchen door, she turned to Mom, saying, "How are *you* doin', honey? Is there somethin' I can help you with?"

"You're already doin' more than enough. Cookin' for us, takin' care of the kids.

"Aw, think nothin' of it, Ethel. Anyways, the kids, they just go off and play. Don't bother me none. Besides, Lee watches Jacqueline and Billy as much as I do. Just you take care of yourself, honey. You gotta take care of the little one, now." She patted Mom's tummy and closed the door lightly behind her, only to open it again and say quietly, "Now don't forget, school starts right after Labor Day. I've got some clothes for the kids, gathered from neighbors around. Should fit pretty well. Nancy Pettry's boy is a year older than Lee and Herman. Gave me some right nice overalls. And Sue Olson had dresses for Jacqueline. They're a little big, but you can take them up a bit. They'll be just fine."

*   *   *

They had saved a little money when Dad was working, but with Lee and Jacqueline needing clothes and shoes for school and the everyday needs of running a household the meager savings had been used up quickly. There was **no** income until Dad began receiving a worker's compensation check of $69.52 a month for a family of five, soon to be six.

When the first check came, more than three months after the accident, Mom danced with joy. She tore into Dad's room waving the check back and forth. "Clifford, now at least we know we have something coming in," she exclaimed. "It's not much, but you'll see what I can do with $69.52." She was on her way to the store right then.

But Dad knew just how little $69.52 was. He knew that no matter how she stretched it, it would never be enough. This worried him. He hated *watching* as his family became more and more dependent on charity.

9

Looking Back

Dad had a lot of time to think as he lay on his back day in and day out wishing with all his heart that he had back the life he'd had before the accident—before all his hopes and dreams had been shattered around him. He yearned to be able to walk, to hold, to touch, to see, and to smell those things that were now beyond him. He tried to hide his feelings of despair, but Mom often found him sobbing. She knew she could not succumb to her own grief, so she aimed to help him get beyond his misery as best she could.

She drew him into conversations by asking him to tell her about his childhood, what his life was like before she knew him. She listened as he recalled his past, his childhood days, the good times and the bad.

*　　　　　*　　　　　*

His parents, Odie Opie and Rosabelle Hurst White, whose families had descended from the British Isles, came from fourth generation farmers who had settled in the Lashmeet area in Mercer County. Opie came from a long line of Whites, most of whom had huge families. He himself was the youngest of ten. Rosabelle descended through the Hursts and the Baileys, both well-known names in the area.

Even as a young girl, Rosabelle stood out. *Everyone* knew Rosie and found delight in her conversational skills and her diverse interests in so many things. She'd been schooled and had been fortunate enough to learn to read music, to play the organ and to sing.

Opie found Rosabelle's charming wit and natural beauty hard to resist too, even once or twice attending services at the Primitive Baptist Church—though he wasn't much on going to church—because he knew Rosabelle sang solos in the choir. Figuring she was a good catch, Opie pursued Rosabelle, 'til one day *she* caught him and by then it was too late. They married on March 30, 1892 and had their first born, a son named Corbitt, in the year 1894.

Getting started on the small farm given them by Rosabelle's parents was easy. Opie worked the land and Rosabelle tended the garden and the farm animals, and when called upon extended her nursing skills to others in the community. The children came regularly two years apart. Soon there were six of them with names beginning with the letter "C"— Corbitt, Connie, Cova, Clifford, Coy and Claudia. As was the custom of many from her religious faith, Rosabelle wanted her children to begin their lives as Christians and the letter "C" at the beginning of their names signified that before all else they would be first a Christian.

By the early 1900's, industrialization had already caused sweeping changes in the economy and farming a small piece of land, as a viable way to make a living, was soon becoming a thing of the past. The coal industry was opening new ground in southern West Virginia. Mining communities, with all necessary conveniences of shelter, a company store for food and clothing, company doctor and post offices were springing up all over. Some mining camps had more elaborate buildings including saloons, boarding houses, barbershops, schools and churches. Men, enticed with the thoughts of big wages, decent housing and a good way of life for their families, came from all over to mine the coal.

In the summer of 1906, Opie and Rosabelle realized that they could no longer provide for their family by farming and Opie said he must do something about it. With reluctance, he took his family and a few precious belongings and left the pastoral life of Mercer County's gentle rolling hills and long, wide valleys to follow other family members to the coalfields of neighboring counties: Raleigh, Mingo, Logan and Kanawha. In these more rugged and steeper mountains lay the coal that was going to transform their lives. They traveled by means of horse and wagon, using the dirt roads that paralleled the meandering rivers or the railroads that hugged the bottoms of the mountains. Migrating from one coal community to the next, they looked for the favored one—the one that would provide reliable work and regular income for their family.

But, they were duped. Though mining jobs were to be found, the quality of life was not. Pay was minimal and given mostly in the form of "scrip" which could only be exchanged at the company store. Like other miners in the same situation, they soon found themselves indebted to and at the mercy of the coal company.

With no means to better their condition, coal miners had begun the process of unionization, which brought on mining wars and much discontent. Opie believed strongly in the movement and soon became a leader among union sympathizers. But, once identified as a union promoter, he was duly harassed. At one job in Mingo County, mine officials stopped him as he left work one day and told him that he had best be out of town by daybreak. Not easily intimidated, Opie looked his messengers in the eye and said, "Well, fellers, I don't know just when daybreak will be, but I'm not leavin' 'til I get my paycheck." His check was delivered on the spot and Opie reasoned that for his safety and the safety of his family he had best leave town. It was on this move that two-year-old Claudia came down with diphtheria and subsequently died. Her death left the family terribly distraught. Dad was six. He missed his baby sister and did not understand what had happened to her.

Opie cursed the God who would allow this to happen to his family, but Rosabelle hushed him saying that God's will was not to be questioned. She suffered immensely, but could not bring herself to blame God. Her faith was far too strong.

As they moved from one mining community to the next, Opie was often forced to sign a "yellow dog" contract before he was given a job. The contract was the coal operator's way of extracting a promise from the miner who was seeking employment that he would not be a troublemaker, that he would not be seen with more than two miners at any one time and that he would not join the union. It broke Opie's spirit but he signed the contracts, always assuring himself that it would be temporary. He had to have work. However, he could not compromise his beliefs for long and one day crossed the line. "Those mine operator's detectives were down on me quicker than the strike of a rattlesnake," he told his wife. Opie and his family were forced to move again. That his actions resulted in a forced move for his family concerned him greatly, but he said he just could not let his fellow workers down.

*　　　　　*　　　　　*

Loading the wagon and hitching his team of horses, Opie became frustrated. "Confound it," he said, "this is one hellacious way to live. We've just lost a child; Rosabelle is ready to have another youngin, and we're havin' to move! This minin' will be the death of me yet. We're not a lick better off than we were over at Lashmeet, farmin'." And Rosabelle agreed. She hoped and prayed that some day they would return to the farm. Her heart and soul belonged there—with her kinfolk, her church, and a way of life she considered worth living. But Opie said it would be no use. Returning to the farm would only set them back even more he said. There would be no going back.

They headed to Raleigh County. Opie had learned from other miners on the move that mine operators there were more sympathetic to the coal miner. They got as far as the outskirts of a place called Brooks before Rosabelle said, "Opie, you need go no further. The baby's coming tonight. I know it is."

"Rosie, I'm sorry as can be. Ain't no way for a woman to have a youngin' I know, but by hang we'll do the best we can." Rosabelle was less concerned. She knew just what to do. She had no fear of childbirth. "Stop along the river bank," she told him. "Find some nice shade trees. We'll set up camp and make do 'til we can travel on. You'll have to deliver the baby, Opie."

The weather was accommodating, actually pleasant for mid-July, though the flies were annoying. Rosabelle gave the orders. The wagon was quickly made into a birthing room, complete with a rope for Rosie to pull on when the contractions came too hard. A fire was built and a kettle of water was kept boiling. When Rosabelle was satisfied that all necessary items were prepared and placed nearby, she gave the final instructions and cautioned Opie and the kids to get some rest. She'd waken them when the time came.

At about 4 a.m., when she could endure the pain no longer, Rosabelle shook Opie's shoulder. "Opie, the baby is coming," she said. "Wake the kids and get ready." Opie knew she gave him little time, so he hustled as he worked by the light of a lantern. Corbitt and Connie took their jobs seriously as they kept the fire hot and the water boiling so that they could keep sterile cloths ready to pass to their dad. Cova positioned herself close by her mother where she could wipe her brow and keep the flies away. Dad and Coy were left to sleep.

Rosie puffed and breathed rhythmically while holding onto the rope when the pain became too much to bear. Finally, after all were nearly exhausted, the baby just seemed to pop out all at once. Cova cried out, "It's a girl!" Corbitt and Connie came running to see but quickly turned away as they were repulsed by how the baby looked with all the birthing fluids still on her.

Rosabelle gave further instructions and then lay resting as Opie severed the umbilical cord, tied it off and then held the baby upside down as he administered a spank to which the infant responded with a loud squeal. Then the baby was laid across Rosabelle's breast for a brief spell before being handed over to Cova for cleaning. Opie pushed hard on Rosabelle's abdomen until all the afterbirth was out. He then went to bury all the birthing materials while Cova assisted her mother. By daybreak, the only thing different than the day before was the squeal of a newborn baby girl named Cora. Dad and Coy were allowed to hold her. Corbitt and Connie declared that she looked a heck-of-a-lot better than she had looked when first-born.

As soon as Rosabelle declared herself and the baby fit to travel, they packed up their wagon and proceeded on into Raleigh County. Their first stop was at Winding Gulf where after only a few months time work slowed down, and they then moved on to Sanderson, in Kanawha County where in the year 1912 Charles was born. A year later they moved to High Coal in Boone County.

It was a common occurrence for a miner to move to a new community and, within a few months time, be told that work was declining because the coal was running out. When work began to run out at High Coal in 1915, just after their last son Clarence was born, Opie declared he'd move once more and it would be his last! After nine years of being on the road, living in one coal community after another, and not one being any better than the last, he said he wanted his family to stay in one place and be a family.

Opie had heard some of the men at work talk about the town of Blakely, a decent-sized community with a population of approximately 450. He liked what he had heard. He made up his mind that he would go to Blakely, settle there and make do no matter what. And so it was that he prepared his family, in the year 1915, for what was to be their last journey—a move from High Coal, in Raleigh County, to Blakely, in Kanawha County.

He loaded up all of the essentials they would need: clothing, bedding, food and cooking utensils, water, and Rosie's prized possessions of things she had kept with her throughout all their travels, things like quilts and feather ticks. As Opie hitched the wagon to his team and prepared to leave, Rosabelle, who always had lots of friends wherever they lived, went to say her good-byes. Then she called all the kids to board the wagon.

Opie, seeing that the family was now too large for all to ride in the wagon, what with all the other stuff they had to transport, directed the older boys to take turns walking. Nothing, he said, was going to hold them back. Full of hope, they headed off to a place unknown to them. "We're goin' and we're stayin' come hell or high water," Opie declared. "I'm tired to death of movin' around, accumulatin' nothin' but kids and trouble! I want some peace."

The first day out they made camp alongside the Coal River in a beautiful setting of large shade trees. Cova and Cora minded Charles and Clarence while Rosabelle cooked a vegetable stew over the open campfire. The older boys swam and played in the river. Opie, at peace with the world, sat under a tree and smoked his pipe. "It don't get any better than this, Rosie," he wondered aloud. "Why don't we just linger here a few days, give ourselves a chance to feel like human beings again." Rosabelle said nothing as she smiled to herself and went on with her cooking.

That evening they rested comfortably under the dark night sky, down amidst their feather ticks and down coverlets. The older kids had made a soft bed of leaves on which to lay their bedrolls and then lay talking and singing until the last dying embers of their campfire signaled time for sleep. Rosabelle had let them be and just lay listening. She was her happiest when she heard the lovely voices of her children ringing out the melodies she had taught them over the years. Opie basked in the peace he hadn't felt for so long.

But, before the sun began its ascent in the eastern sky, Rosabelle awakened Opie and gave warning: "Opie, I feel it in my bones. There's a storm brewing somewhere. We'd best head out of here." Opie, who had learned to trust Rosabelle's instincts, climbed from his bed and began giving instructions to bleary-eyed kids to break up camp. "We're out of here before daybreak," he said. "You can sleep on the way."

"But, I thought we were going to stay here to fish and play," Corbitt said as Connie moved in to give him backup. "Don't ask any questions, just do as I say," Opie said. "Your mom has a feeling, a bad feeling. We'd best get going."

They worked together in synchronism, as they'd been taught to do, hastily putting everything in place, and by break of dawn they were on the move. The sky had an ominous color as it soon broke forth with rain—heavy rain. Trying to get ahead of the bad weather, Opie drove the horses hard while Rosabelle remained with the kids. But the rain quickly made the ground soggy and the wagon's wheels began to sink into the slush. With not a minute to spare, Opie and Rosabelle began giving urgent directions.

"Stop the wagon, Opie," Rosabelle called. She got out of the wagon and ordered all the kids to do the same: "Corbitt, put Charles on your back; Connie, put Clarence on yours. Clifford, take as much as you can carry into your arms. Cova, you and Cora do the same." Then she gathered up what she herself could carry, and Opie was able to get the wagon moving once again.

As they trudged on ahead, the waters of the river rose higher and Opie knew they must get to higher ground as quickly as possible. Everyone and everything was soaked from the torrential rain, which only made the load heavier. Opie had to make a decision. "The water tanks," he said, "the water will have to go." Corbitt and Connie put their charges down and turned the water tanks on their sides. As the tanks emptied, the wagon became lighter, but it still rolled sluggishly and Opie could make no headway.

The river swelled rapidly. Folks who lived along its banks could be seen heading to higher ground, taking with them the essentials they could carry. Opie made a split decision. "We're going to higher ground," he said. "We'll carry what we can, save what will be saved. The horses will go; the wagon remains." And so, with each carrying as much as they possibly could they began their ascent, going straight uphill. When they had reached a level beyond reach of the flooding waters, they stopped. With nothing to do but wait it out they huddled and cuddled to keep warm, trying to shelter the younger ones amongst the older ones and shushing the crying babies to no avail.

The rushing water pushed fallen debris down the river. The sound of it left a pounding in their ears—a sound they would not forget anytime soon. Rosabelle lamented the loss of some of her more prized possessions as she watched their wagon fall apart and wash downstream—especially the quilt her Grandma Bailey had given her as a wedding present. "But, we're lucky to be alive," she proclaimed to all around her. "No possession is worth the life of one of our family."

Fortunately, the rain was not accompanied by thunder and lightning, and it stopped after two hours of a steady downpour—as quickly as it had started. The sun came out and the river slowly began to subside.

As the drenched and shivering family looked about, they saw that they were not alone. A group of ten or more stood nearby. A pathetic lot they all were, sopping wet and forlorn looking, saddened over the loss of their homes and possessions. The children wailed as parents walked toward one another to seek what small comfort they could find in the sharing of their losses. Only one among the group had a house still standing and once the waters had subsided sufficiently, it was to this house that they all took shelter. Scrambling to find food items among their combined, salvaged possessions, the women in the group prepared johnnycakes.

The women washed and dried clothing; the older girls looked after crying babies, and the men discussed what to do in the aftermath of the destruction. For Opie, it was not an easy matter. He had no wagon and very little money. He went to the nearest mining community and was grateful to find work and housing for his family. They began all over again, though Opie vowed it would be his last. "Rosabelle," he said, "don't waste a penny. We'll do all we can to get out of here and on to Blakely as soon as we can."

Two months later, Corbitt, who was barely of age, volunteered for military service. And Connie, who declared he would never set foot in a coal mine, went to work as a railroad engineer. Rosabelle, saying she could use the extra money, took in two boarders to replace her two sons. All the while, Opie cursed his life in the coal mines.

But Rosabelle had her faith. Again and again she said: "God will see us through this, Opie. He will. I know He will." In the meantime, she wasted no time making herself known in the community. Before long, she was attending church, delivering babies and nursing the ill. Opie never figured her out. "Rosie, you're some woman," he'd say. And she would smile, believing in her heart that God would make a way for them in the near future.

Opie played poker whenever the opportunity presented itself even though Rosabelle was completely against gambling. But there was one time that he played poker and she said nothing. It was on a cold January night in 1916. Opie trudged through the snow to the boarding house where a game was already underway. He hung his coat on a hook near the door and rubbed his hands to warm them as he looked around for a table to his liking before sitting down to play. His money dwindled quickly and he feared that this was not to be his night. He was coming down to his last few dollars before he was dealt a good hand. He knew he had to make it count. He played his best poker he said when the pressure was on. The hand came down to Opie and one other player, who with no money left had put up his wagon. Opie decided that if fate were ever to be favorable to him that this would be the time. He put all he had in the pot and then held his breath as his three kings beat the man's three jacks. Opie walked away with a very nice wagon.

For the first time ever, Rosabelle did not complain about Opie's poker playing. For some reason, she decided that God had answered her prayer and that she was not to question it. Although she felt remorse for the fellow who had lost his wagon, it did not last long. "Opie," she said, "take one of the horses and go to look for our place. I know it's out there somewhere. God didn't give you that wagon otherwise." Pleased to have Rosabelle's blessing, Opie saddled his horse, and went out on his own. After five days on the road, he came to the place (Wills Hollow, an outlying area near Blakely) he decided his family would call home. He liked what he saw: forest, farmland and streams. An ideal place for all his needs, he said.

Opie found work in the nearby coal mines, a house big enough for his family and, for Rosabelle, land enough for a cow, a barn and a garden. He went back for his family.

Wills Hollow proved to be a pleasant place for Rosabelle and the kids. Though his teenage years were full of upheaval, Dad said he always liked Wills Hollow. "It took all of us to keep things running there," he said.

*   *   *

"Cliff, you and Coy take the wheelbarrow and head over to the barn," Dad heard his mother call. "We're going to need four or five loads of manure on the vegetable garden." Rosabelle was on her way outdoors with Charles and Clarence heading in the direction of the chicken pen. Cova and Cora were left to tend to household duties.

"Oh, look," Charles said as he stumbled over an exposed root. His eyes were locked on the old Dominicker hen proudly strutting about the pen with her brood of eight little biddies. Recovering quickly, Charles threw a handful of chicken feed their way and watched in shock as the bigger chickens swooped upon it, pushing the biddies aside.

"Won't do, Charles," Rosabelle said. "The little fellers don't stand a chance. Round them over here to the side where we can separate them out. We'll give them some special biddie food." With no time to waste, Rosabelle used every opportunity for teaching and learning. Her brood of young ones had to be of help to her. There was a multitude of work to do each day.

Dad said it was easier and a lot more fun to help each other with the chores. It made the time go faster and got the chores completed sooner. And the sooner the chores were done, the sooner he could get out to hunt, fish or trap. So, as Coy fed the horse and slopped the hogs, Dad filled the wheelbarrow with manure and then they both headed out to fertilize the vegetables. Their concerted effort earned them at least an hour of leisure time. Both boys set out to do what they liked best.

Finger fishing was often what Dad chose to do. Kneeling beside the creek, he cupped his fingers and slid them under the ledges of rocks along the shore and waited for fish to become trapped beneath. He caught a lot of fish that way. Sometimes enough for supper.

The day was often too short for all Dad wanted to do, and Rosabelle had her agendas as well, as all too soon she would call: "Clifford, round up Coy. We'll be off to church directly. Dust yourselves off. Wash up a bit."

Dad would often find Coy off playing in one of the large open areas of the combined coal camps in some rough-and-tumble game with few rules. On occasion, Coy would be involved in a scrap with another boy, and Dad would have to pull Coy away as the other boys called after them.

"Sissy, Sissy, going home to Momma," Dad would hear while trying to find enough reasons for not going back and taking matters into his own hands. But facing Rosabelle could be worse, so he figured it wasn't worth it.

Saying that team sports were too wild for his tastes, he left them to Coy. Dad preferred being a spectator or engaging in less aggressive games like marbles where he had some control of the situation.

Hunting, fishing and trapping were more to his liking. Hunting, fishing and trapping put food on the table. He was one of the breadwinners for the family.

*　　　　　*　　　　　*

Rosabelle put schooling, religion and chores first, mostly religion, but Dad still found time for fun and sport.

At school is where he first saw my mother. She sat in the second row with the young ones, and he in the fourth. Dad said her beauty and demeanor intrigued him. He'd lose his place in his lessons while he watched her pretty shining, dark auburn hair bounce around as she moved her head from side to side. He'd end up getting his knuckles rapped as he received sharp reprimands from the teacher, but he said he didn't care because it usually resulted in Mom turning around and giving him a soft look of sympathy.

The two had a budding interest in each other, but they weren't destined to have a romance so soon. Both had some growing up to do.

Actually, Dad's youthful freedom ended early. Just four months after he turned thirteen, Opie began to take him and his younger brother Coy into the coal mines to help him load coal. Miners were paid for each car they loaded, and Opie could never load enough cars to make the money he needed for his family. So he took his sons to live with him in boarding houses as he moved about to find work—though Will's Hollow remained their home place.

"Boys," Opie told his sons, "I've got no choice. Too many mouths to feed, too many shoes to buy."

Since child labor laws were not yet in effect, Dad and Coy were able to travel with Opie wherever he found work and help him to make the extra money the family needed. "It's a man's world out here, boys," Opie informed them. "Stay close to me, or close to one of the men you can trust. Safety is your number one concern. Men get hurt or killed all the time. Boarding houses can be rough, too. Won't be like your mom's cooking, neither. But, we won't be gone long now. We'll make some money and get on back here, help your mom out on the farm. She needs all the hands she can get."

Dad and Coy each earned fifty cents a day. The money went straight to the family coffer.

Dad's first job in the mines was to keep an eye on the little bird. "You never wanted to see a dead canary," he said. A dead canary meant a gas leak and the possibilities of an explosion.

Dad found lots of "mine sayings" during his work with Opie. He said his hard hat saved his head more times than once, as he often forgot that he was stooping for a reason and would suddenly stand up only to meet up with a low ceiling. He never knew what it was like to have back pain until when for the first night or two in the mines he couldn't straighten his back. He learned what "pitch dark" meant, 'cause in the mines, there was no light except for the carbide lantern he wore on his hat, which sometimes went out on him and he couldn't see his hand in front of his face.

He dreaded hearing the words "Fire in the hole" that meant someone was putting off shot somewhere in the mine and there would soon be a big explosion. Once a blast deafened him for a brief period of time and left a ringing in his ears.

He didn't mind the cold and dampness inside the mountain too much. At least, it was the same temperature year round. Wearing long underwear helped to keep him warm.

He and Coy stayed awake many a night after hearing the ghost tales. Many lives were lost in the mines, and it was not uncommon for some-one to claim to have seen the ghost(s) of the dead miner(s).

The story that bothered him the most was *The Ghosts of the Gulf,* a story often told at the mine at Winding Gulf in Raleigh County. As the story goes, a slate fall and cave-in happened soon after the mine opened. Men and their sons were trapped deep within the mine, in the left entry of No.16 after a cave-in had sealed them off. Though an attempt had been made to dig them out, another timber had collapsed causing another cave-in and the rescuers had been forced to abandon their mission. Once the coal operators decided that there was no way the miners could be rescued, the men and their sons were left to die though their faint cries for help could still be heard. The entrance to No. 16 was sealed off, but work still continued in surrounding areas. Men working in these nearby areas often reported seeing shadows on the walls, shadows they said looked like two big strapping miners carrying young boys on their backs. Some claimed to hear faint screams for help and mournful cries as they entered the area. Some lost their jobs because they refused to work in that part of the mine they called "*hainted*."

Even with the tales of ghosts in the mines, Dad said that working in the mines soon grew natural for him and Coy. They saw lots of their buddies there working right alongside them. "In school one day, the mines the next," Dad said.

He took up smoking and Coy took up chewing tobacco while living at the boarding houses where they were just one of the men earning money, playing poker and learning about the ladies of the night— which sure did not please Rosabelle.

"Opie," Rosabelle quarreled, "you're ruining these boys. They're but kids. If you want to smoke your pipe and play poker 'til your hands bleed so be it but not Cliff and Coy!"

"Rosabelle, we do what we have to do. You need the money. We'll make the money and we'll send it to you. Cliff and Coy are big boys. They can handle it."

"Opie, they haven't finished their schooling yet and what about church? Are you taking them to church? Are you?"

Rosabelle was a farmer with class, tall and commanding and stylishly dressed when she wasn't in the fields. She had sparkling blue eyes and dark, wavy hair which she normally kept swept back in a bun exposing favored earrings that had been handed down from her mother. Her children reflected her good tastes as well. At least for church they were always clean.

"Rosie, you do have a handsome bunch," Mrs. Pickering used to say as all the kids filed into church and headed for the front pew where Rosabelle could keep a good eye on them. The front pew was also an easy place for them to stand for singing. Rosabelle rehearsed them at home and paraded them at church.

"Here comes Rosie with her chorus of songbirds," one churchgoer said, finishing up with a teasing mock, "When are you going to get that Opie in church? He's got a front row seat whenever you get him here."

Opie never attended church though Rosabelle often prayed aloud for him when she was there. "Oh, Lord," she prayed. "I pray for Opie's soul for he knows not what he does."

*   *   *

On paydays, Rosabelle was especially alert to Opie's whereabouts. Though not above going to where she thought he might be, she, nevertheless, always met him at the door.

"Opie, I know you've been playing poker," Rosabelle once scolded scornfully, knowing that he had been playing for hours on the rocks outside the mines at Wills Hollow. "I see the blood stains on your hands. Gambling with your hard-earned money. Did you win?"

Sighing, Opie handed his gambling money over to Rosabelle. The amount was slightly more than his pay would normally be. "Rosabelle," he said, "don't I always bring you the money? Have I ever kept it for myself?" Opie loved and respected Rosabelle, but she made life hard for him.

Firm in her convictions, Rosabelle remained steadfast. She stuffed the money in her bosom and commenced with her churning, her hands rising and falling rhythmically as she began to hum and sing, hum and sing. Opie became more aggravated.

"I don't say a word about all the time you spend out there delivering babies, do I?" Opie said. "Or goin' off to church all the time, or all the time you spend nursin' all the kids in the neighborhood—do I?" Opie tried hard to draw a comparison. "You're busier than a hornet, Rosabelle, out there taking care of people, milkin' your cows, feedin' the chickens, plowin' and hoein' and—and churnin' butter!" he sputtered while Rosabelle's hands continued to rise rhythmically up and down over the churn. "Why do you care so much what I do with the men?"

Rosabelle stopped churning and looked wistfully at her husband. "Opie, you're a good man. You're a good provider," she said. "You do your best. But you go against God, and I fear for you. You'll be punished. God don't take to men gambling with their hard-earned money. How much money did you take from the poor souls this time?"

"The men and I like playing poker," Opie said. "It brings us a little pleasure after workin' so hard." Becoming impatient he donned his hat and started for the outdoors where there was always a chore to be done. He knew he wasn't going to change her thinking anyway. "Besides," he muttered to himself as he made his way down to the barn, "don't I always play long enough for them to get some of their money back?"

Opie was correct on all counts regarding Rosabelle. She was quite active in the community. Folks respected her opinions and relied upon her for many services as they recognized her good upbringing and appreciated her education. She was a farmer, midwife, notary, nurse of sorts and an elder in the Primitive Baptist church where the sermons roused her passion for saving the sinful and the choir gave her the outlet she needed for the expression of her soul.

*   *   *

"Rosie, you always have a hint of a smile and a glint in your eye," Mrs. Pickering said one day as she came onto the porch for a little visit. Statuesque Mrs. Pickering was a neighbor and dear friend. "Rosie, you are one strong-willed woman," she said. "You get more done in a day than I do in a week. Give me just half your energy."

"I appreciate the compliment, Mrs. Pickering," Rosabelle lamented, looking away from her friend and off into the distance, "but right now I've got a burden in my life and I'm going to need the Lord's help with it. I wish I was powerful enough to change it, as you say I can."

"Why, what is it, Rosie? I've never seen you like this."

"It's my boys, Mrs. Pickering," Rosabelle said, as she eased herself down into a porch rocker and leaned forward. Her fingers twisted loosely in the folds of her apron as her eyes remained focused on something far away. "Opie's taking them off to the mines," she said. "They're gambling, playing poker, smoking, chewing tobacco and Lord knows what else. I'm worried sick. They've not finished their schooling. Opie don't take them to church. Coy is not even a teen, and Clifford is acting like a man."

Mrs. Pickering sympathized. "Rosie, it's happening all over. Folks just can't make it anymore on one man's paycheck. If the miners got paid for a honest day's work, it wouldn't be this way. The men are getting cheated out of their hard-earned money. We all know the coal operators are weighing the cars low. Takes a man and two boys just to make a day's wages. It's not fair."

Rosabelle knew in her heart that Opie would not take his boys into the mines unless he felt he had to, but she suffered just the same. She simply had no authority over the matter and was forced to take the much-needed money for the family and allow them to work. She prayed long and hard for her husband and sons.

*   *   *

WWI was nearing an end, and Corbitt returned home from active duty. His tales of war made for exciting conversation around the dinner table as he told of bullets whizzing over his head, of the foxholes, of the trenches and of the horrors of seeing his compatriots injured, maimed and killed. He told of the dread of the mustard gas and the trials of communicating with the French soldiers he fought alongside. Dad said he found it hard to sleep afterwards and was filled with a hunger for a similar adventure. The tales served to arouse in him a sense of patriotic duty. He wanted to serve his country and to fight for the cause of freedom everywhere. So, it came as no surprise to

Rosabelle when he announced his intention to enlist in the United States Marine Corps.

"You can't! You're not old enough, Clifford. I will never sign for this!" Rosabelle contended. "Opie," she said, venting her frustration on him, "hang your head in shame. See what you've done, taking this boy into the mines, making him think he's a man when he's but a lad. How can you just sit there and smoke that old pipe when your son is talking so?"

"If he's old enough to stay in a good poker game 'til the end, he's old enough to make his own call about this too," was all Opie would say as he settled his hat on his head and walked out the door. He would never get into it with Rosabelle. She never let up, just going on and on 'til it nearly drove him crazy.

Rosabelle fought tooth and nail, but late in the year 1918 as WWI was coming to an end, Dad, at fifteen years of age, was inducted into the US Marine Corps. He was sent to Camp Lejuene in North Carolina and Paris Island in South Carolina for basic training, after which he was immediately shipped to Haiti where a civil war was underway. The Haitians were rebelling against the oppression of the French rulers and were savagely killing, maiming and brutalizing whites. The Marines were sent to Haiti to quell the uprising, and Dad was one of those Marines.

After only a short while in Haiti, he came down with malaria, sometimes referred to as "yellow fever." Contracted from mosquito bites, the illness was known to reoccur time after time throughout a victim's life, leaving the victim completely debilitated with severe chills and flu-like symptoms. *"I'm slowly dying,"* he wrote to his mother. *"Men are dying all around me. You must get me out of here and back home or I will surely die."*

Rosabelle sought legal assistance and worked diligently to obtain a discharge for him. Her stubborn persistence finally paid off, and Dad was allowed to come home, released from the Marines. Upon arrival, he was, in Rosabelle's words, "as thin as a rail and white as a sheet, just a shadow of himself."

She put him on a pallet on the floor behind the kitchen cook stove where she could keep the chills at bay and nurse him back to health. "Spoon fed him soup and used a lot of my own remedies. Even gave him that quinine they were giving him in the military. And, we offered up some powerful prayers for his recovery at church, too!" she said.

But Rosabelle anguished, nevertheless. "And, just as soon as he was able, and against my wishes," she said, "he went right back into the coal mine. Opie and three of my boys were working in the mines. And bloody mining wars breaking out all over. People were getting killed and shot up, and my men were right out there in the midst of it!"

Miners had seen no progress since previous attempts to unionize had failed so miserably, and Opie was especially sympathetic. "Now, Rosabelle," he said, "I'm not going to let my fellow workers down. They have families just like we do. I know for a fact what those heartless thugs did to the sympathizers over at Cabin Creek and Paint Creek when they set out to unionize a few years back. Throwin' them out of their homes. Layin' all their belongings out on the street. Leavin' them homeless. If not for the union they'd have been without a place to sleep and nothin' to eat. Nothin'!"

"Opie, my heart goes out to them, you know it does. We're praying for them at church and planning ways to help, but Opie, I just feel like I'm losing all my boys to the mining wars. A mother should not have to do that."

"Rosabelle, I know a mother loves her sons, but a man's got to do what a man's got to do. And that's the way it is."

In Mingo and Logan Counties, the coal operators had bought off the local police and were using them to their advantage while fending off the miners who continued their efforts to unionize. The sheriff of Logan County had also deputized the Baldwin Felts Security force out of Bluefield, allowing them to do his *dirty* work. Some men in the security force had been in prison for murder and other heinous crimes and were thought to be completely ruthless, without feeling.

Opie recalled seeing the thugs, as he called them, at Cabin Creek and Paint Creek in earlier years when he had been a witness to a drive-by shooting. "I saw the thugs take aim and shoot right over their tents," he said. "They didn't give a hang about women or children. They just shot their guns and rode off laughin'."

Because of these and other atrocities, Opie, Dad, Corbitt and Coy all became staunch union supporters and joined the United Mine Workers of America. As members, they were active participants in at least one revolt.

Opie enticed his sons. "Boys, its time we show our support. There's miners in Logan and Mingo Counties that are not getting a chance to organize. It's just like Cabin Creek all over again. They have no rights, and they're being dealt with unfairly by the coal operators. The operators won't allow any union sympathizers into the counties. They have their own private army. The sheriff has deputized these Baldwin Felts thugs and has them workin' for him, against the miners. We need to go. Nothin' good is going to happen for miners until they all ban together. There's a group of union men leavin' out of Charleston tomorrow. We'll want to be among them."

Opie's speech was enough to convince Dad and Coy of the merits of joining the march. "Who will be going besides the four of us?" they wanted to know.

"Just about all the men I'm workin' with," Opie said. "They're armed and ready to go. Taking their sons with them, too."

Dad and Corbitt said they had no problem with that. They had guns and ammunition. They were prepared to do battle.

"We'll need to stick together with the Pickerings and the Johnsons," Opie said. "It's going to be a shootin' fight, not just a talkin' fight. This is not going to be just a demonstration. This is going to be a battle. They're armed and dangerous."

The next day the four men joined the ranks of thousands of armed miners as they traveled by train and by foot the sixty-five miles from Kanawha County to Mingo and Logan Counties. They moved through small mining communities and larger towns, gathering strength and local support as they went.

At Blair Mountain, the miners were stopped and could go no farther. The sheriff of Mingo County had a line of defense entrenched on the ridge of the mountain so the miners had no way to get across except to fight their way in. It became an actual battle, with armed confrontation, firing and shooting with people on both sides getting killed. Opie, his sons, the Pickering boys and the Johnson boys stayed together, and though they were openly fired upon, they suffered no casualties. They did, however, see men get killed or seriously injured, some maimed for life. Corbitt said it was a lot like some of the battles he had been in during WWI.

It took 2,000 federal troops and threats of bombing to bring resolve to this revolt. The union leaders finally declared a halt and sent the miners back to their homes in defeat. It was said to be the largest insurrection of its kind since the Civil War. The miners believed the effort was worth it, though it would be many years before they would actually realize the opportunity to unionize and bargain for safer working conditions, better pay and a higher standard of living.

It was a spiritual thing, Dad said. A binding connection between men who sought to save the very soul of the coal miners who had for so long been brutalized at the hands of the coal operators. Even though the coal operators responsible for the brutality were later brought to trial, they were not found guilty of the crimes of which they were accused. The mining wars ended with little to be had for the effort, but Dad said he was always proud that he was able to participate in a piece of history making.

*   *   *

A handsome and dashing young man, just out of the Marine Corps and having a steady job as a coal miner, Dad was one of the most eligible bachelors around. Many ladies pursued him. Unfortunately, one of the ladies was my mother's schoolteacher. Rosabelle saw the young woman, who was as young as the oldest of her pupils, as a "fine catch."

"Clifford, she'll make you a mighty fine wife," she beseeched. "She's a schoolteacher, refined, and a good churchgoer, good singer and pretty as a rose."

But Dad had not forgotten my mother and the spell she had cast on him earlier in the one room schoolhouse. As soon as she was old enough to date, Dad began courting her and only her. A serious conflict then arose between my mother and her teacher. School became a daily battleground between the two, with Mom being in the inferior position.

Ms. Elswick chose to embarrass Mom whenever she could by saying: "Ethel, you talk too much back there. Move up here on the front row with the little ones. They won't be interested in what you have to say. You're keeping Mary Elizabeth from doing her work," or "Ethel, maybe you know the answer," when the question was extremely hard.

The harassment finally became too difficult for Mom to handle, and she made her decision to resolve the problem once and for all. She dropped out of school at the age of fourteen and soon married Dad who was eighteen.

Rosabelle expressed her concern, but Dad was steadfast. Grinning wickedly he told his mother that he knew he had a child bride, but that she was beautiful and smart and that he had loved her for a long, long time, leaving Rosabelle to ponder just how it was he had known her for so long.

Rosabelle was watching her son leave the nest again against her wishes. She had serious doubts about his decision to marry one so young, but she did not let her feelings get in the way of her love for him. "I'll pray hard for your marriage to work, Clifford," were her parting words.

She did pray long and hard for him and asked her congregation at church to do the same. "My son Clifford has gone and married a young, young girl," she told them. "I fear he is making a mistake and he's going to need the help of the Lord and many prayers. Please pray for him."

Mom's older sister Orphie, with whom Mom had lived for several years prior to marrying Dad, was more understanding. She had married young herself.

She helped Mom get a pretty red dress. Red was Orphie's favorite color, as she believed the color red "turned men on." With a hint of romanticism in her voice, Orphie encouraged Dad to take Mom into the city (Charleston) for a little honeymoon. "Then you and Ethel can stay here with Johnny and me and the kids 'til you get a start," she said.

All too soon, the day came when Mom approached her sister. "Orphie," she said, "we're going to be leaving. We're going over to Raleigh County, to a place called Marfork. The mines are working good over there."

"But Cliff has a job here!" Orphie was alarmed that her young sister would be leaving Charleston and its rapidly developing chemical plants. Her husband Johnny had worked at Dupont for fifteen years. And, there *were* coal mines too, though she said she never understand why Dad chose to work in them.

"Clifford says he'll make more money," Mom said. "We need to move on anyway, Orphie. We've been here long enough as it is. You barely have enough room for your own family."

Orphie's bright-eyed smile pushed her cheeks upward, giving her face an impish look. She recognized that feeling of excitement when going it on your own. She recalled her early days with Johnny and how it had been for them as they had begun to make a life for themselves.

"Besides," Mom grinned. "Clifford's got to make more money. I'm going to have a baby, too!"

"Oh, Ethel, you're too young! You might have trouble having a baby so young," Orphie said. She was distraught at the idea of Mom having a baby, but, nevertheless, she sent them away—off to Marfork—with her blessing.

10

September 28, 1933

Dad loved telling Mom about his family and all the good and bad times they had experienced. He enjoyed reminiscing about the early years of his marriage to her. But, the closer the day came for Mom to have the new baby, the busier the household became and the daily talks with Mom had to be put on hold.

Grandpa White, Opie, was there. Just came in on the train one day. Said he'd come to stay 'til the baby came. Now that his children were grown, he was fulfilling his lifelong dream of being a professional gambler. He traveled all over the country wherever the game took him although he returned from time to time to visit and mend and repair, and he always sent Rosabelle money from his gambling gains.

"I want to die with my boots on and playin' poker, Cliff," he told Dad, who grinned sheepishly and asked Opie if he had selected a place yet.

Opie attempted to keep Dad's "spirits up." They spent much time in conversation and sometimes, though not often, if Dad felt up to it, they played card games like "rummy" or "setback."

On the evening of my birth, they did not play cards. Everyone in the household was nervous and anxious, knowing that Mom was going into labor. Dad said little, but suffered quietly, remembering how previous times of giving birth had been so hard for Mom and in particular he remembered her intense anguish over Lonnie's death.

All this weighed on his mind as he lay in bed frightened and worried and *watching* as his dad Opie, who was notorious for making light of a situation, tried his best to ease the tenseness in the household.

Dressed in his usual attire of white long-sleeved shirt, dark pants, suspenders and dark-rimmed glasses, Opie sat astride a straight-backed chair, hooked his feet inside the front legs and rocked it back and forth a few times before finally securing it against the wall opposite the foot of Dad's bed. He had only a few light gray hairs remaining and these he kept slicked back over a now shiny pate that most of the time was kept covered with a hat anyway.

"Cliff, it won't bother you none if I smoke my pipe in here now, will it?" Opie asked as he tamped down the tobacco in the bowl of his pipe and struck a match to light it with or without permission.

As he toyed with his pipe, he commenced to spew forth a constant chatter of small talk that mostly reminisced about days gone by. Dad barely listened, as he was too weak and worried to carry on much of a conversation.

"Cliff, you remember how Mrs. Pickering used to come by and try to get me to go to church," Opie chuckled. "I know your Mom put her up to it. Boy, those people sure did think I was a sinner, didn't they?"

Dad grinned, only slightly cheered, as the talk did divert his attention for the moment and he did remember. He told Opie a story about the time he and Coy had stayed at play a bit too long, and how, when Rosabelle came looking for them, Mrs. Pickering had rushed onto her porch in a hurry to say where they had run off to. "Rosie, they went by here about an hour ago. I suspect they're over yonder at Blue Creek. Pretty girls over there," he mimicked. Mrs. Pickering sure got him into some messes, he said.

Dad smiled and Opie laughed aloud, but the awful screams from the other room quickly recaptured Dad's attention and he looked away, fearful and anxious. He didn't want to talk small talk. He wanted to be by his wife's side, as he had been for all the other births of their children.

The kids had been "farmed out" to Mrs. Coots. "Now Ethel," Mrs. Coots had said, "don't you worry none about the youngins. One or two more won't matter at my house. I'm just like the *Old Woman in the Shoe*, I'll spank them all soundly and put them to bed!"

Dad liked Mrs. Coots. He often cackled when he'd hear her come to the porch and call for her children in rapid cadence—William, Henry, Herman, Mildred, Joe—Bob!" He would then call out, "Ethel, get ready!" For he knew that his own kids would be coming home, too. He recounted some of Mrs. Coots' antics to Grandpa, who was more than eager to listen. Opie had been around a lot when Rosabelle delivered babies as a midwife, and he believed that keeping a steady conversation going was a big help to the men.

Aunt Orphie was there. Nervous and anxious, she paced from room to room, stopping occasionally to wring her hands or chew on her fingernails as her right elbow rested on her left hand. A frown creased her forehead. The usual perpetual grin and mischievous gleam in her gray-blue eyes had faded. She was earnestly worried. Things were not going well.

With apprehension finally overtaking her, she walked directly into Dad's room and looked fretfully back and forth between the two men. Suddenly her hands dropped hopelessly to her sides and she nervously blurted out, "Cliff, do you think Ethel's going to make it? She's havin' an awful time! The doctor's not here yet! What if he don't get here?"

Grandpa Opie was on his feet. "Now Orphie, I believe it's about coffee time for you." He led her into the kitchen and proceeded to pour her a cup of his "special blend." When he saw that the offer of coffee was not enough to relieve her anxiety, he offered her a draw from his pipe. "Here, maybe this will calm you down some. It always works for me." He gave her one of his most mischievous grins, but the grin did not console Orphie. "Oh, Opie," she said with a look of disgust. Her mouth turned upward on one end and her eyes rolled heavenward as she pivoted sharply and with a backward swipe to her skirt made a hasty retreat to her sister's side, where she remained until the doctor arrived.

Orphie met him at the door. "Oh, thank God you're here," she said. "She's having an awful time of it, Doc."

Quickly preparing for delivery, Dr. Williams tried a calming approach. "Now, now, little lady," he said to Mom, " you just lighten up a bit. We've got us a baby to deliver." But, Mom was close to giving birth and was holding nothing back.

Though the atmosphere remained heavy with concern for my mother, there was excitement too, since there would soon be a new baby to coo over. *If only she would get here.*

When finally I was born, after fifteen hours of hard labor, Mom called out with as much volume as she could muster in her weakened condition, "Clifford, it's not a girl, but we'll keep him!"

After the cheering, Grandpa Opie pulled out a gold pocket watch he had won at one of his poker matches and proudly announced the time of my arrival: "7:30 p.m., September 28, 1933." Much to everyone's delight, the watch chimed. Shaking her head and rolling her eyes, Orphie gave Opie a smile and a look that said she forgave him for his earlier antics.

Although Mom had really wanted another girl, she was not disappointed with her little boy. In fact, she would later tell Dad that she was overjoyed as she felt an immediate and spontaneous connection the moment I was laid against her breast.

It would seem to some that another baby would be all that was needed to push this family to the brink. Dr. Williams must have thought so, too. "Ethel, you and Clifford have so much to bear right now. Why don't you let me have this little fellow?" he asked. "I promise you my wife and I would love him and take care of him as we would our own. You'd never have to worry a day about that."

Tears formed in Mom's eyes as she looked at the doctor with sympathy flowing from her heart. She knew how badly he wanted another child and she also knew that he must know that it would be a tremendous strain on her family to care for an infant at this time, but she just could not bear the thought of giving up her child. "You know we can't do that, Dr. Williams," she said weakly. "But I appreciate your concern. It won't be easy, but we'll find a way to care for him."

Dr. Williams looked around. "The little guy is in the best of hands," he said. "There's enough love in this house to keep him alive, but I'll be around to check on him now and then, anyway."

Giving away babies was not uncommon during the Depression. Some families in the coal fields were so impoverished that they could not give realistic and necessary care to their newborns. Without a lot of help and intervention, Dr. Williams believed that this would be true for our family, too. Indeed, had there not been assistance from relatives, caring neighbors and the church, Lee, Jacqueline, Billy and I would most certainly have been separated. Dr. Williams' intentions were humanitarian. He only wanted to give the new baby a fair chance at life and to help the family at the same time.

As soon as I was cleaned and blanketed, Orphie carried me in to see Dad, who by now was overcome with joy and relief. Seeing that Dad's eyes were misted over, Orphie said, "Now Clifford, don't you start cryin' on me too!" She grinned at Opie and winked. Then, she laid me next to Dad and stood back with a smile as she teased, "Well, now that you've got a boy, what are you plannin' to name him? You can't use any of them girl names you and Ethel had picked out." Dad thought for a moment. Then he looked in the direction of Dr. Williams, and, without consulting Mom, said, "We'll name him for the "*good doctor.*" And so, I was named, *James* Edward White. The good doctor said he was honored.

I soon became the new love object as the focus changed from the tragic slate fall accident that had consumed the family with worry and suffering for a quarter of a year to focusing on a blending of both Dad's tragedy and my birth. He needed constant care, and so did I. Our lives were intertwined from that day forward.

11

I Just Want to do Something

Knowing that he had been released from the hospital with little or no hope of living left Dad with mixed feelings. He was grateful to be alive, to have his family, a new baby son to hold, his children nearby and a lovely wife to cherish, yet he felt sad and frustrated because he couldn't do anything. He was still very, very weak.

He loved having visitors—for he was definitely a people person—but he hated for them to see him with all his entrapments, his sons sharing his bedroom and his wife tending to all his personal needs. He knew many, perhaps **all** of his visitors, believed that he would not be around much longer and he found this very frustrating although he managed to keep that feeling inside.

Mom continued to climb onto his bed where she rubbed his back and shoulders and hugged and kissed him. She could not bear the thought of him dying. He was, in her mind, still a man who would again someday bring to her the physical pleasures she had once enjoyed, and she did not want to think of their relationship in any other way.

But Dad did not want to talk about the intimate side of their lives. He saw no point in dwelling on something he could do nothing about. "Ethel, that part of our lives has come to an end," he told her. "We'll just have to make the best of this sorrowful situation. Do the best we can."

And they did the best they could as both adamantly denied to themselves the possibility that he might soon die.

Mom often nestled me up close to him while she went about her daily routines. "Here, Clifford," she would say, "mind Jimmy for a bit. I've got other things to do." She teased him but she also knew that it made him feel useful and helped to keep his mind from dwelling on his terrible plight even though he still was trapped and could only watch.

He *watched* as his still-young wife got up at daybreak to start a fire in the cook stove with the kindling wood Lee had brought in the evening before. He knew that she would soon have the coffeepot perking, something cooking for breakfast and the house warm enough for Lee and Jacqueline to eat and dress for school. And he wished with all his heart that he could be the one to walk them out the door and on to the waiting school bus.

It troubled him to be so helpless and to know there would be zillions of experiences he would perhaps never have again. He was trapped. Confined to a bed in a small room with only the barest necessities. Mom tried to keep the room cheerful and pleasant, but Dad ached to be able to get up and get out of there. It was hard to keep all his feelings hidden inside, but he somehow managed to put his best face on as he continued to *watch*.

He *watched* as Mom dressed and fed Billy. He *watched* as she took me from his care so she could change my wet clothing. He *watched* as she pulled a rocker close to his bedside and proceeded to nurse me. And, he would *watch* as his loving wife tended to all *his* personal needs. Oh, how he longed to be able to change the tragic circumstances. At night he went to sleep with tears in his eyes, as his sadness was sometimes overwhelming.

12

Finding the Good

Although Dad believed with all his heart that he would someday walk again, he had come to accept the fact that he also may not. For his own good and the good of his family, he realized that he could not allow his feelings of frustration to consume him. So, he deliberately set out to focus his attention on the positive aspects of his life—whatever they might be—and slowly began the process of living for the day and for the moment by deriving small pleasures from whatever came his way.

"Do you feel that bright warm sunlight, Jim?" he would say as I lay nestled close to him. I had found my feet and had just begun to kick, but I still did not roll about so Dad said it was a pleasure to have my company. "Listen, Jim," he'd say. "Do you hear the birds chirping? That one's a robin. I can tell. She'll be pulling a big fat worm from the ground to feed her baby." Mom would stand in the doorway and smile.

Dad enjoyed helping Lee and Jacqueline with their homework and frequently posed problems of his own for them to solve. Mom would come into the room. She liked it when the whole family was together like that. "Here, Clifford," she'd say, "let me prop this pillow behind your head. You can see better." He felt he was important again.

*　　　　　*　　　　　*

Being kids, Lee, Billy and Jacqueline often fought, sometimes as the result of normal sibling rivalry, and sometimes over the frustrations of the circumstances in the home. With Lee having so many other chores to attend to, Jacqueline was often asked to "look after Billy and Jimmy." Billy was now an active four-year-old and I was just beginning to walk and get into things. This must have been very difficult for Jacqueline, because she was herself only seven. "Sometimes," she said, "I yearned to just go sit somewhere all by myself and play with my paper dolls or go next door to play with Mildred."

Given responsibilities not of her choosing, Jacqueline sometimes reacted in contentious ways, sometimes getting into scrapes with kids in the neighborhood. More than once she was sent home from the home of a playmate for fighting. This concerned Dad because Sissie was his little girl. He would say to her, "Now Sissie, little girls just aren't supposed to fight." He knew that she was most likely embittered of others because they had a normal home situation while hers was different. And, it was different. We had so little. Our clothes were all hand-me-downs, given by neighbors or relatives whose own kids had outgrown them. There was never money for frivolous expenditures. We had only the essentials for living and almost nothing to play with other than what we created for ourselves. Dad knew that these were hard situations for us to deal with, but he had resolved that all would strive to make the best of the situation.

Once when Jacqueline was sent home from a birthday party for throwing ashes on the floor, Dad asked her why, after her mother had cleaned her up so pretty and sent her off to have a good time, she would do such a thing. She just tightened her face and blurted out, "I just don't like the way that girl acts. I just don't like her."

It bothered Dad to see his daughter having difficulty getting along with her peers. "Look at your mother," he appealed. "She gets along with everyone." But, when he saw that Jacqueline wasn't interested in "getting along," he admonished her for reacting as she did, and said to her in his ever gentle way, "Now, Sissie, if you just look long enough and hard enough, you'll find something you can like about her."

The idea of finding the good in everyone and everything became a way of life for Dad. His zeal to always find the positive side of things often frustrated others, but it never failed to bring *him* peace of mind.

Knowing that his family was experiencing trying times and that more difficult times lay ahead, he set out to do his part to provide the moral and spiritual leadership his family needed. He sought to be a positive role model and establish standards within his household for all to live by.

Psychologically on the mend, he began to accept the circumstances in which he found himself and attempted to make the best of it. By so doing, he found that he was no longer just watching. He was becoming involved, doing what he could from his bed, seeking to derive some worth from everyone and everything, if he "tried hard enough!"

His optimism became contagious in our household. It became a challenge to make do with what we had, and to make any situation better, if we could.

13

A Blue Ribbon Baby

For Dad, time slipped by slowly. "Like waiting for cold molasses to drain from the jar," was the way he expressed it. But it was his plight and he would live with it. As for his wife, he felt differently.

"I saw that Ethel was spending a lot of her spare time doting on Jim," he said. "Always brushing and curling his hair. She loved his blonde, curly locks. She'd wet his hair and then take all this time wrapping strands around her fingers until she had little curls all over his head. Then she'd ask me how I thought he looked. 'Lovely, just lovely, Ethel,' I would tell her. And one day, old Jim just got tired of being fussed over. He wanted to get down and rough house."

Indeed, as Dad recalled, I was clearly ready to escape the mother-baby routine and hit the dirt, so to speak. I yearned to be outdoors more. It was summertime. I was two. All the kids were outdoors, playing and yelling. I could hear them. I'd stand in the kitchen doorway, open the screen door an inch or two and then slowly let it close again, all the time keeping my eye on Mom. "I see you Jimmy," she'd say, watching as always, from the corner of her eye.

"It won't be long, Clifford, before he opens it all the way and slips on out."

"He's growing up, Ethel. The call of the outdoors is beckoning."

Dad was delighted to see me make my move and he did his best to pave the way. "Ethel, take old Jim out for awhile. Take him for a walk; go see Bessie. Give me a chance to get a little shut-eye."

Mom wanted to go. "Clifford, are you sure you'll be all right?"

"I'll be fine, Ethel. It's not likely I'll fall out of bed! Besides, I can holler loud."

So Mom and I began our little outings. Within a short while, I was allowed out for short periods of time on my own, so long as I stayed inside the fence.

I also became Mom's helper, following her wherever she went. Washday was a favorite time for me when we were in and out of the house and up and down the steps from the porch to the yard. I put my hands in the soapy water and helped with the washing. I held the clothespin bag and handed Mom clothespins, as she needed them. I hid behind the big fluffy sheets as they dried on the clothesline and danced in the sudsy water as Mom scrubbed the porches with the used laundry water.

I treasured my independence and when I wasn't doing something with Mom I had a special little place in the yard where I could play by myself with a big spoon and a pot and pan. I played in the dirt and loved it. Mudpies were my specialty.

On one of my outdoor adventures, I spied the traveling photographer, "the picture man," we called him. He was coming down the lane, stopping at all the houses, calling up all the kids and their parents, "Picture man's here. Get ready. Fancy up a bit." When I saw he was going into the Coots' yard, I knew he was too close for me. I heard Mom, who loved having her picture made, saying to Dad, "The photographer's coming! Let me get my hair brushed. Oh, where is Jimmy? He'll have to be cleaned up." She was on her way out to look for me.

The picture man was finishing up at the Coots' and I was feeling very uncomfortable. I ran for cover and tucked myself into a little spot under the corner of the house where I could keep an eye on the picture man and at the same time remain *hidden*.

Mom had a worried look on her face as she called for me. "Jimmy. Jimmy. Has anyone seen Jimmy?" I thought that I should come on out, but when I saw the wet cloth in her hand, I knew she was planning to do the "scrub routine" and I decided to stay put. I lay low, but I guess blonde curls are easy to spot because she soon had me. "Jimmy, come out from under there!" she scolded as I pulled one way and she the other. Giving in, I crawled out and with lowered head accepted the scolding. "Look at you," she said, "The picture man's here and you've got dirt all over you."

Trying to escape the picture man was futile, but I did not have to like it. "Stand right up here beside your Mom now, Little buddy," he said, as he placed me on a straight-backed chair up next to the side of the house. Then he stood behind the black curtain and called for us to look at the tweetie bird." He tried all his cute little sayings to bring on the smile, but I held firm and only gave him a frown. I was finally let go, but the photographer kept on talking to Mom as he made his pitch for the baby contest to be held in Whitesville on Labor Day weekend.

"You ought to enter your little one in the Blue Ribbon Baby contest, Mrs. White. He's a blue ribbon baby if ever I saw one. With them blonde curls, he's a sure winner. You don't see a baby like him every day." Listening to the photographer, Mom got all giddy and proceeded to get all the details which included filling out some papers.

Labor Day was a big day of celebration in Whitesville. The many and varied activities, sponsored by the United Mine Workers of America, brought together all the mining communities in the surrounding areas.

Dad wanted us to go. "Take all the kids," he said. "It'll do you good, Ethel, and help you too." He loved using that expression. He wanted Mom to go and have fun and if entering me in a contest would do the trick then he was for it. He told Mom that it was no wonder that I was such a pretty baby. "Look at yourself, Ethel, " he coaxed. "He takes after you."

"Clifford, we don't have a penny to spare and you know it. We don't even have the train fare."

"Well, write to Orphie. She's always telling you that if you need any-thing to let her know."

"Oh, Clifford, I ask her for too much already. Besides, she'll want to spend the day with her own family. But, I'll do it. It would be nice to go." So she wrote to her sister and asked for the favor.

Aunt Orphie drove over from Belle, arriving the evening before the day of the celebration, full of apologies for arriving so late. "I thought I'd never get on the ferry at Marmet," she said. "I waited on that thing for two hours! And then I get over here and Clear Creek's all swelled up and I can't get cross *it* 'til it goes down some." She threw up her hands in disgust. "I was lucky I didn't blow a tire."

Mom felt wretched. "Orphie," she said, "I shouldn't of asked you to do this." But Orphie, already over her despair, only said, "Now, Ethel, you know I wouldn't want to see you miss something this nice. We'll go and have a good time. Won't we kids?" She saw the look of excitement in our eyes and gave us one of her *winks*. We liked Aunt Orphie.

The next morning we were all up at daybreak. Orphie fixed breakfast while Mom got all us kids, especially me, dressed for the big day. I was dressed in a little blue sunsuit and white shirt, my locks all in place. Mom had found a neighbor to look in on Dad. "Have fun! Good luck!" Dad said as he waved us out the door and we climbed into Orphie's big, old Pontiac.

We saw numerous activities throughout the day, including top enter-tainers, politicians, beauty pageants, and all day boxing matches. There were contests of all sorts. All of the miner's union groups participated in areas of competition among themselves, such as which team could handle the safety equipment the fastest. There were carnival rides. And food booths were everywhere, but we couldn't splurge on food. We had a picnic lunch with us. We didn't have money to spend like most of the people around us, but we had a grand old time. We went all over and saw all the happenings, and then I was entered in the Blue Ribbon baby contest.

The picture man must have told everybody in Ameagle about the contest because we saw a lot of our neighbors in line with their little ones too. "Why Ethel, I see you've brought Jimmy," one of them said. "He sure is a cutie. At least he has blonde curls. They usually like them blond curls." There were other prizes, but I won the Blue Ribbon! And Mom was happy. So happy that she took part of my prize money, which was $10, and treated us all to cotton candy.

Dad *knew* the moment we walked through the door. Beaming, Mom went straight to his room, holding onto me with her left hand and waving the blue ribbon with her right. "Well, I reckon we have us a blue ribbon baby," he said proudly! I smiled too as Mom hung the ribbon prominently on the wall in the living room. Though young, I had gained an understanding about entering contests, but more about winning contests. It was the winning that seemed to make people so happy.

It had been a grand day for all of us. And Dad declared that he had enjoyed his company, too. "Old John and me talked and played cards and listened to a baseball game on the radio. We had us a grand old time!"

After that Dad encouraged Mom to take more frequent trips away from home and, of course, I was always with her. We saw all the Clark Gable movies. Aunt Orphie saw to that. She'd say: "Now Ethel, I've come all the way over here from Belle to take you to the movies. And you're goin'! And take a hankie!" She knew Mom always cried.

Dad would grin broadly. "Tell me all about it when you get back, Ethel," he'd say. "I'll have a dry hankie for you!" He loved having Mom recount her experiences because she always made it as exciting as she could, and she would cry again, too!

This is also about the time Dad began talking sports to me. He listened to all the baseball games and boxing matches. And though he often had adult company with whom he could converse, he seemed to want to tell me all about the events too. I can't remember a time he wasn't talking to me about something. I was definitely a good listener, though my hands could well have been occupied doing something else. I helped Mom a lot, but I listened to Dad.

Dad read the newspaper daily, combing it from one end to the other. I got so I knew how to comb the newspaper thoroughly, too. He'd show me pictures and tell me the stories behind the pictures. We talked about world events. He drew pictures of where the oceans were and the continents and the countries, so that I could have an understanding. We didn't have books with pictures, but we had the newspaper. I learned a great deal from the newspaper: sports stats, ABCs, addition and subtraction. At one point I started asking questions and we began having what Dad referred to as interesting interchanges.

14

Evaline's Coming, A Gardening We Will Go

Except for Dad's modest Worker's Compensation check of $69.52 and whatever we could somehow garner for ourselves, we were completely dependent upon the charity of relatives, neighbors and the community at large. At critical times, a relative would come to stay and help us out. They helped in ways that counted even though they were sometimes as bad off as we were.

Mom's mother, Evaline Smars, a matronly, heavy busted woman with an oval shaped face of clear, unblemished skin, big glassy blue eyes and straight gray hair she pulled back into a bun, was one who came. Her own living conditions were dire, so she had nothing to contribute in a monetary way. What she did have was a talent for gardening, and this talent proved to be the biggest asset we could ask for. She took my brothers, Billy and Lee, and my sister Jacqueline up a steep hillside about a quarter mile from our house to "put out a garden."

"She was the gardener from Hell!" Billy said of her.

Grandma chewed tobacco and she could spit a respectable distance. "She could knock your eye out at ten paces," we kids would teasingly say. In the house, she carried a "spit can" around with her, but outside, she just let it fly! She had two brands that pleased her, Apple and Brown Mule.

"Now, kids," Dad said once when he overheard us talking bad about Grandma. "Grandma was a lady in her time and a real pretty woman. She's had a tough time of it. Been dealt some hard blows, but she's a hard working woman, here to help us put food on our table. Now you mind her and don't let me hear you talk that way again." It was true, and we knew it was true, but to us Grandma seemed coarse and crude. She was so unlike our mother that we sometimes wondered if she really was our grandmother!

Dad liked Evaline. She joked with him a lot, saying things like, "Cliff, if you weren't so lazy, you'd get your ass out of that bed and help out around here." Then she'd laugh heartily. It was not just her company or her crude humor that Dad liked so much; he truly appreciated what she did for the family.

"Evaline is a hard, hard worker," he reiterated often. "She's always willing to do what has to be done so that we have food for the winter coming up. We must show our appreciation, for we don't want to go hungry, do we?"

Evaline didn't seem to mind the hard work, but she also had plenty of help. There were no idle hands when Grandma Smars was around. Not a minute was wasted. We gardened, watered, picked, pulled, scrubbed, canned and preserved, pickled, dried, washed, chopped and carried— whatever! And though we kids did not show Evaline a lot of love and affection, we came to appreciate her, as our parents did, for we knew what her visits meant to our family.

"I know what tough is, Cliff," she once said to Dad. "I've been there many times over. I figure the best help I can give Ethel is to teach her all I know, help her to make do with the hand she's been given." So, she taught Mom how to dress a hog, how to wring a chicken's neck, how to can and process food, how to garden (especially garden) and how to identify the wild greens that were plentiful in the area.

Each spring and into the summer, Mom frequently took us little ones in tow and we'd go to "pick a mess of greens" for dinner. Upon our return, Dad would call out, "What's the fare of the board tonight?" Mom had learned to identify all of them—plantain, poke, dandelion, mustard and dock, among others. "Just toss them in a little bacon grease with a splash of vinegar," Grandma used to say. "They'll be the best thing you ever tasted."

The first time I went to garden with Grandma was a thrill. She liked me right away and said I was a willing and hard worker. I remember how she carried with her one jar of water, which she allotted sparingly. A drink of water was to be earned; it was not given freely. She left the water jar down in a little valley between two ridges where there was a tiny rivulet of water running much of the time. This small rivulet of water provided two necessities: (1) it kept our drinking water cool and (2) it provided water for the plants in the garden.

There was a huge mulberry tree down by the rivulet, and this is where we kids would go for respite from the heat and from Grandma's prying eyes. We sat under the branches to rest and cool off. As the day wore on, it became increasingly harder to leave the shade of this wonderful tree and get back to the task of gardening. We were, after all, just kids. We wanted to play. But, out of fear we stayed until Grandma reluctantly gave up.

She would say, "As soon as we get all these potato plants watered we'll be finished." So we would then take turns carrying buckets of water, again and again, up and down the hill to water those potatoes. It seemed an endless task. Each plant was dutifully given two dips of water from the gourd dipper—or whatever the taskmaster said they needed that day.

Grandma preferred the boys and often shunned Jacqueline. Sometimes she would withhold water from Jacqueline for giving her "smartmouth," or for not working fast enough. Once I saw her give Jacqueline's hair a good yank to try to hurry her up. And sometimes she would use one of her choice expletives to try to shame Jacqueline into being more cooperative.

Jacqueline declares that gardening with Grandma Smars was the bane of her life, though she also recalls the times the two of them went for walks, looked for four leaf clovers and made clover necklaces.

Grandma had a way of making work fun, too. Once when the flies were especially bad, a time right after she and Mom had canned a whole bunch of peaches, Grandma commanded us all to get towels. "We're going on a "fly kill!" she said. We went from room to room swatting in every direction. Dad egged us on. "Here's one Jim. There's one Billy." We had fun on the fly kills. We didn't stop until every fly in the house was done in!

Grandma also gave us lessons about nature. On our return trips from gardening, she taught us how to identify different trees, plants, berries, roots and nuts and how they could be used as food sources or in medicinal ways. "When we get back, we'll make us some sassafras tea," she'd often say. When I think about it, life was never dull when Grandma Smars was around!

We kids got used to Grandma and her colorful ways. By following Mom's lead, we soon paid little attention to her coarseness. Mom would just grin and wink at us kids; she understood. This was a special trait of my mother's. She had a knack for making all kinds of people feel completely comfortable.

15

He's knocked out cold!

In the summer before I turned three, I was mobile, walking and talking, and because I could entertain myself for longer periods of time, Mom now had more time to be with Dad. Sometimes I was taken outside to play with the other kids so that they could have their private moments. Once I came back inside to find Mom sitting on Dad's bed, running her fingers through his dark, curly hair.

Chuckling lightly, she said to him, "Clifford, your hair is so unruly!"

"No one would believe they used to call me Curly, would they." Dad smiled as he moved his hand back over his thinning, yet still wavy hair. Mom smiled too and ruffled his hair again as she reached over and changed the radio station, stopping when she heard Ernest Tubb singing *I'm walking the floor over you.* "Oh, I like that song," she said and began swinging her legs to the sound of the music and singing the lyrics along with Ernest. Dad, with all smiles, just looked at her. They appeared so happy. I was quite young, yet I somehow felt that I was intruding.

Recognizing my presence, Mom asked, "What is it, Jimmy?" Before I could answer the screen door flew open and Lee's friend, Herman Coots, burst inside. "Mrs. White, come quick!" he gushed. "Lee's hurt. He's knocked out cold!" He turned abruptly and rushed back outdoors, his right arm motioning Mom to follow.

Mom called out to me as she ran behind him, "Jimmy, stay here by your dad!" She was gone.

Herman did not slow down. He directed Mom to where Lee lay injured and then ran the whole mile or so down the road to get the doctor. I believe he thought that Lee was dead and because they had been playing together at the time that he was probably responsible.

The accident happened about three doors down from our house, in a backyard where a neighbor had built a merry-go-round of sorts. He had balanced a large-sized plank, measuring about 3" X 8" X 10' over the middle of a tree stump and drilled a hole through the center of the plank and into the stump. Into this hole he had placed a metal pipe which served as the axis for rotation. Because both the pipe and the stump were kept well greased, the plank swung round and round very fast.

A few of the older kids in the neighborhood had been playing on the merry-go-round. Two sat or knelt on the plank while two pushed. It probably was not uncommon for kids to fall off. I'm not sure whether Lee was pushing or riding or whether he fell or stumbled, but he was hit in the head with a mighty blow. He had a gash in his upper lip that extended almost to his nose.

When Mom arrived on the scene, she found Lee bleeding profusely. and just as Herman had said, except for a slight spasm, he was "out!" She knelt over him and began calling out to him, "Lee, Lee, wake up. Wake up, Lee." Lee did not respond.

"Move out. Move away," Mom commanded the bystanders. Someone handed her a cloth, which she pressed tightly against Lee's wound. She wanted to bundle him up in her arms, hold him and cry. She had been through so much the past few years and Lee had been right there with her helping her all the way. It was heartbreaking for her to see him hurt; yet she knew that at a time like this she had to "take hold of herself" and do what was necessary.

News of the accident spread quickly throughout the camp. Billy and Jacqueline were among the ones anxiously asking what had happened to Lee. Mom sent them home. "Go tell your dad what's happened and stay right there with him and Jimmy until I get back." They came straight home, frightened out of their minds, both afraid that Lee was going to die or may already be dead.

Jacqueline was nine and Billy six at the time. As instructed, they informed Dad of Lee's condition, and I heard him say softly to himself, "It must be pretty bad."

Nevertheless, he spoke as calmly as possible, "Now Sissie, you and Billy just come on in here with me and Jim. Your mom will take care of the situation. He's just knocked out, that's all."

Billy was not so easily consoled. "But, he's got blood all over him," he exclaimed. His huge blue eyes, framed by long dark lashes, pointed brows and a shock of curly coal black hair, looked like marbles frozen inside his ghostly white face. He was so frightened.

Dad was afraid, too. But he did what he must do and began "taking hold" of his end. "The doctor will stitch him up," he said.

"Sissie," he continued. "You can start fixing dinner for your mom. Go ahead and peel the potatoes. And Billy, you go get some kindling and get the fire going. That way the stove will be hot when your mom gets back."

Although Jacqueline did as she was told, Dad's effort to divert her attention was to no avail. "Is he dead?" she kept asking, "Is Lee dead?"

"Now Sissie, let us wait 'til we hear from your mom and the doctor." Dad tried to ease her mind, but he could not. With drawn face and knitted brows, she stood near his bed looking directly at him. Her thin brown hair, wet from the running and playing she had done earlier, lay plastered against the sides of her head. Before long, we were all huddled near Dad who made every effort to comfort us, but he was as worried as we were.

Meanwhile, the news continued to spread and soon the whole backyard where the accident occurred was filled with curious onlookers seeking to see the now infamous merry-go-round. Talking among themselves and to their kids, the remarks flew:

"This could have been you."

"Oh, thank God, you're all right."

"I don't want to ever see you on this contraption ever again, you understand!"

And, to the neighbor who had built the merry-go-round, "You ought to have knowed better than to build such a contraption. It's a wonder some kid hadn't already been killed on it!"

There was a rush of sympathy too. "Poor Ethel. She's been through so much." They all knew of Dad's condition, and they felt sorry for Mom who by now had become adept at handling the tough situations. Regardless of her inner feelings and her desire to sit down and sob, she continued to do what she hoped would help Lee to awaken and respond to her. She left the emotional outcries to others.

Lee still lay unconscious when the doctor arrived. He had not responded to Mom as she called out to him, and he did not respond to the doctor. "Mrs. White," the doctor said, "we'll need to take Lee down to my office." In the doctor's car she held Lee's head on her lap and prayed silently with all her heart.

In his office the doctor stitched the open cut and checked Lee for responses. In time, Lee awakened and seemed to be okay. "We'll take him on home now," Dr. Williams said. "He's had a hard, hard lick to his head. I'll need to check it out a little later on."

Herman Coots had paced the outside of his house a thousand times; his mother had done the same inside. Both showed elation when they saw Lee get out of the doctor's car. Herman fairly danced for joy. "Hey, Lee," he called. "I'll see you tomorrow." Mrs. Coots came to the porch, smiled and waved, but decided to keep her thoughts to herself for the evening.

Billy ran to greet Lee. "It's Lee, he's okay! He's not dead!" he called. He and Jacqueline were both amazed that Lee was alive and walking, though his lips were blue and his face horribly swollen. He walked slowly into the house with Jacqueline and Billy at his sides and Mom and Dr. Williams trailing behind. I remember looking up at Dad and seeing the look of relief on his face. I then clasped my hands and jumped up and down as I sensed I was supposed to show elation, too. I was young but I knew that things were better. Our family was back together, and I began to feel secure once more.

"Put a cold compress on his face to keep the swelling down," Dr. Williams told Mom as he prepared to leave. "Keep him awake for the next few hours." The doctor left with a worried look on his face, instead of his usual, happy smile.

Dad felt Lee's swollen and bruised head as he directed Billy to get a towel and put it in the icebox on the porch. "There won't be much ice left," he said. "Delivery man comes tomorrow. While you're there put up the marker so he'll know how much ice to leave."

In the meantime, Dad gently asked Lee to tell him just how the accident had happened. Lee was apologetic as he blamed himself. Like Dad, at the time of his mining accident, Lee felt shame for being "so stupid." The ground was "slick" he said and he was running too fast.

Dad did not admonish Lee for playing recklessly. He knew that not all accidents were caused by carelessness. He recalled how he had felt when the slate fell so unexpectedly onto his back. For now, he just wanted to be able to help. So, in an effort to keep Lee awake, he engaged him in conversation.

Mom's friend Bessie came to help. "Ethel, I've brought something for dinner. I know you're exhausted, dear." Bessie stayed through dinner and then left after assuring Mom that she would come back if needed.

Mom and Dad stayed up with Lee for a long time. The rest of us were put to bed.

16

"One more clean shirt might do me!"

Dad had lingered now for close to three years in a state of healing, and he now knew he *wasn't* going to die. He had made at least one important gain during this time: he could pretty much schedule his bodily functions, which gave him a small measure of independence, much like a child growing from diapers into training pants.

He could sit up higher in bed as long as he had pillows propped behind him. Several times a week I'd climb up onto the bed with him and make myself comfortable, making room for both of us. Mom would bring us the comics to read.

"Now find us all the A's," Dad would say, as we began our lessons. We'd scan the page for all the letters before we would actually read the "funnies." School time went on as Mom brought us the necessary supplies. We counted, added, subtracted. When we finished or I got tired, Dad would tell Mom, "Ethel, Jim's the smartest pupil I ever had." He'd have a big grin on his face, and I'd smile, too. I felt important.

While the others were in school, I was Dad's "gofer" and partial caregiver. "Jim, fetch me a glass of that good cold water," he'd say. I'd run to the water bucket, crawl up on a chair and using both hands fill the dipper almost full and pour the water into a glass. Then I would carefully carry it into Dad. "Look at that, Ethel" Dad would say. "Didn't spill a drop."

I also delivered his mail. Since he could now care for himself when he had bowel movements, he would call out to me, "Jim, I need to write a letter." I knew what that meant. I would go get an old newspaper and bring it to him. When he got through he would call out again, "Jim, here's a letter to mail." He would have it wrapped tightly in his special way, somewhat like the shape of a coke bottle. It had no smell. I would take it from him and run from the house and down the path to the toilet where I would mail his letter!

I was Dad's constant companion, but he had other visitors to talk to as well. Bummy Bumgardner was one. Bummy frequently dropped in on his way home from his shift at the mine. On his way through the kitchen, he'd help himself to a cup of coffee or tea. Then he'd walk right on into Dad's room, take up a seat somewhere near the foot and to the side of Dad's bed and commence talking. Bummy kept Dad abreast of what was happening at the mine and in the community and Dad kept Bummy abreast of what was happening in the world.

One mid-summer day, when Bummy, still wearing his "bank" clothes, came to call, Dad had just finished bathing and was donning a clean shirt. "Cliff, how goes it today?" Bummy said. It was his traditional opening remark.

"Oh, I think one more clean shirt might do me," Dad retorted with a glad-to-see-you smile.

Bummy, who had a long stride for a little fellow who was permanently stooped from working so long in the coal mines, laughed at Dad's humor as he strode on into the bedroom. Making himself comfortable, he straddled himself backward across a straight-backed chair and took off his hat, revealing a white dome in sharp contrast to his face which was blackened with coal dust, creating a look much like the Chinese symbol for yen and yang. He took out his pipe, one of those pipes that had a big dip in it, and lit up as he commenced talking.

"Just come from a union meetin'," he said. "They're talkin' up a big strike down at the mine. McGarly says he won't be a part of it. Says it's too hard on the miners and their families. Says he can't do without that long. Says the company store'll take back everthing he owns."

Dad, always quick to take the side of the union, replied, "Miners are going to have stick together. They can't afford to lose all that they've fought for. The union has been good for all of us."

They didn't get much further into their conversation before Mom interrupted. "Clifford," she said. "I see Reverend Pindar just leavin' the Coots' house. He'll be here next." She wanted to make sure Dad and Bummy didn't plan to have a little toddy of some sort.

Bummy got up to leave, but Dad put up his hand. "No, stay Bummy. He'll just be a minute or so. Besides, it'll be good for your soul!"

With glowing countenance, the reverend strode into the house and on into Dad's room before Bummy could take leave. He greeted both men with a broad grin and said in his resonant booming voice, "Good day, fellows."

Dad, with a rather large grin of his own, pointed toward Bummy as he greeted the reverend. "Well, Reverend," he said, "looks like you timed it just right this time. And, you've got a real sinner here. His soul just might be worth saving." The reverend laughed as Bummy, clearly uncomfortable, shifted in his chair.

"Now, Clifford," Bummy mumbled, "the man is here to work with you and you know you need it worse than I do. Anyways, I'd better be runnin' along, wife's expectin' me, ain't been home yet." He started to say something else, but the big, burly, red-haired, charismatic Irish preacher didn't make it easy. "Bummy," he said loudly, "you stay right there. You're in good company—me, you, Clifford, and the Lord! Let us pray!"

I could see that Bummy wanted no part of it. I felt like inviting him to hide with me behind the living room sofa, a place I scooted to every time the reverend came. But Bummy got away on his own which left me by myself to listen in terror as the reverend prayed loudly with much enthusiasm telling Dad how mighty and powerful God was and that he was always watching over us and knew our every need. I wasn't sure I wanted God to know all that went on in my mind and certainly not all of my *deeds*!

Nevertheless, Dad seemed comforted and strengthened as the reverend read scripture and spoke fervently about the Bible's intent and his belief in his God. "Clifford," he said, as he prepared to leave, "do you have a Bible? I never thought to ask you. You read so much."

"No, Reverend, I don't," Dad said. "And I'd sure like to have one."

Reverend Pindar left him one on the spot. Years later, Dad would say he had read that Bible many times over, from "kivver to kivver." He referred to the Bible as the *Good Book*, and quoted from it, too—whenever it served his purpose.

Dad read everything that was brought to him. Reading sharpened his mind. He couldn't get up on his paralyzed legs and walk, but he figured he *could* expand his knowledge. He became quite learned in many subjects so he had plenty to talk about when visitors came.

Bummy was one of Dad's favorite visitors because Bummy liked to read, too. He'd sometimes bring an article or book with him and say, "Cliff, I'd like you to read this in your spare time and tell me what you think of it."

Dad would take a cursory glance at the material and lay it aside, with his own comment. "Give me a few days on this Bummy. I'll have to fit it into my schedule." They never had a dull conversation that I'm aware of.

17

Hope

Dad never wanted pity. He just wanted to get his life back together. After close to four years of lying on his back, with only minimal activity, his muscles had begun to atrophy, leaving him in a very weakened condition. He had begun to think that maybe he would just shrivel up like a little boy. It frightened him to think about it.

But, something began to happen which brought new life to him. One day he called to Mom in a highly excited voice. "Ethel, come here," he said. "Touch my leg below my right knee there." She did so, and he winced as if in pain. "Oh glory, Clifford, did you feel that?" Mom looked at him in disbelief.

"No, Ethel, I didn't really, but I have been feeling some funny sensations in my legs. Just about every day now for a week. I think the feeling is coming back!"

"Really, Clifford?" Mom asked with great surprise.

"Really, Ethel!"

Mom started for the door "I'll go get Dr. Williams, right now!" she said.

But dad stopped her. "No Ethel," he said. "Let's be patient. He'll be by in a few days. If I'm still feeling something, I'll talk to him about it then."

Mom saw no point in waiting. She sent word to Dr. Williams that very afternoon and the next day the good doctor made one of his unscheduled visits. "Clifford, what's this I've been hearing about you having feeling in your legs?" he asked Dad spiritedly.

Dad enthusiastically described for the doctor the funny sensation he was feeling in his legs, certain that Dr. Williams would be able to tell him what the *delightful* pain meant, but the doctor said he could not.

"Clifford, I'm as ignorant as the next person about this kind of pain. It could be sympathetic pain and it could be real, I don't rightly know. But, tell you what I'll do. I'll look in my medical books and journals and I'll bring you any information I can find on the subject, let you read for yourself." He looked around at the pile of books and magazines he knew Dad had devoured. "You're right scholarly now. Probably be good reading for you."

After this incident, Dr. Williams visited Dad more frequently, each time bringing with him whatever research he could find on the subject of spinal injuries. On one of his visits, Dad said, "Doc, I've read here in one of your journals about a place called the Mayo Clinic. Says they're doing research on spinal injuries. I think I need to go there and have them take a look at me. Might be the pain I'm feeling in my legs is real."

Dr. Williams leaned back in his chair and smiled broadly. His gray eyes sparkled and as he spoke his voice had a ring of adventure to it. "Clifford, I know of no reason why you shouldn't do just that," he said. He admired Dad's courage and spirit, but unfortunately he didn't know anything about the program. "No more than what you've read for yourself, Clifford," he said. "But I'll do what I can to help you find out."

The next day Dad put his good penmanship to practice and wrote a letter to the clinic requesting that he be allowed to be a part of the research. Dr. Williams also wrote a letter in Dad's behalf, and they both waited eagerly to hear from the clinic.

The response came much sooner than expected. Mom hurried home from the post office, waving the letter in her hand and handed it over to Dad, who fairly ripped it open. "They want me, Ethel, they want me!" he exclaimed with animated excitement. "They say I sound like a good candidate for the research. And it won't cost me a nickel—just have to get myself there, that's all!"

Resting her elbows on the edge of Dad's bed, Mom gazed upon him in hopeful wonder. "Oh, Clifford," she said, "won't it be something if you can walk again."

"Now Ethel, don't get your hopes up. There's a chance though. A chance. The pain I feel has got to mean something."

He hardly slept that night, and his enthusiasm still ran high as daylight came creeping through the windows. Mom brought him a bowl of warm water and a towel. He quickly freshened up and then said he was ready for coffee.

Watching politely as he poured his coffee into a saucer, Mom asked, "Clifford, how on earth are we ever going to get you to the Mayo Clinic?"

"I've been thinking about it, Ethel. It's not going to be a piece of cake, but no reason for me to give up hope. I'm sure I'll find a way."

Feeling optimistic, he mentioned the trip to everyone who visited in hopes of finding a way to somehow get to the clinic. But no one he knew, not even Dr. Williams, nor Rev. Pindar, nor any of his kin, knew of a way to get him there—though they all cared deeply and wanted to help him. "Well, Ethel, maybe its just not meant to be," he said sadly one day after the reverend left and there seemed no one else to appeal to. "Now, Clifford, I've never known you to give up hope once you started on something. There'll be a way." Mom refused to let him become discouraged. She also had been seeking help. Bessie was hard at work on it too, but times were too hard. Even someone who had a car could not take the time off from work to take him. And no one had the kind of money it would take to get him there by other means.

Dad and Mom both prayed. God had not forsaken him in his darkest hour, Dad said. "And he won't forsake me this time either. This is just not meant to be easy, Ethel," he said. "We'll just put our faith in God and if it is meant to be, then he will lead us toward that way."

Weeks went by. And the Mayo Clinic pretty much slipped into the recesses of their minds—*not meant to be.* Then one day, Mom came dancing into Dad's room with Bessie on her heels. "Clifford, you're going. You're going to the clinic. Bill and Bessie are going to take you. And I'll be going too!"

Dad looked up at the two beaming women and sighed loudly. "Well, I guess the good man upstairs is looking out for me after all."

"You mean the good man down the street, Clifford!" Mom took his hand and perched herself on the side of his bed and allowed Bessie to explain further. "Clifford," Bessie said, "Bill and I have prayed over this, and we've decided that with the help of the church and some of our family that we will be able to take you to the clinic. We know it won't be easy, but we're committed and we're going to do it. Bill will come over after work to talk to you and Ethel more about it."

Dad said he tingled *all over* at the news, saying he was never so excited about something in his life. He and Mom talked at length after Bessie left. They busied themselves making all the necessary arrangements. Mom said she would ask Orphie to stay with the kids. And Evaline would help, too.

Bill Legg was tall and lanky and wore dark rimmed glasses, which gave him a studious look. As an electrician for the coal mine, he was one of the few in the community who had a stable job with a good income. He had more than the average coal miner. He had a car, which he kept down at one of the garages. His wife Bessie was Mom's best friend and a stalwart figure in the community. Bessie worked diligently with the Presbyterian Church and spearheaded much charitable work in its behalf. She had been aware for some time of the difficulty Dad was having securing some way to get to the clinic, and though she had worked persistently through the church to get help for him, it had not been enough. She finally decided that if it *were* to happen, then it would be up to her. "Bill," she said to her husband one evening after she had prayed hard all day, "you know we are about the only ones around who could take Clifford to the Mayo Clinic. Do you suppose we could do it?" She looked pleadingly into his eyes. "Miner's vacation is coming up soon. We could use that time."

Bill took time to light his ever-present pipe. "Yes, Bessie, we could," he said with a sigh. "I've been thinking about it, too. If no one in his family can do it, then it seems we're the only ones left. We'll have to. We can't just sit here and let that man not have the benefit of knowing whether he might walk again when we can do something about it. I'll talk to the mine superintendent tomorrow. He'll have to give me some extra time off work. Even if we go during miner's vacation, I'll still need extra days." Then he gave Bessie a hug. "Bessie, you are a sweet and caring woman. I'm a lucky man to have a wife like you. Everyone in this community is lucky I have a wife like you!"

Bessie smiled happily. "No Bill," she said. "I'm the lucky one."

Dad and Mom talked. "Ethel," Dad said, "we don't have a penny to spare. We'll have to beg and borrow from everyone we know to get money for this trip."

But Mom said not to worry. "I've talked to Bessie. She's had a fund going for you for quite some time now, 'The Clifford White Fund.' They've had nickel-a-spoon-dinners at the church, put donation jars at the company store and had people selling things. She's getting some money together."

"But," Dad said, "we need to help. Get me my pen and paper. I'm going to write to Mom, let her know. She might be able to help some too."

Mom said she would contact her family, also.

Reverend Pindar called on Dad before he left and explained just what the church had done and how the church would continue to do what it could to help him. Dad said he would be eternally grateful. The reverend said that making such things possible was the work of the church. "It is our mission," he said. "We'll be praying hard for you, Clifford."

✶   ✶   ✶

Dr. Williams came to give assistance in helping Dad and Mom prepare for the trip. He made sure they had all the medical supplies they would need and gave them instructions on how to care for Dad along the way. He knew it was going to be a rough experience, but he was highly excited about it and said he wished that he could be going with them.

✳   ✳   ✳

"Now Cliff, it's going to be a real tough journey," Bill said. "Rochester, Minnesota, is over a thousand miles from this little old coal camp in West Virginia. It'll take a long time, maybe a week, just to get there. We may hit every red light between here and Minnesota. We'll have blowouts along the way. Might have engine trouble. Lots of things can happen. But buddy, we're goin'! Ain't nothin' goin' to stop us!"

Dad admired Bill's spirit. "You and Bessie are making a great sacrifice for me, Bill," he said. "I won't ever forget it."

"Cliff, we're just doing what we figure you and Ethel would do for us if the shoe was on the other foot. Now, I've rigged the car to accommodate you as best I can. Laid the front seat back some and put a leather strap in so you can buckle yourself in place. Strapped two spare tires to the top of the car, stocked up on patching materials. Won't be no luxury ride. Probably won't be many places along the way where we can stop for the night or to get us a bite to eat."

"Ethel's packed us a bundle to eat," Dad said. "As long as we have a can of potted meat and a loaf of bread, we'll survive." He would allow nothing to get in the way of this adventure.

✳   ✳   ✳

It was a long and arduous journey. The highways offered no direct routes, which meant they had to go through all the small towns between here and there and over much wide-open country. Fortunately, the weather was decent most of the time. But, mechanical problems, flat tires, pot holes, detours, long waits during road construction and strug-gles to find some form of accommodation each evening left them weary. Conveniences for handicapped people did not exist. It was a make-do trip.

Having Bessie along helped when it came to getting accommoda-tions. She had a way of expressing their needs. "We've got a crippled man in the car," she'd say sweetly. "Had his back broken in the coal mines. We're on our way with him to the Mayo Clinic. They may be able to help him walk again." Her tender optimism helped to spawn more generosity toward Dad's needs among the hosts on the road. But even so, there were times when they had no other choice than to stop along the road in the shade of a big tree where, after assisting Dad with his personal needs, Bill, Mom and Bessie would lay out the bedrolls to rest their exhausted bodies.

*   *   *

"Cliff, we'll have to sleep in the car tonight," Bill said on the third night out. "I can't find a thing out here."

"I can suffer through it if you guys can," Dad said as he attempted to keep their spirits up. "Just give me something I can use to fight off these bugs." Mosquitoes concerned him as he still had an occasional relapse of malaria, and it worried him that something might happen to prevent him from keeping his appointment at the clinic. But he remained in good cheer. "I'll have mustard on my dog," he said with a grin.

On the fourth day into their journey Bill was able to find a tourist's camp with an available cabin. He looked longingly at the cots, the table and chairs, the lantern, the common bathhouse. He was so hot and tired.

"Got us a place here, Cliff. We'll get a bath and a good night's rest. Have us a good meal for a change."

"Sounds like heaven to me," Dad said. Bill did not tell Dad that the establishment had first refused him. The owners weren't entirely insensitive. They just were not used to seeing a crippled person out traveling. Cripples stayed at home or in hospitals. "We have no suitable accommodations," they'd told Bill. "You can see the cottage is up a little hill. That's a hefty walk as it is. And, he won't be able to shower."

"Well, you don't need to worry about carrying him up the hill. I'll carry him up the hill. And his wife will help him with his bath. And, I'll carry his food out to him, if you don't mind."

Bill struggled with his temper, but he maintained a courteous tone. "Look, fellows, I've got my neighbor in that car. He's paralyzed from a slate fall in the coal mines. We're on our way to the Mayo Clinic, hoping he'll get treated so he can walk again. His heart is aching to walk again. We've been on the road for four days and we need a rest and some decent food. We've got the money to pay just like any one else."

His earnest pleas persuaded the owners to rethink their position. They prepared a meal for Dad and even helped Bill get him into the cottage.

"We really do appreciate this, fellows," Bill said as he returned the dishes. "A good turn will come your way some day."

*   *   *

Refreshed from a good meal and a night of complete rest, the party of four quickly recaptured their enthusiasm and started off again on their journey of hope. About three times a day, Bill, Bessie and Mom helped Dad to stretch out on a blanket and elevated his feet, which were swollen to three times their normal size. The swelling worried them.

By the time they reached the outskirts of Rochester, they were all greatly fatigued, disheveled, hungry and smelly! Bill was so weary of driving he was beginning to nod at the wheel. The others forced themselves to stay awake and keep up a lively conversation. Dad chose politics.

"Bill," he said loudly, "they say the miners are getting the shaft again. Say that Roosevelt's New Deal's not working for the miners. John L. Lewis is talking big time strike." Bill was roused. "Hell, if them miners don't get a backbone, they ain't ever goin' to get ahead," he said. "Roosevelt's doin' all he can do," he continued. "People just have to do somethin' for themselves." Both Bill and Dad were staunch democrats and believed that had it not been for Franklin Roosevelt the country would have been in shambles. Both were for the common man, whose plight they thoroughly understood.

Dad managed to keep Bill alert until on the outskirts of the city they found an accommodating cottage that also had a small restaurant. As they pulled up to the cottage door, Bill looked at Dad and Dad looked at Bill. They began to laugh uncontrollably. It must have been a miserable sight; the two of them looking for the world like two escaped prisoners.

A loud "Whoopee!" went up from all of them as the car rolled to a stop. Bystanders stopped in their tracks as they turned to stare at the two funny-looking men and the two pretty women. "We've done it, Cliff," Bill said. "We've arrived. We're here, in Rochester, Minnesota, and tomorrow morning at eight you're going to be checking into the world famous May-o Clin-ic!" Mom and Bessie, all smiles, embraced one another.

Dad was happy, but also nervous. Just being there, in Rochester, was exhilarating. Not knowing just what to expect made him anxious. But he reserved his anxieties for later and gratefully allowed Bill to carry him into the cottage where a nice clean bed awaited.

"Cliff, I believe I can get you down into this tub with a little water in it," Bill said as he examined the bathtub.

But Dad said no. "Bill, I want nothing more right now, but I believe I'll wait to see what they have to say at the clinic first." Dad ached to be able to get into a tub the way Bill did, but at least he had the comfort of some good clean linen and a nice wipe-down.

Bill, Mom and Bessie all freshened up and made plans to eat. "No potted meat sandwich tonight!" Bill said. "It's time to splurge." Dad knew it would be awkward for Bill to take him inside the restaurant. "Now, you guys go on and enjoy yourselves," he said. "Me, I'm plumb tuckered out. I'll just get me some shut-eye while you eat. Bring me back the fare of the board." Mom thought she should stay behind, but Dad said no.

When Mom returned to the room with a sumptuous home cooked dinner of meatloaf with all the trimmings, Dad was rested and prepared to eat. "My stomach is rumbling," he said. Mom propped some pillows behind his head and assisted him with the meal. "Compliments of the owner!" she proclaimed proudly. "She liked your story. Said she's real proud to have you stay here in her cottage. Said her husband died a few years back from an accident, and she's all sympathy for you. Her name's Mary Wilson."

Fact was, Mary was so impressed with Dad's story that she took a personal interest in his behalf, coming to the cottage to make sure that his accommodations were suitable and even coming to the car the next morning to give him a big sendoff. "Cliff," she said, "when they finish with you over at the clinic, you come back by here and we'll celebrate! Whiskey and all!"

Dad really wanted to see that day come. He gave Mary the biggest grin he could muster, thanked her profusely for her hospitality and caring ways, and the five of them slapped hands as Bill revved the motor up for the trip to Mayo!

Bill carried Dad into the clinic and waited until he was properly admitted before locating the rooming house where he, Bessie and Mom would stay—compliments of the Clinic.

Over a period of seven days, Dad was given a complete evaluation by the best team of neurosurgeons in the field. He struggled to understand all that was being done to him, but never gave up hope. In the end, the diagnosis was that the sensation Dad felt in his legs was merely sympathetic pain and that he would **not** be able to walk again.

The news was terribly disappointing, but with the bad news came some good news. "Mr. White, you've shown marked improvement in your circulation in the short time you've been here," the doctors told him. "Though you won't walk, you are clearly ready to begin a training program to improve your upper body strength. We want you to exercise and rehabilitate those muscles. Retrain them. You need not fear further damage to your spine."

Dad was given a specific exercise program to follow and the equipment necessary to carry it out. "If you follow the regiment of exercises our therapists lay out for you, your upper body should be as strong as it was before the accident. Now it won't happen overnight. And, you'll get discouraged sometimes, but if you do as we say and never falter, you can do it," the doctors stressed.

"And more good news," they told him. "Once you have that upper body strength back, you should also be able to stand and move about with the help of braces and crutches."

Dad found the news uplifting, giving him a new burst of energy. He could now exercise without worrying about further injury to his spine, or more extensive paralysis. He could live a semi-normal life again!

Eager to begin, he raised his level of expectation and began preparing himself mentally. He now knew that a day would come when he no longer had to lie in bed and *watch* the world pass him by. He **would** strengthen his upper body and he **would** get out of that bed!

*　　　　　*　　　　　*

The return trip was also long and arduous and had all the inconveniences, trials and tribulations as the trip up, yet the party of four made it back without delay, though tattered and torn and eager to have the trip behind them.

Jacqueline and I were the first to see the car. We rushed to the front gate, calling out to Lee and Billy who were out in the neighborhood. Bill blew the horn, and as the car came down the dusty lane it soon had an entourage of children, barking dogs, and curious onlookers.

Aunt Orphie had spread the word that when Dad returned he might be able to walk. So by the time the car got to the gate, a crowd had gathered. Billy had hitched a ride on the running board and was hanging onto Dad's neck as the car came rumbling to a stop.

We all converged at the same time with hugs and kisses for Dad and Mom. Other than when Dad was in the hospital, our family had not been separated, so for us it was truly a joyous reunion.

Uncle Coy was at the house, on furlough from the Navy. He lifted Dad from the car and carried him inside and placed him on his bed as the rest of us began asking the hard questions. Dad tried to smile and greet his welcoming party graciously, but he was too tired from his weary journey to stay upbeat for very long.

We had already guessed that he would not be delivering the news we had hoped for. We had set our hopes so high that we even envisioned him coming back able to walk in what could only be interpreted as some form of magic. Dad saw our looks of disappointment and said he felt somewhat guilty that he hadn't been able to deliver the goods. "After I have me a good rest, I'll tell you all about it," he said.

The first hours at home were hard for him, but he was back in the security of his home, which made him happy. Mom knew how tired he was. She was exhausted herself, but she quickly shooed everyone away so she could freshen him up and make him as comfortable as possible. Dad's voice trailed after her, "Sorry folks, I'm just too pooped to pop!"

For the moment, Dad needed a rest. But, tomorrow would be another day. He now had a head full of ideas and an amazing feeling of confidence that he could move forward.

He had become somewhat of a celebrity, since he had been places and seen and done things that most people in the community could only be in awe of. Most had never heard of the Mayo Clinic, much less talked to someone who had been there. Dad's travels would serve as opportunies for exciting and lively conversations.

Orphie had baked a cake and planned a little celebration of sorts, but she downplayed it now as she invited everyone into the kitchen for a home-cooked meal.

"Orphie, that's music to these weary ears," Bill said. "A big plate of your cookin' might make us all members of the human race again."

Coy took his meal in the bedroom with Dad. Mom sat with Bill and Bessie. Orphie was eager to hear all about their trip. "I won't be able to sleep tonight unless you tell me everything that happened," she said. Dad called from the bedroom, "Go ahead and tell them all about it, but leave the good stuff for me!"

We all gathered around the kitchen table, where Mom, Bill and Bessie gave us a good overview, but *left the good stuff for Dad*. Coy joined us, leaving Dad to rest. "Coy," Bill finally said, " there were times when Bessie and Ethel and I thought we couldn't go it another day, but Cliff just kept plugging along. He never seemed to tire. He's going to be all right, that man. We've known all along how tough he was. But now we know he's tougher than nails."

Bill and Bessie left. Coy and Orphie stayed the night.

Coy, who had hoped to have his brother back as a *whole* being again, was disappointed. But, he quickly resigned himself to "Cliff's fate" after hearing the *good stuff* from Dad the next morning. "Cliff, this is good news. You'll be able to feel like a person again, be up doing things like everybody else. Just 'cause you're crippled don't mean you can't do things. Why you can use your hands and you've got a good mind. God, you read all the time. You must know about everything there is to know by now."

Amused at his brother's assessment, Dad said, "Coy, I figure once I'm out of this bed I'll be able to do at least half what a regular man can do!" to which they both laughed enthusiastically.

Coy left the next day to return to the Navy. "Cliff," he said upon leaving, "I'll soon be retired from the Navy, and I'll be back here to see you, brother. Heck, if you do everything those doctors told you to do, you might be up on your feet when I get back. We might take us a walk!"

Dad watched his brother leave. He wished they'd had more time together. Coy was an inspiration, a lifeline, so to speak. It helped to know that Coy expected him to make great achievements. He couldn't disappoint him.

18

The Shuffle

Dad wasted no time getting into his new exercise routines. I stood nearby watching in awe at his ability to pull himself up on a bar that was suspended over his bed.

"Jim," he'd say. "Get my chart. Write this down. I did two extra reps today."

He looked forward to his daily regiment of exercise. Though it was a slow and exhausting process and he could have become disheartened at times, he was making headway. He knew he was getting stronger, and it excited him.

Still, he had his setbacks. About once every two or three months he would waken in the middle of the night cold and shivering; an attack of malarial fever was coming on. I'd hear him call out to Mom, and she would go quickly to his side. She knew what to expect. He'd had bouts of malaria three or four times a year since they'd married. Mom would layer blankets on him and then go to the kitchen for a bowl of cool water because later he would be hot and sweating.

I often helped Mom by doing what she or Dad instructed me to do. My help usually consisted of alternately covering him when he shivered and wiping him down when he was hot and sweating. The attacks usually lasted for hours, leaving him weak and spent for two to three days afterwards. I worried about Dad, but I had seen him suffer like this many times before. He always managed to pull through. He'd say, "Jim, that was a tough one. Wasn't sure I'd make it through the night. Must've been the good care I got from you and your mom."

A few days later he'd have his strength back, and slowly the color would come back into his hallowed cheeks. His smile would return. Then, he would resume his regiment of exercise again. The malarial attacks offered tremendous setbacks and feelings that he might have lost all that he had gained; yet he never deterred. It was something over which he had some control. So, every day that he was able, he pushed himself to complete his routines.

Like the tortoise in *The Tortoise and the Hare*, Dad exercised and exercised and exercised and he became stronger and stronger until the day came when he was ready to try sitting in a chair. I remember how excited he was. "Jim," he said, "Go get your Mom and Lee. I think I'm going to sit in the chair today." I rushed to get everyone! Lee and Mom were at the kitchen table, peeling and dicing potatoes. Mom had a habit of collecting the peelings in her apron, and when I made the announcement that Dad was going to sit in the chair, she sprang up from her seat with a cry of amazement and the peelings went flying. She and Lee looked at each other as if to say, "What?" Lee dropped his knife, grabbed a chair and away they flew. I knew this was going to be a "big one." I didn't want anyone to miss out, so I ran to find Jacqueline and Billy who were playing outdoors.

"Dad's going to sit up!" I exclaimed. "In a chair! Hurry!"

We kids rushed inside the house just in time to see Lee and Mom lift Dad from the bed and help him to ease down onto the chair. He looked funny, deformed, top heavy. His upper body, which by now had regained much of its former athletic look, was a sharp contrast to his legs which were small and thin, like little round white sticks joined together at the joints. As he settled down into the straight-backed chair, he began to laugh nervously. The sensation of sitting upright after all this time made him giddy.

"I feel like I'm floating on air," he said. We all joined in the laughter!

The straight-backed chair just wasn't going to work. He couldn't get a grip on anything. But, he wasn't discouraged. With his mind going at full speed, he asked to be transferred to Mom's rocker. He had been watching Mom for years and had taken note of how she seemed to shuffle the rocker from place to place instead of getting up each time she needed to move. He figured if she could do it while holding a baby in her arms and diapers under her chin, then he could surely do the same. "Wow," what a difference. Although he said he still felt like he was floating, he now had some support for his arms—thus he had the control he needed to keep himself in place.

The first try was a hard one. It took a lot of effort, but he managed to move forward an inch or so by *shuffling* the rocker as he had seen Mom do. The rest of us watched in wonder, behaving like a cheering squad, cheering him on—every inch of the way!

He stayed in the rocker for fifteen minutes or so, every so often making an effort to inch forward. But, soon his energy waned and he asked to be helped back into his bed. Although physically tired, the smile never left his face. His goal to get out of bed had become a reality and he was highly encouraged.

Each new day became a stepping stone to covering greater distances as he added more inches until one day he managed to shuffle the rocker out of the bedroom and into the kitchen. It was a struggle for us to watch as he slowly shuffled the rocker inches at a time. We all wanted to just push him, but he waved us away, saying, "No, this is something I must do for myself." So Mom, Lee, Jacqueline, Billy and I watched curiously from a distance, tears filling our eyes as he bravely inched his way out into the room, stopping now and then to steady himself. He'd lift one leg at a time and place it about six inches in front of the rocker after which he shifted his weight from side to side and shuffled the rocker forward. Each step was repeated again and again until he was finally out of his bedroom and into the kitchen. It seemed to take forever, but he finally made it to the middle of the room. Beads of perspiration gleamed on his forehead, but pride shone on his face as we applauded his accomplishment. "Jim, I believe I could use a big glass of water," he said.

While I hastened to get the water, I thought Mom was going to hug and kiss him to death. "Clifford, I thought I'd never see the day," she said through tears of happiness. "This calls for a celebration."

"Yes, Ethel, this is truly a magic moment!" Dad reveled in his conquest as we all enjoyed a little snack.

After this momentous step forward, Dad shuffled every day that he was physically able. His heart rate increased and his circulation improved. He had gotten stronger. But best of all, he was up and about again. When friends came to call they no longer had to see him in bed with all his medications and personal entrapments. The verbal interchange became more positive. Even Dr. Williams exclaimed to him, "Clifford, you're going to outlive us all!"

Of course, Mom was really excited to see him regain his former physical appearance, even if only from the waist up. "Clifford, you truly are a handsome and charming man," she said with a smile as she placed a blanket over his lap to keep his legs warm. "And now that this handsome and charming man is up and about he may as well make himself useful. There's plenty to do around here. You can start by looking these beans." She laid a package of pinto beans on the table, within his reach. He leaned toward the table and began to carefully sort through the beans, looking for the tiny stones that would need to be removed before cooking. Dad took his good old time. "No need to do a rush job," he said.

All of Dad's first chores seemed to have to do with beans! Beans were a staple at our house. Almost every day we had beans in some form. And Dad was now the "man behind the scene" and loving every minute of it. "I see beans in my sleep. I *look* beans, *string* beans, *snap* beans, *shell* beans and *cook* beans. I am the bean man," he said laughing at himself. "I'll move on to peeling potatoes tomorrow."

Now that he could help in small ways he began to regain a lot of his self-respect. As he showed that he could endure being up for longer periods of time, he was given additional responsibilities of things he could do while sitting in one place. He helped with food preparation, mended, sewed on buttons, wrote letters, and if Mom noticed he had nothing to do, she'd say, "Clifford, keep an eye on Jimmy." I was constantly by his side. We were big buddies.

I was almost five, Billy eight, Jacqueline eleven and Lee almost sixteen. For so long we had seen Dad only in his bed. That he could now join us in activities was a time to rejoice. We were a happier family.

19

Forks of the Road

Dad quickly made up for lost time. "I've read so much my head aches," he said. "I'm ready to do something. I know I can do more than look beans, peel potatoes and sew on buttons! Put me out there at the forks of the road, I could make a living just telling people which way to go!"

Over the years, Dad had taken home correspondence courses on repairing watches, radios and small appliances and now he dug out the manuals. "I see no reason why I couldn't do repair work of some kind," he said.

"Clifford, there's nothing to keep you come from doin' some of these things," Mom said. "You've read these manuals from cover to cover a dozen times over. You must know them by heart. You might even make some money fixin' things for people."

"Then, we'll have to put a little money aside for awhile so I can order a few supplies," Dad said, picking up on Mom's enthusiasm.

"Clifford, you know I'd go without food to help you get started," Mom said as she left the room. Returning with the catalogs, she said, "Here. Make your first order. I've already put a little money aside. But after this, you're on your own!"

"Ethel, how is it that you always seem to be a step or two ahead of me?"

"I handle the money in this house, that's how! Now, get on with it before I go and spend it on myself!" Dad looked at his wife in adoration and smiled a joyful smile.

*   *   *

A new neighbor, Harry Kinder, was the first to give Dad a job. "Cliff, I got this old watch. Ain't worth a damn. If you can fix it you can keep the damn thing."

"Harry, I'm not interested in keeping it. I just want to practice on it. If I fix it, you can use it!"

Dad fixed the watch and Harry was confounded. "By damn, Clifford, that old watch has laid around here for a coon's age. How'd you do that?"

"It only needed a new stem," Dad said, amused at Harry's feigned astonishment.

Though awkward at first, with ample opportunity from family members and obliging neighbors, Dad quickly proved that he could do small repair work though he had a difficult time viewing it as work. He said he just did not feel comfortable charging a fee for what he said was truly his pleasure. "I'm just practicing," he would say.

But Mom thought differently. "Clifford, if someone wants to pay you for fixin' something, you take it. We can use the money. I might even get me a new dress!"

Dad smiled at the thought. "Well, Ethel, if I do begin to charge, will you make it a *red* dress?"

Blushing, Mom pinched his cheeks, shook his head and hugged him. Before the hour was up, she had informed Mrs. Coots that Dad was now willing to accept a little pay.

"Good as done, Ethel. The word is on its way."

Mrs. Coots was Dad's first paying customer. "Now, Clifford, you need this money more'n I do," she declared after Dad replaced a tube in her table model Philco radio. "You take this money and get you some more supplies." Dad said he was grateful.

"It's a start, Ethel," Dad said. "Here's what I'm going to do. Half of everything I make, I'll keep in one jar to be spent only on more supplies. The other half you put in your jar for that red dress."

Mom laughed. She loved fantasizing about having pretty things. But they both knew that she would spend any extra money that came her way on a toy for each of the children for Christmas.

Christmas of the year that Dad made a little money was one of the best we ever had. Mom had Lee go to the woods and chop us a small tree. With Dad's help, we all made decorations while Mom busied herself in the kitchen baking gingerbread and sugar cookies that made the house smell so good, so warm and spicy.

We made paper chains and cut pictures from magazines and newspapers to hang on the tree as ornaments. Christmas music poured from the radio, and we sang along. Mom popped corn, and she and Dad both helped us thread needles and make popcorn strings for the tree.

On Christmas Eve, just as the radio announcer had predicted, the snow came down in big, dry fluffy flakes, the kind Dad said made the best snow ice cream. We kids quickly gathered several cups of only the cleanest snow and Mom added a little canned cream, some cocoa, a bit of vanilla flavoring and a little sugar to our cups. I made an extra cup for Dad and Billy made one for Mom.

As we ate our ice cream, Dad said that he thought he heard carolers. Carolers always came to our house. We had a shut-in. Mom opened the door and we stood around Dad in the kitchen as we listened attentively though the cold air was chilling. Mom invited the carolers in for gingerbread, but they said they had more houses to go to. Dad thanked them for coming. We all wished them a Merry Christmas, and they wished us the same.

We continued to sing along with the radio for awhile, and then Dad read *The Night Before Christmas,* after which we hung our stockings, the biggest ones we could find, on the wall just behind the tree. Then, off to bed we flew with the fantasy still alive in our imaginations. Mom said she'd stay up for a while to bank the fires to keep the house nice and warm. As soon as all was quiet and we were close to sleep, Dad quietly declared that he thought he heard reindeer on the roof though the snow made it hard for him to know for sure. We all listened, the quiet deafening, and one by one we heard the reindeer too. Dad said we'd best keep our eyes closed, take no chances, and let Santa do his job.

On Christmas morning, we kids awakened nearly at sunrise to a cold house before the fires were built. We jumped from our beds in our long legged flannel pajamas and flew to see what Santa had brought us. It would have been a great picture except we had no camera.

Each stocking was filled with a toy, an orange, an apple, some nuts and some hard Christmas candy. My toy was a Lone Ranger outfit, complete with fringed gloves, mask, gun and holster. I cocked the gun and began shooting at imaginary Indians right away. Lee was less exuberant, but he was happy. He was older now. He didn't get a toy, but he got a real pocketknife. Jacqueline got a doll, and Billy got a set of toy soldiers. I ran in and showed my Lone Ranger outfit to Dad, who declared that he was going to have to watch his every move, what with me having a gun around the house. I wondered why Santa had not left something for Mom and Dad, but I said nothing and went back to playing.

Mom made hot chocolate for everyone, and we kids played and played as the house warmed and Mom went about fixing what she called a special breakfast, being it was Christmas Day. But we kids weren't enticed. We ate the orange, the apple, the candy and the nuts. We only licked the candy, occasionally putting it aside, hoping to make it last all day.

Dad stayed in bed a little longer than usual, saying he would like to be served breakfast in bed. He turned the radio on, and again we had beautiful Christmas music. Mom opened the curtains in Dad's bedroom and raised the shades so he could see how the snow had covered the trees and bushes in a most beautiful way, giving them definition and charm. He sure did love the snow. Mom had her breakfast with him.

After Christmas Day and things were back to normal, Dad began his repair work again. He didn't make much money, but he sure did delight in the conversational interchange he had with those who came to see him. He seemed to get more out of the conversation than being paid for any work he did. Still uncomfortable with taking money for his services, he'd say nothing until he was asked, "Well, Cliff, what do I owe you now?" Then he would say, "Oh, just whatever you think it's worth." He said he was never shortchanged.

Before long, people began to barter with him, and this he found delightful because it required even more intellectual dialogue. It was a way of getting something that perhaps he needed or that someone in his family could use. He called bartering a "win-win" situation with both sides getting something they wanted or needed and most times with no money exchanging hands.

"Everybody walks away from the deal happy if it's a good trade," Dad said.

*   *   *

Dad's steady hand made it easy for him to perform tedious fine motor activities. I remember that he wore a magnifying glass over his right eye when he fixed watches. His tools were quite tiny as the springs and pieces he used for repair were unbelievably small. Occasionally, he dropped a piece, and it became my job to locate it.

"Jim, come quick; I've dropped a piece," he would call out. I always searched until I found whatever he had dropped because I knew the supplies were limited and every piece counted.

"I don't know how I could do this without you, Jim," he'd say with a real serious look on his face. "We're in this business together." I felt really important.

In time, Dad gained a reputation as the neighborhood "fix-it" man. Folks would say to one another, "Oh, take that on over to Clifford, he can fix it."

Funny thing, as people began to notice how effective Dad was at repairing things, they began doing some of his thinking for him—moving him along so to speak. Neighbor and friend Charles Gillespie was a barber-turned-coal miner who had been cutting Dad's hair for years. One day he said, "Cliff, it seems to me with all the hair to cut around here you ought to learn how to do it yourself. I'll give you the tools and teach you how."

I was the first guinea pig. "Come on, Jim," Dad said, "let's give it a try." I didn't run right over as I figured that I might regret it later. But my curls had been gone for some time now and I didn't want Dad to feel bad, so I lowered myself cautiously onto a small stool within Dad's reach and sat very still, pretty much holding my breath.

Charlie led Dad through the process, giving instructions along the way. I listened intently, hoping Dad was paying close attention. "Cliff, hold the scissors at an angle now. That's the way. You're doing fine. Pull the hair up between your fingers. Right! By golly, you've got it! Now take the clippers and even things out." That remark scared me.

"All right, how'd I do?" Dad asked as he finished and I scooted off to see what damage had been done. Fortunately, I wasn't so old that I was ashamed of my haircut, but Dad got better in a hurry and was soon cutting all of our hair, including Mom's.

Not long after beginning to cut hair, Dad also began repairing shoes. Grandpa Opie brought him the cast iron lasts in varying sizes. He also supplied him with the other necessary tools of a supply of leather, an awl, a sewing machine, leather thread, big needles, glue, and an assortment of tacks. Dad had a miniature shoe shop!

Mom was impressed. "Pop, when you do something, you sure do it right. Clifford will be repairing shoes 'til doomsday."

"Nothin' at all, Ethel." Opie told her. "Just had a run of luck at poker, that's all. Figured since Cliff is up and about, he might as well be doing something useful. Everybody needs shoe repair."

"Mine need fixin' right now," Lee said. "Got a hole big as a barn down near the toe. Can't get the paper to stay over it."

"Well, what are you waitin' for boy? Put it on up here! Put Cliff to work!" Opie grinned as he lit his pipe and settled back to watch. He wanted to see how well Dad could repair the shoe.

Dad first determined which last was size-appropriate and then fitted the shoe on the last. "It's going to take more than glue," he said, eyeing the gaping hole. He looked around at his supplies, pulled a piece of leather from the stack, and measured off a piece. The first job, he figured, was for practice so he wasn't concerned for looks. Lee may have been concerned for looks, but he didn't say anything.

Herman came by. "Hey, Lee," he said. "Slop the hogs?"

"Not now, gettin' my shoes fixed. Come on in and see."

Herman joined the onlookers as Dad worked at his newest skill. "Well, I'll be," he said. "I've got to tell Mom about this. She'll be thrilled to high heaven to have someone in the neighborhood who can fix shoes."

I was thrilled to high heaven that my dad could do these things. I figured this would make him really important around the neighborhood.

*   *   *

Once, when we kids were playing football with a ball that belonged to my friend Buddy, the ball popped open at the seam. I saw the look of disappointment on Buddy's face and immediately realized I could do something about it. "Let's take it to Dad," I said. "He can fix it. He has the stuff to do it with." Buddy looked impressed. We took the ball to Dad, and he fixed it in no time.

"Can he fix shoes, too?" Buddy asked as we sped away.

"Sure, he fixes most anything," I said proudly.

Word got around. Shoe repair was a necessity. To make one pair of brogans last a whole year was a tough job. Everybody I knew had holes in the soles of their shoes sooner or later. By spring, cardboard lined the inside of most of my friend's shoes.

Word soon spread throughout the community that Dad could repair shoes, even making its way to colored town. Ottaway Chambers, a man who had once worked with Dad, came by to get some papers signed. Noticing that Dad was now repairing shoes, he said, "Colored folks don't have no way to get their shoes fixed, either, Clifford. Would you mind if I brought you a pair of shoes?"

"Bring them on, Ottaway!"

"Now this ain't going to be charity, Clifford. I intend to pay you."

"And I intend to charge you," Dad said. Both men laughed as Ottaway waved his signed papers high in the air, said goodbye and walked away.

He was back the next day with three pairs of shoes, one pair for him, two pairs for his neighbors. "No hurry, Clifford," he said. "I'll be back in a week or so. You take your good sweet time."

*   *   *

During most of the '30's our community was fairly isolated. There were no roads in to it from the Beckley direction, and the road to Whitesville was not paved. Since only a few folks had cars, taking the train or bus was the accepted form of transportation, and then used only when necessary. Rather than making a trip out of the area for services, many sought help from among each other when it came to medical, dental, legal or other significant issues of concern to them.

It made sense that folks began to consult with Dad regarding some of these needs. He was informed; he was always there, and over the course of time, some began to rely on him solely for particular services.

"Cliff, how 'bout you read this here paper for me. I can't make heads or tails out of it," I heard one man say. "Its been layin' there on the table and me not knowin' what to do with it."

Some also came for medical advice. Dad had knowledge of right many folk remedies that he had acquired from his reading, his parents and his mother-in-law, Evaline. Except for emergencies, no one in our family ever saw a doctor. And, folks in the community were always consulting with one another before going to the company doctor anyway. Doctors were used more for delivering babies and the real emergencies.

Dad had a remedy for just about everything. One day as I came up on the porch for a drink of water, I heard him giving a woman from the neighborhood a surefire cure for a big carbuncle she had about halfway up her left arm.

"Get you a milk bottle," he said. "Place it in boiling water for a minute or so until its very hot, hot as you can stand it, and then place the head of the bottle directly over the carbuncle and leave it there until you feel it drawing. Do it a number of times. It'll suck that poison right out of there."

She was back in a few days, "Cliff, you're as good as any doctor," she declared.

His medical remedies must have worked because people did return for help again and again.

My experience with Dr.Cliff was not so pleasant. It was summertime and I was playing hide-and-seek in the yard with some neighborhood kids when my bare foot caught a splinter as I ran across the walkway on my way to my selected hiding place high in the peach tree. The splinter, about a quarter inch wide, went right under the ball of my foot and came out at my heel. I screamed like a stuck pig, not only from the pain but also from the gory look of it. Dad was sitting on the porch and saw the whole thing.

"Stay right there, Jim," he called, with fear in his voice. "Stay put, 'til I can get someone to get to you."

Bill Evens, who was cutting his grass across the lane, saw the incident and came running. He carried me up to the porch.

"Bring him on in the house. Put him on the table under the light so I can get a good look at it," Dad told him.

Kids came running onto the porch to peer through the screen door to see what was going to happen. Mom shooed them away. "He's going to be all right," she told them.

Dad saw that it had skimmed the bottom of the foot. He reasoned that because the sole of my foot was thick like a piece of callus there would not be many nerve endings in it. "It looks worse than it is," he told Mr. Evens. "I can take care of it. Get me a single-edged Gillette razor, Ethel."

But Mr. Evens thought differently. "Cliff," he said, "this boy needs to go to a doctor. I'll take him on down."

Mom was horrified. "Clifford, maybe we'd better take him to the doctor, like Bill says. It looks bad to me."

"Yeah, take me to the doctor," I cried.

But Dad prevailed. He worked the blade carefully down the sole of my foot, saying occasionally, "Now Jim, tell me if it hurts." It hurt all right, but I bore the pain. He had sterilized the blade like he did when he lanced boils and things. When he finished, he said, "Jim, this is going to sting, but it will be over quickly. I screamed louder than any pig ever did, but the splinter was out.

Dad bandaged my foot up and said; "Now Jim I'm not going to charge you for these services, seeing as to how brave you were."

I propped my foot up high and endured the throbbing pain as a real Tom Sawyer/Huck Finn type would, glorying in the attention I received for the rest of that day.

Jacqueline watched me as I winced in pain from time to time. I could tell she was interested; she always felt my pain. I suffered, but mostly it just kept me off my feet for a few days. I sat on the porch with Dad and listened to baseball games and to folk's conversations as they dropped by to discuss their needs with him.

    *   *   *

By the late '30's, Dad was definitely meeting a need for the community while filling a void for himself. I was so proud of him. I saw all these people coming and going and I remember thinking that he must be a really important person, maybe the most important person around.

Being important was fine but being important in and of itself didn't add much to the family coffer. Mostly, being important provided an outlet for Dad.

    *   *   *

During the warmer summer months, Dad positioned himself on the porch as much as possible. Here, he was visible to all who passed, making it easier for folks to stop for a friendly chat or have him help them out in some small way.

I recall a day when I was five or six, when the tinkerman came. We called the tinkerman Homebud because he always called out, "Anybody home, Bud?"

Dad and I were listening to a Cincinnati Reds baseball game as it was broadcast live from Crosely Field in Cincinnati, Ohio. The Reds were playing the Brooklyn Dodgers, and Dad was giving me a running commentary.

In his younger days, he had been to Crosely Field to see the Reds play and he liked to tell me about those times. He told me all about the old timers: guys like Ty Cobb, or the Big Train, Walter Johnson, Babe Ruth, and Cristi Matseon. He was really impressed with how one particular pitcher, whose name has escaped me, could pitch either right or left-handed and during a double-header, used both.

I was all ears, sitting there dangling my legs over the side of the porch, really getting into the game and Dad's commentary when I heard the familiar jingle, the rattling and tinkling of pots and pans, and I knew Homebud was coming. I jumped up and ran for Mom. She always had something that needed fixing.

The tinkerman stopped his truck near the front gate and bounded up the sidewalk and onto the porch. He could hear the Reds game coming from the radio. "What's the score, Cliff?"

"Neither team has scored yet. The Reds have three men on bases right now," Dad told Homebud. Then he put up his hand. "Whoopee!" he cried. His favorite team, the Reds, had scored a run.

"I remember one time when my brother Coy and I went to Cincinnati on an excursion train with 500 people from Charleston to see the Reds play," Dad stated proudly.

"Hey," Homebud said, "I always have wanted to go down to see one of them games, Clifford, but I never have the time. My wife keeps me on the road. 'Get out there and make a living,' she tells me." Homebud laughed, Dad laughed and I grinned.

Dad and Homebud always had plenty to talk about. Dad was up on all the news: sports, politics, local, national and worldwide. He was never at a loss for a good conversation. Sometimes he would include me, "Old Jim here," he might say, "likes baseball. He's going to be a baseball player one of these days." I felt like one of the men.

Mom knew Homebud would be around for a while so she brought him something to drink and something from the bread drawer. (Everyone knew about her bread drawer. Even strangers!) Then she'd go get the pot or pan, scissors, knife, or whatever needed repairing. The tinkerman didn't come all that often, and she knew Dad would end up doing a little bartering so she planned to get as much done as she could.

Homebud was a jolly, pleasant-mannered man who was graying at the temples, but you couldn't really tell because he mostly kept his hair covered with a baseball cap. He was rather short and pudgy and had a little roll at his mid-line where a button always seemed to be missing, showing a little of his navel, but his appearance never got in the way of his disposition. His good-natured comments kept everyone around him smiling. Mom loved to hear him say, "Ethel, there is no better gingerbread in this valley than right here at your door!" And he would go on, "Clifford, you've got yourself the prettiest woman this side of the mountain." Dad would break into a big toothy smile. "I certainly do think so, too," he'd say. Mom would turn several shades of pink, but she loved it.

Men seemed to take a liking to Mom, though she never flirted or anything like that. She took a lot of pride in her appearance, and in her cooking, and she never tired of having someone compliment her on either one.

Homebud gathered all that Mom had for him to do and headed back to his truck to complete the job. He didn't take long because he wanted to get back to the Reds game, but he did the job well. He knew he had better please Mom.

I was wondering what Homebud was going to have Dad do for him, when he finally went to his truck and hauled out a radio, declaring on his way back, "Clifford, I've had this old thing for a while now. 'Bout ready to throw it away, but I thought I'd let you have a look at it first. Never know, the old thing might be worth salvaging."

He brought it up to the porch and Dad immediately figured it needed nothing more than an amplifier tube, which ended up being a fair barter between the two of them. Dad called it a win-win situation as both parties left happy!

I thought Homebud came out ahead. He also got some of Mom's delicious gingerbread and a nice glass of water.

20

"Tell Them I'll be Right Back!"

Dad knew that he would be able to get around better in a wheelchair, but he also knew that the shuffling he was doing in the rocker was helping to strengthen his upper body to such a degree that he would someday be able to try walking—with the help of crutches and braces.

I heard him say to Mom once when she was in one of her progressive moods, "Ethel, there's no need talking about it. We have no money for a wheelchair. Besides, I'm getting on just fine with this rocker." Mom wanted desperately for Dad to have a wheelchair, but the raw fact was that he had no money for a wheelchair, or crutches, or braces. So, for the time being he simply accepted what he had, and made do.

Dad had put having a wheelchair out of his mind since it seemed beyond his reach, but others had not. And, sometime near the end of the '30's, Dad got a wheelchair. It probably took the involvement of a lot of people through a lot of donations, and most likely help from churches far away, but the day Reverend Pindar came waltzing in with that wheelchair is a day I'll never forget. Dad was like a little boy getting his first bicycle. The wheelchair had three wheels, two big ones on the sides and a little one in the very back, making it easy to turn. "I could turn on a dime!" Dad exclaimed.

He was so overjoyed with the wheelchair that he fairly flew through the house, going to each room again and again. "Come on

Jim, let's take a ride," he invited. I rode with him, feeling a little awkward, but enjoying it just the same as I placed myself between his legs with my feet on the footrests.

That night, we kids joined Dad around the radio as we listened to our favorite radio programs, *The Green Hornet*, *Amos and Andy* and *Inner Sanctum*. During commercials, Dad would wheel off to the kitchen for water, calling over his shoulder as he left, "Tell them I'll be right back!" He'd been the tortoise. Now he was the hare.

*   *   *

Reverend Pindar was happy for Dad and on one of his visits he proclaimed in his booming voice, "Now Clifford, I know this affliction has changed the course of your life, but the Lord may have had something different in mind for you than you had for yourself. Take a good look at what you have learned. Look at all the people who have come to you for guidance and help. You must see this affliction as a turning point and see what it is that the Lord wants you to do."

"I see it the same way, Reverend," Dad said. "I've got to make the most of what I have."

"Praise God," the reverend said.

Dad had suffered much, not being able to do things. He'd had plenty of time to think and he knew he would somehow find a way to someday rise above his troubling circumstances.

Having a wheelchair opened new avenues for Dad. Like a child first learning to walk, he approached each new day with a bright new outlook, looking about to see what he could do this day that he had not been able to do the day before. Opportunities were limited. He was still confined to the house. Only occasionally when someone visited who had a car did he get out. But he was happy with his newfound freedom. To see him happy made me happy.

I was growing right along with Dad, and like a sponge I absorbed all that was around me. Dad being handicapped gave me a different perspective on life. I had a life of my own, but at home my life was entwined with Dad's. Being one of his caretakers, listeners, "gofers," and entertainers proved to be one of my life's greatest blessings.

21

The Fit

Our family had adapted to our life-style and we lived peacefully within its confines. We were accepting of the hand-me-downs, visits from family members who came to help, and neighbors who dropped by to have Dad do something for them.

By the year 1939, Mom decided that since I was in school and Dad was doing so well with his wheelchair that she would look for a job. Her friends helped. "Ethel," Mrs. Coots said. "They're startin' a hot lunch program at the grade school at Long Branch. You go on down there and ask for a job. You're a good cook, won't be nothin' for you to cook for those kids, you do it all the time."

Mom was hired first among several applicants. I knew she could do it. I was pleased to see her in the kitchen at school, serving a nice hot lunch. *Mine was free.* She was allowed to bring home some of the leftovers and even some of the government commodities like cheese and powdered milk. I couldn't wait for her to get home, to see what she would have.

She also washed windows occasionally at the Presbyterian Home School in Colcord, a job Reverend Pindar helped her to get. Though both jobs required walking several miles each way to and from, she said that getting the little extra spending money for her family made it worth her while.

Mom wanted desperately to be able to buy something new for Jacqueline. "Clifford," she said, "There's this beautiful white coat with a red collar down at Hall's Department Store in Whitesville. I'm going to get it for Jacqueline. I'll have it paid for by the end of the month. She'll have it in time for Easter."

"Now Ethel, don't you go feeling bad about how Sissie looks," Dad told her. "You're a mighty fine seamstress, and Sissie has always looked good in her clothes. Even the clothes people give to her you make over to fit her real nice."

"But I've never got her anything new," Mom said. "Orphie gets her a dress at Easter, but I've never got her anything. This will be her first store-bought coat."

"You have a heart of gold, Ethel. Sissie will be the prettiest little girl around here."

The day Jacqueline got her new coat she strutted all over the neighborhood showing it off. To be the first to wear it and to know that it had been purchased just for her made her feel so special. Dad said he was proud of Mom and of her love for their children.

*   *   *

Dad got used to Mom being away a good portion of each day, and because he knew how hard she worked, he did his best to relieve her of some of the cooking chores. We all liked his cowboy stew that was made with whatever he could find in the way of leftovers. Graced with his special blend of seasonings, it was a hearty and filling meal.

We moved right along in our own little world, content and accepting of our fate. Dad did his things. Mom had her jobs. Billy delivered newspapers. Jacqueline did some baby-sitting. Lee continued to help with all the manly chores. I helped Billy with his newspaper route.

And then one night our world shattered again. We woke to Dad's urgent calls for Mom. "Ethel," he screamed, "hurry!" Mom, Jacqueline and I jumped from our beds and hastened to his room.

The sounds were hellish. Lee was growling, moaning and thrashing. Dad was halfway up in bed trying to get to Lee. Billy hung close to the wall, wild-eyed and wringing his hands.

Mom ran to Lee, but could only watch helplessly as his legs and arms flailed and he foamed at the mouth and gnashed his teeth. His body grew rigid, then relaxed as he fell into a deep sleep. It was like a tornado had run through Lee's body, leaving him totally spent, soaked with perspiration, and the bed linens drenched.

None of us had seen anything like this before, and we were frightened beyond belief. Billy began pacing back and forth. I thought his eyes were going to jump out of his head as they were so wide. Jacqueline was sniffling and clinging to Mom, and I went to Dad's bed and stood as close to him as I could. He reached over and put his hand on my shoulder, offering a wee bit of comfort. "He's had a fit," he finally said.

Mom, with no understanding of what had happened, was crushed to see Lee in such a condition. "Clifford, what should we do?" she asked.

It was late at night and Lee seemed to be all right, so Dad suggested that Mom wait until the next day to consult the doctor. He knew about "fits." He knew that for now it was over, but figured that there would be others. Lee slept soundly throughout the rest of the night and had no recollection of the seizure when he awakened the next morning.

Dr. Williams, who still helped our family in emergencies, and yet never charged for his services, diagnosed Lee's "fit" as a *grand mal* seizure and said it was serious. "Lee needs medical attention," he said. He prescribed Phenobarbital, supplying the initial prescriptions free of charge.

Lee responded to the medication favorably. His life remained pretty much normal, though he did continue to have an occasional seizure, almost always at night. Mom moved him to the living room where he had a cot of his own. I was moved into Dad's room to sleep with Billy.

Mom implored Dad to help her to understand Lee's seizures. Dad made an effort to learn as much as he could about epilepsy, figuring that ignorance was his worst enemy. Dr. Williams helped. He supplied reading materials.

Mom remained distraught and Dad did his best to bring her comfort. "Ethel, the Lord does not give us more than we can bear," he said.

"But, Clifford, it just don't seem right. Lee is so good. He helps me so much. It seems like God is punishing him."

Dad's beliefs were much like his mother, Rosabelle's. "We will get through this, Ethel," he said. "Just as we have before. The good man upstairs has not failed us yet."

Dad's idea was that they would control what they could in their lives, and let the Lord help them with the rest.

He asked Dr. Williams if the hard lick to Lee's head from the merry-go-round incident years before might have triggered the seizures. The doctor said it most likely was the source.

22

"Boys, go make your tracks!"

It was always at the time of the first snowfall, and it didn't matter if it was early morning, late evening, a school day, a holiday, a light snowfall or one that was two feet deep as soon as Dad discovered it, he called out, "Boys, go make your tracks!"

Billy and I knew what that meant. Usually in bed and just waking, we'd jump out in a hurry and make like the wind to the great outdoors. Barefoot and clothed only in long-legged flannel pajamas, we made our tracks by running without stopping as we encircled the outside of the house. Our squeals of delight sent neighbors to the windows—though none came to join us.

Before going back inside, we would indulge ourselves in a small snowball fight which meant also rolling in the snow until we were thoroughly wet or wetter, depending on the quality of the snow. Sometimes we had a dry, powdery snow, and sometimes we had one of those awful wet ones. I liked the wet ones the least.

Mom would be calling for us before we finished. It upset her every time Dad had us do this. "Clifford," she would say, with a look of disgust, "those boys will get their death of cold. Why do you do such silly things?"

But, Dad thoroughly enjoyed the whole show. Watching from his bedroom window, he cheered us on. We'd wave to him on the first trip around the house and blast his window with a snowball on the second while relishing the powerful feeling it gave us.

We consumed the rest of the time in our own delights as Dad watched with his face contorted from the effort to conceal his mirth. He was remembering days gone by when he, too, as a young lad had frolicked in the snow with his brothers.

"Now, Ethel," he would say, with a touch of warmth in his voice. "It'll do them good and help them, too," using his favorite expression.

"It won't be good, and it won't help *those* two!" she'd come back at him. "Just you wait 'til they're sick with cold. I'll remind you of this."

"They won't get sick, Ethel," he'd retort. "It's a boy thing. They'll be back in directly."

"I know you think it's just a boy thing. But look at them. They'll be ice cubes when they get in here." She'd be hiding a smile by now as her hands were busy stirring hot chocolate on the stove, and consoling Jacqueline who wanted to join us. All Jacqueline ever managed to get from Mom was an, "Absolutely not! Don't be ridiculous!"

Dad stayed out of that one. He'd laugh though, knowing he was winning the battle for the men!

"Besides, it's time the boys braved the world," he'd say.

"Oh, yes!" Mom would retort. "Look at them. They're out there wrestlin' in the snow. Jimmy's going to get hurt and Mrs. Coots thinks they're crazy. (Mrs. Coots had left the window and was on the porch. She probably did think we were crazy.)

We wouldn't last all that long. The cold would get the best of us, and we'd head back in, all cocky, knowing that Mom, for all her talk, would have some steaming hot chocolate and warm towels for us. Jacqueline's looks of envy made us feel bigger than ever.

"Now see, Ethel," Dad would say while we continued luxuriating by soaking our hands and feet in warm water. "They'll be stronger for it. This is the kind of thing that makes a man of a boy."

"A man!" she'd scoff. "It's tom-foolery and you know it."

"No," Dad would say. "Boys need to know they can make it in this world. They need to know how to be tough, to get by. If boys are coddled too much, they won't take risks and they won't know how to weather the storm."

I'm not sure Mom understood this. She was more interested in getting us dry and warm again. But, Billy and I did. Dad had already begun a series of man-to-man talks with us. (Especially Billy, since he was beginning to venture from home and try to make some money.)

Billy began his endeavor into the business world with a newspaper route, which Dad, through his acquaintance with Sam Thompson, had helped him to get. "Old Billy," Dad would say, "is tough as nails. Look how he gets himself up in the wee hours to fold those papers and take off at daybreak to deliver them. He'll be a good one, you can bet on that." Billy *was* good. He caught on quickly, and with Dad's added advice about how to market himself with his customers he was soon saving a little on the side.

Billy always had a few extra newspapers that he used for leverage to help him acquire new customers. For three consecutive days he'd leave one of the extras at the door of someone who didn't subscribe and on the fourth day he'd ask, "How'd you like the paper, folks?" I'm not sure whether it was Billy's charm or the fact that folks really liked the paper, but Billy got a lot of new subscribers this way.

Billy wanted to give his earnings over to the family, but Dad and Mom refused. They wanted him to learn not only how to earn money but also how to budget it as well, saving some and giving some to charity. Dad said what he gave to the family was the charity! He liked getting a free newspaper each day.

Billy learned to spend wisely, buying mostly essential things, though he occasionally treated himself to a sweet at the company store if he felt so inclined.

He delivered his papers by foot, until one day he lugged home an old, but sturdy, bicycle frame he had found near the dump—a place near the end of the community where people frequently discarded their unwanted items and junk. We often scavenged there for scrap metal that we would later sell.

Billy was not proud. He had learned to make do with what he had, so he reckoned that with a few spare parts he could restore the bike to working condition. He dug into his savings, and with assistance from Dad and the Sears and Roebuck catalog he ordered all the additional pieces he needed. Ultimately, he made himself a serviceable bike.

The bicycle made delivering papers a cinch for Billy. He ended up with spare time on his hands and began looking around for something else to do. He was never one to be idle, particularly not since he'd begun making money.

Quick to notice the change in Billy, Dad said to him, "You know, son, the world is larger than this coal camp." Billy took this to be Dad's permission for him to expand his paper route.

In order to expand his territory, Billy figured he would need to be able to carry more papers. After some problem solving, he reasoned that if he added a basket to the front of his bicycle and saddlebag baskets to the back, he could carry enough papers to pretty much double his customers. So, as Dad advised him to do, he invested some of his savings back into his business by ordering the baskets from Sears and Roebuck and was soon into delivering papers big time. He expanded his territory and in a short time had a route that extended all the way down into Ameagle and on into Colored Town, a round trip distance of about two miles.

It thrilled Dad to see Billy work through and solve his problems this way. He got a kick out of watching him rise early and organize his newspapers for his early morning run, though oft times Billy needed an assist.

"I can't get all these Sunday papers in my baskets," he'd say. "Jimmy's going to have to help me." So I ended up taking his New Camp route on Sundays—on foot, I might add.

Delivering newspapers was a hard job. Billy saw lots of his fellow carriers fall by the wayside as they became disillusioned and frustrated with the early and late hours, bad weather, and putting up with customers who claimed not to have the money. Billy often heard, "I'm a little short this week, catch you next week." It caused him many repeat trips to collect, but old Billy just hung in there and got better and better. The more money he made, the happier he became. He was a natural entrepreneur.

Billy met a lot of people too. Some would say, "Aren't you Clifford White's boy?" and Billy would beam with pride that Dad was recognized and respected in the community.

Anyway, this is the way Billy began to make his tracks. He learned a lot from delivering newspapers.

As for me, I stayed close to home and continued to be Dad's sidekick, absorbing like a sponge all that he was able to share. From these talks, I learned that it was important to be a hard worker, to complete the task, to give my all, to be fair, and to never take advantage of the underdog.

I learned about the world of sports, about competitiveness, about being the best. Dad's favorite sports were boxing and baseball, and he was quite knowledgeable about both. He'd played baseball a little in his day and he had boxed some, too, while in the U.S.Marine Corps.

Talking about sports helped Dad to experience vicariously what he missed being able to do physically. He loved reminiscing about the greats of his day, John L. Sullivan, Jack Dempsey, Gentlemen Jim Corbitt. He knew them all.

I became his listener and his entertainer as he gave me pointers, showed me techniques and then had me demonstrate them for him. He figured correctly that I would someday do well in sports. "You should've seen old Jim," he'd say to anyone listening. "He took all the punches old Joe gave out and stayed on his feet." I'd feel like I'd really boxed with Joe Louis.

We listened to all of Joe Louis' fights. Dad would jab right along with Joe, and so would I, and when the fight was over, both of us would be pretty well spent. Dad got a kick out of this, saying, "Jim, I need me a big drink of water. What about you?" We'd have our water, with me usually sitting in a straight chair leaning against his bed, legs sprawled, wondering what we'd do next. It was always like this. I knew more about the nature of sports than about anything else. I couldn't seem to get enough of it.

23

Do You Good and Help You Too

Dad's two younger brothers, Clarence and Charles had a habit—a drinking habit, that is. They came now and then to visit—mostly, as they said, "to see that Old Cliff gets a good stiff drink." They were the sociable ones, loud and upbeat, and usually with a glow when they arrived. They came with a repertoire of humorous tales or off-color jokes to entertain and amuse Dad. I was duly impressed and would station myself nearby so I could hear it all until Dad would catch on and send me away. "Jim, you run on out and play now," he'd say.

Clarence and Charles weren't like Opie and Coy and Connie and Cova and Cora, or Orphie or Evaline, who came to help the family in some more serious fashion. Clarence and Charles didn't come to fix the chicken pen, paint the house, or help with the garden. Their form of help was always entertainment and mirth. They laughed and joked and cajoled, but they were fun and as Dad would say, "We need fun in our house, too!"

Though Mom adored both of Dad's brothers, she monitored their activities closely. Clarence, a plumber by trade and especially good-looking, had a nice build, great blue eyes, a shock of black curly hair, and always a ready smile. He was a charmer, and the women around loved him. Mom dreaded the times he came because she said she never knew whom he might end up with. There was at least one child in our neighborhood purportedly fathered by Clarence.

As a young lad, Clarence had once taken a dare and jumped from a train trestle, jamming his hip and leaving him with a slight limp. So, he always appeared a little tipsy even when he wasn't.

He had a nice car and weather permitting, he'd say, "Let me take old Cliff for a ride, Ethel."

"No, Clarence," Mom would say emphatically. "You're in no condition to take anyone for a ride. You'll take Clifford out there somewhere and get him hurt."

But Clarence never took no for an answer. "Now, shucks, Ethel, you can come along too. Then you can make sure we don't get into any trouble." Clarence tried his charm, but it didn't matter anyway, because Dad would already be at the door waiting for Clarence or Charles to carry him out. "Ethel," he'd say. "Things will be all right. We'll be back directly." Dad knew he'd have a good old time. He would never pass up an adventure.

Clarence especially wanted to make sure Dad had some of the manly pleasures he was certain he was missing. When he saw how well Dad was getting around in what he referred to as "that old wheelchair," he decided that he'd help Dad get back into making his own "home-brew", the term they used for homemade beer.

Dad didn't need the recipe for this process, but he did need the supplies: hops, malt, brewer's yeast, and some bottles and caps. Clarence eagerly obliged, giving Dad a generous amount of what he needed. So, by the end of the thirties, Dad began making home-brew again though he had to be careful because it was illegal to make beer.

Being illegal didn't bother Uncle Clarence. He just said, "Well, Cliff, how else are you going to get yourself a drink? You sure can't buy it!"

Dad didn't argue with Clarence's logic, for he sure couldn't buy it! But he was excited and thrilled and really looked forward to having his own magic moments once more.

I distinctly remember the beer-making because I helped with it. Dad and I started the process on a Saturday while Mom and Jacqueline were washing windows down at the Home School. Billy was out delivering papers. I don't recall Lee being around.

We first laid out a plan. Laying out a plan was a big thing with Dad. "Before you do anything, always first lay out your plan, Jim," he would tell me. I could see that a plan was probably necessary for making beer because Mom wasn't going to approve of it anyway.

First in the plan was to locate a place for the beer to be housed during the fermentation process. We did a little problem solving, with me doing most of the thinking. Dad was all smiles. *I was making my tracks!*

At my suggestion, after mixing the first batch according to the recipe, we put it in the well on the side of the cook stove in the kitchen. After all, it had to be in a place that was consistently warm, and Dad agreed that there was no better location in the house.

Mom was furious. "I've a good mind to dump all this crap out in the yard. Clifford, you shouldn't have done this. You shouldn't have made that stuff. What will people think of us? It is against the law, you know."

But Dad prevailed. "Now, Ethel, there won't be any problems. Nobody's going to know. It is in our house, you know. It's not like I'm bootlegging. I'm not going to be selling it. I'm going to be drinking it."

Mom finally gave in. "I guess we'll be lookin' for a house up in Sand Lick," she said with good humor. Sand Lick hollow was where all the moonshiners lived, and where she was certain Clarence took Dad on his little outings. But Mom said she knew Dad's pleasures were few and she also knew that he would be discreet about his beer making. She said she just couldn't see denying him this little pleasure. He had few enough.

Dad and I watched our batch carefully until the day it was ready for bottling, which coincidentally also fell on another day when Mom and Jacqueline were not around. But Billy was, and he was a big help. Dad said that Billy reasoned as well as I did, and he made a lot over Billy's suggestion that after we bottled the beer we should store it under *our* bed.

Occasionally, one of the quart-sized bottles would explode—usually in the middle of the night—at which time Billy and I would awaken with a jolt and bolt upright in bed, sometimes in unison. Once we almost knocked each other out, or maybe we did; our heads bounced off each other. I looked at Billy and said, "Billy, did you see those stars?" He just groaned and went back to sleep.

Poor Billy, he was always getting his sleep interrupted. He'd say, "Jeez, can't a fellow get some sleep around here. I gotta get up in an hour!"

Loss of sleep would make Billy grumpy, but he kind of liked the idea of making the beer, so he didn't complain too much. Neither of us ever really got used to the explosions. It was like being shot at with a gun again and again. We never mentioned it outside the home, though. This was not your typical "show and tell" story for school.

After an explosion, with the sweet pungent smell of the beer permeating the room, Mom would come in to see how much damage was done. If it wasn't too bad, she'd say, "I'm just going to let you beer-makers lie here and smell this all night." Then she'd look at Dad with a crooked smile and say, "Clifford, the great beermeister. You'd better be glad you can't get out of that bed and clean up this mess!" I could sense Dad grinning in the dark.

Mom worried about visitors—especially Reverend Pindar, who still came to call regularly. The height of embarrassment would be that a beer might explode just as Reverend Pindar was offering up one of his powerful prayers. "That won't happen, Ethel," Dad said. "The good man upstairs looks after us." He'd laugh and Mom would be miffed.

"And how about Dr. Williams?" she asked.

"No, he would just sit here and enjoy one with me, Ethel." Dad just wouldn't let anything interfere with his beer-making.

Though he shared an occasional beer with a visitor, he chose his recipients carefully. His brothers, Clarence and Charles, were always allowed to imbibe, and imbibe they did. Dad was always eager to show off his batch, and his brothers were just as eager to share it. There was a time when the three of them got a little drunk, joking and laughing while they played cards, just happy-go-lucky guys having a good time.

Mom was furious. "All you boys do is get Clifford all worked up. He's silly enough already!" She referred to Dad's antics as "silly" whenever she saw that he was losing control. The men just laughed her off, and proceeded, all of them, to get a little more intoxicated.

After Clarence and Charles left, Dad just sat all giddy and smiles. Mom decided he'd been up long enough and said: "Clifford, you go on to bed, now. You've had enough fun for one day." Dad wheeled off to his bedroom. Mom and Jacqueline followed with plans to give him an assist into bed, but he motioned them away, saying, "It's okay. It's okay. I can do it. I think I can catch it (the bed) the next time it goes around." Mom was disgusted. She and Jacqueline put him into bed.

Dad didn't imbibe so carelessly after that. He wanted to stay on the good side of Mom, so he behaved. But Billy and I had witnessed the drunken scene and we were intrigued. It seemed like a manly thing to do.

We chose a Saturday when Dad was napping and Mom and Jacqueline were off cleaning windows. I had already sneaked the bottle out and had it hidden up on one of the rafters in the coal bin. I figured correctly that the coal bin would be a good safe place because Billy and I were the only ones to ever get the coal. Besides, the coal bin was right next to the doghouse and old Sparky would bark ferociously if anyone other than one of us came near. Lee was away. He wouldn't know.

Billy wrapped the bottle in one of his newspapers and we went whistling off toward the creek. It was a nice fall day. The leaves were still intact on most of the trees, though the colors had changed to various shades of yellow, red, and gold. We considered ourselves lucky to have such good cover as we meandered casually along the creek bank, finally selecting a place where the creek made a nice curve giving us visibility from several directions and where the bushes provided plenty of protective camouflage. Over from the bushes jutting out into the creek was a big, boulder-like rock that had a wide, almost flat area on top.

Settling down Indian-style on the flat part of the rock, we began our little adventure. I don't remember who went first, but we began drinking, passing the bottle back and forth without stopping, and yes, before long, we were silly too. We started laughing and carrying on, and it didn't take long for one of us to almost drop the bottle before one of us did drop the bottle, which shattered on the rock. "Uh-oh, what do we do now?" Billy was first to speak. Of the two of us, he was the more responsible, but worried less about consequences. I knew that we had better clean up the evidence and so we did. We buried the broken glass in the soil around the rock.

We might have planned another little adventure like this one had it not been for the aftermath. On the way home, totally unaware that we were staggering—what drunk doesn't believe that he is in complete control of his gait—happiness overtook us. We were men of the world, throwing caution to the wind, no longer worried about being discovered—just silly and brazen and loud, even letting out an occasional "Whoopee!"

Billy was the first to stumble, and then I fell over him. We laughed at first and pretended to get into a little scuffle, which resulted in some grabbing and holding as we began to roll around in the grass.

"I'm getting sick," Billy said, grabbing his stomach. I followed with a lurch, unable to even say how I was feeling. Then we both let go. It was awful. Vomit spilled all over our clothes, and neither of us was able to stop. "Oh, oh," was all either of us could say.

We lay there for some time, with the good fortune of no one noticing us; and then we headed home, where to our dismay we met up with Mom's best friend, Bessie Legg. Mrs. Legg was just leaving our house after having discovered that Mom wasn't at home. She took one look at us and became seriously alarmed.

"Oh, my goodness, boys, what has happened?" she asked.

Drunk as we were we knew better than to tell the truth, but on the other hand, we were in no condition to converse either, so we just shook our heads and headed in.

Dad was up. He took one look at us and at Mrs. Legg, who had followed us into the house, and he knew. He knew the smell of a drunk. "Boys," he said sternly, "You had better get yourselves cleaned up fast, before your mom gets home." And to Bessie, he said with resignation, "They're drunk."

Dad used his words sparingly, often conveying a big message with but one or two words.

Mrs. Legg got the message. She knew our family well and she knew that this problem would get resolved expediently with the proper consequence applied. She headed on home.

Sensibly, Dad waited until the next morning to deal with us. As we awakened, he said, "Boys, stay here." We sat on the edge of our bed and faced him, expecting a strong reprimand. Speaking in measured tones and holding back a smile he asked. "Boys, did you enjoy that batch or was something wrong with it? It didn't seem to go down well." We both responded with a low moan.

In his wisdom, Dad counseled us about the dangers of what we had done, and the risks it had put us all in. We could see ourselves sitting in jail, along with Dad in his wheelchair, and Mom and Jacqueline coming to visit us. We were breaking the law, and Dad wanted us to remember that part of it well.

And remember I did. I remembered how sick and silly I felt. I wanted to crawl back into bed, but Dad said, "No, your mom will want to know why you're sick. You'll just have to be men now and go on out there and face the day." And so, we did.

As for any future drinking, Billy and I weren't concerned as Dad had made it clear to us that we could have beer anytime we wanted it—so long as we drank it with him! He'd simply said, "Having a little drink now and then will do you good and help you, too." Which he said meant drinking responsibly. In our case, it would be at home, with his blessing. It was a long, long time before either of us had another beer, but we did still help make it.

As for Mrs. Legg, she never let on that she had ever seen anything. That's the way it was with our families.

24

Rich Man, Poor Man

It was a colorful October day, just a few weeks into the school year. I had just gotten off the school bus and was flying off after three bigger kids, all about Billy's age, who had quite quickly gotten way ahead of me. They had been teasing and heckling me since we got on the bus. Now, they were laughing, pointing back at me and calling out, "You look like Raggedy Ann's brother. Where'd you get all them patches? You ain't never had any new overalls since we know'd you. Don't nobody ever get nothin' new in your house? Them ole things look like they been wore to death."

Mom had been watching for the school bus and had seen it all. Out of the house she came, with Dad's words of "Now, Ethel, kids will be kids," trailing after her. Dad figured that the boys were just getting their jollies by teasing me, but Mom was angered. She was on her way to collar them for picking on a boy smaller than they were.

The boys took off when they saw Mom and were soon beyond my reach, leaving me to give up with a "I'll get you, just you wait and see." They knew they had the best of me—though I had the last say as my rock bounced off a fence post and grazed the ear of one of them.

The three of them wore bib overalls, too. It was the style. However, their overalls were newer and had only a few patches, while mine were not only threadbare, third time hand-me-downs, but also ill fitting and all but covered with patches. No holes, but lots of patches.

I looked down at my overalls and I was suddenly ashamed. I felt something I had not felt before, and I tore off for home, passing Mom on the way and upping my speed as she attempted to get me to stop. I stormed into the house and fled to my bed where I quickly buried my head in my pillow and scrunched it up to wipe my tear-streaked cheeks and hide my embarrassment.

Dad wheeled into the room but said nothing until Mom came popping back into the house.

Fuming, she asked, "Jimmy, what was that fracas about?" Dad put his hand up to quiet her. He knew I wasn't yet ready to talk.

I was in second grade and had begun to be a little on the scrappy side, especially when it came to my family. I knew we had a harder time than the other families around us, but up until now no one had ever teased me about it, and it hurt. It hurt terribly.

Work had really picked up during the late '30's and early '40's, and everyone around us had someone working in the mine and bringing home a paycheck. They all seemed to have anything they wanted, buying all the newfangled electrical appliances on the market and going places and doing things that only money can provide. Plus, they all got to use the company store for credit when they needed it. Meanwhile, I was still setting our electric meter back each month so that the reading was negligible. The man who read our meter had given Dad instructions as to how to turn it back. Though the meter man knew it was wrong, he said he felt bad charging us for electricity knowing how we needed our every dime. Each time he came to read the meter, he'd stop in to chat a bit with Dad and upon leaving, say, "Cliff, I've read your meter. I don't understand it, but you folks just aren't using any electricity." Then he'd leave, exchanging smiles with Dad.

The electric bill would not have amounted to much but even that little bit of savings helped us. We were still surviving mostly on Dad's monthly check for $69.52 and the piddling little amounts that he made doing odd jobs for people. Besides he bartered so much that he made little money anyway. Mom finally said to him one day, "Clifford, we can't spend toasters. They're not taking toasters on our account down at Roy Flint's grocery store. Please don't take any more electrical appliances for services rendered." Although humorous, it was true. Dad had gotten a little carried away with bartering. The coal miners were buying toasters, electric coffeepots, sandwich griddles, etc. and then trading them off to Dad when they had no cash with which to pay for his services.

Mom made a little from her job as a cook at the grade school and from cleaning windows at the Home School. Lee was away in the Navy. Billy made money with his newspaper route, enough that he could occasionally buy something new for himself, like trinkets for his bicycle. He had more freedom and independence than the rest of us. Jacqueline baby-sat a lot, but she never got paid any money. She baby-sat and cleaned for one family off and on all one summer and when fall came, they bought her a new pair of shoes for school.

I was just frustrated with it all and too young to understand on my own. So as Mom came over to me, I just blurted it all out. "Why do I have to wear these old raggedy overalls all the time? How come I don't get some new overalls like the other kids? They say I look like Raggedy Ann's brother with all these patches. They say, 'You're poor, you don't ever get anything new.'" On and on I went until I finally broke down and cried anew. When I looked up again, I saw the pain in Dad's face and the anger in Mom's face. I fell back onto the bed, ashamed that I had spoken so harshly. I knew the answers to my questions.

We had never really talked about our plight in terms of being poor, but Dad figured it was time we did. "Yes, Jim," he said, "we are poor. But poor is not a dirty word. Lots of people are poor, and many are much worse off than we are. Some don't have a roof over their head or food for their hungry stomach or a warm bed to sleep in at night, or clothing enough to keep warm when it's cold outside. Yes, we are poor. We're poorer than some and better off than many others, but we're surviving and things are going to get better for us. We're not real poor. Real poor is like that old stray dog that wanders around out there in the alley. He doesn't have a home and has to scrap for every bite he gets. Survival is a constant struggle for him. He has no one to care for him, nothing he can depend on. Things just get worse. That's the hardest kind of poor. You, Jim, what do you have?"

He paused long enough for me to weigh his words, and then continued. "To get new things, you have to have money and right now, we have very little money. When you don't have enough money, you have to do without some things. You have to use your money for the things you cannot do without. So, in that way we are poor. But your mom does the very best she can with what we have and with what others give to us. She always has a nice meal for us. She always has a little something in the bread drawer for you when we're hungry. She keeps our house warm and clean. She works hard to keep your clothes mended. Every time she sees a tear or rip she quickly sews it up for you, so you'll have no holes in your clothes. That's what a good mother does; she patches the holes, because she loves you. All those patches on your clothes are little love buttons from your mom."

Mom smiled and glanced at Dad with a loving expression that said, "Clifford, you do have a way with words." I caught a fleeting glimpse of moistness shining through her big, round eyes. She knew that she always did her very best by us and that she was often overly protective, but she'd never thought of her patches as being "little love buttons."

Mom's radiant complexion, now aglow in varying shades of pink, gave me to understand that she had allowed Dad's simple description of her loving ways to calm her inner rage. Her outer beauty majestically blended with her inner beauty and suddenly all I could think of was the nice hot meal she had cooked that day at school. I was so proud that she was a school cook. I gave her a nice warm hug and told her how sorry I was. Dad, too. He was my hero. I thought he could just about solve any problem.

Feeling much better, I now knew that we were poor, but I had some understanding of the different qualities of being poor. Besides, we were rich in love and that counted most in a family anyway. I still wanted better overalls, and somewhere deep inside me I knew that Mom and Dad, now that they knew how important it was to me, would find a way to get them. I also felt that I could handle this problem a little better on my own in the future.

Jacqueline arrived. She now attended junior high school and came home a little later than I did. Right away she wanted to know what had happened, "What's wrong?" she said, "Why is Jimmy crying?" But, she would have to wait. Dad was not one to repeat things and certainly not one to keep something stirred up. She'd just have to bide her time and get her information later—from Mom—which she did.

Jacqueline was more protective of me than Mom was. After getting the scoop, she went into a tirade and verbally bashed the boys who did this to me and vowed to give them a well-deserved tongue-lashing when next she saw them. And you could be sure she would. Kids didn't usually mess with Jacqueline. She had a scathing tongue! She also had friends who supported her when she set out to defend someone. Together, they were a formidable group.

I knew right then that my sister would always be there for me, right or wrong. It was a comforting feeling, one that drew us close. I now knew that she would always come to my rescue. I wasn't worried about the boys anymore. With her as my caretaker, I could take some risks.

In some ways Jacqueline was insecure, always hanging onto Mom, but in other ways she was tough as nails. She had a sense about her that she could take care of all of us. She made a believer out of me.

Dad accepted her behavior for what it was. "Sissie will be Sissie," he said. "Her tongue may be biting, but her heart is in the right place."

By the time Billy came in from delivering his newspapers, things were pretty much back to normal, though Jacqueline let him know just how she felt about his classmates.

"Those boys are too big to be teasing Jimmy like that. They won't run away when I get hold of them. They'll wish they'd a kept their smart-assed tongues to themselves!" she announced.

Billy's reaction was a practical one. He knew the boys. "Oh they're just old silly boys. Don't know any better. They got plenty of patches of their own." Billy was quickly becoming independent, learning the ways of the world and how to deal with troublesome people. He was known to take no foolishness, but he didn't waste his energy on futile arguments. No wonder he was so popular at school, and so well liked in the community.

25

Charlie

Charlie's feeling very bad today. The fever's been in his family now for two months. His younger sister Arnell has already died from it, and the family is fearful that his Mom may be next. The family situation is dire and there seems to be no way out. Charlie is advised by his parents that his best bet would be to head south, where the climate is warmer and healthier. He has an uncle in Texas, and the family thinks he should head there.

He's just turned sixteen, which is supposed to be a happy time, but he is sad that everyone in his family is sick. His family is so poor. He has no way of helping them. His dad hasn't worked in two years. The mills are closing in Illinois where he lives and work is scarce. Charlie can't stay in school. He wants to stay in school, his grades are good, but his family cannot afford to keep him. They want him to go live with his uncle in Texas. Uncle Joe has sent a letter from Texas saying that he can find work for Charlie. The family says, "Go, Charlie, we can't do anything to help you. Go to Texas where you'll have a chance."

Charlie ties up his belongings in a huge bandanna and takes the two biscuits his mother hands him and heads out, promising his mother and dad that he will write as soon as he gets there and that he will send money. Tears fall from his eyes.

Charlie's a good boy. He's never harmed a flea. His head hangs low as he heads down where the hoboes hang out. They'll be able to advise him as to how to hitch a train and where to get food and whatnot he will need.

He has the directions to his uncle's place in his pocket. And two $1 bills, one in each shoe, all that his Dad had to give to him, with instructions not to use it unless he absolutely had to, only under the direst of circumstances. Take it all the way to Texas, if you can, boy, his Dad had said. It'll be quite an accomplishment if you can. You can do this. I have confidence and faith in you. Things will be all right.

The hoboes have a fire lit and they're frying chicken. Chicken! Charlie wonders whose chicken coop was robbed. The smell makes him hungry. He wishes they'd offer him some, but he sees just how little they have.

He settles in with the red faced and grimy old characters, placing his bandanna on the ground to cushion his head. They laugh and welcome him aboard. "Ain't no use you hanging around here, Charlie. Ain't no work anywhere between here and Houston. You be better off going on down to Houston. Ain't nothin' here. Bob here, he's taking off tomorrow. You go along with him. He'll set you on the right track."

Charlie waits around for Bob and takes off with him as the sun rises the next day. Bob hops aboard the train first, like a pro, and Charlie tries to copy the way he does it, but it's not really that easy and his leg gets caught in the ladder on the side of the car. Bob grabs on to Charlie's hand and together they somehow untangle him and get him inside the boxcar and just as he falls forward onto the floor the directions to his uncle's place in Texas fall out of his pocket and fly off into the wild blue yonder. Charlie doesn't notice. He's too scared. He knows he just barely escaped death. He's lying on the floor panting; his heart pounding so hard he thinks his chest is going to explode. Bob laughs and pats him on the back. "All part of the game, my boy," he says. And then Bob rolls over onto a sack of something and goes to sleep, leaving Charlie to think about what would happen next. He looks at all the scenery along the way, the farms, the animals, the cloudless blue pastel sky and he begins to feel better, except he's plenty hungry.

The biscuits are gone, and he's got to figure a way to get something to eat somewhere along the way. The next thing he knows he sees a sign which says: Welcome to Tennessee. The train is coming to a stop. Bob is still sleeping. Charlie tries to waken him, but Bob doesn't stir.

"Okay, boys, take it from there." Dad had started one of his Charlie stories, as he so frequently did when it just seemed too early to go to sleep. *Charlie* stories were a far better way to keep us boys occupied than the rough and tumble stuff we sometimes got into.

Billy and I ate it up. Charlie was a part of our lives. We never tired of the *Adventures of Charlie*.

Billy wanted this one. "I got it," he said, and proceeded to get Charlie into more trouble before he turned it over to me. We got Charlie in and out of all kinds of scrapes: saved him from a vicious dog, found his directions as they traveled via another hobo, got him a small job, found him a place to sleep, fed him, clothed him, wrote letters to his mom, got him sick with the fever, lost his shoes, found his shoes.

Mom came to the bedroom door and stood listening, waiting for a time in the story to interject her needs. "Clifford, it's time to give us all a rest. I know Charlie would appreciate it. Charlie has to be tired. He's crossed two states while I've been standin' here listenin'. If need be, I'll take a leg of the story and get his skinny little, well-traveled butt in bed." She laughed at her own comments. She liked it when we told stories. She let this be one of our man things.

I tried, but I couldn't fall asleep. My mind was racing. I wanted to get Charlie into a predicament that hopefully Billy or Dad would have trouble getting him out of. I knew they would try to do the same.

Storytelling was another way Dad helped us boys to *make our tracks*.

26

A Star in the Window

The smell of chicken frying came floating through the house. Billy stirred and soon I was sitting up. Dad began shuffling, "Ethel, what on earth are you doing? It's two o'clock in the morning!"

"I'm celebrating," she called from the kitchen, and finished with a light chuckle, "David's home."

When David came in on furlough from the Navy, he didn't go to his home first. He came directly to our house, no matter what time of day or night. By now, he claimed us as his family, and he had been adopted by us as well.

Most people called him Deedle, not David or Dave. He answered to whatever, but we called him David because Jacqueline did. He was her beau and had been for about three years. They began dating when he was a junior and she was a freshman in high school.

By high school, Jacqueline had grown into a rather beautiful young lady with a *somewhat* softened temperament. Though several guys were interested, with the help of Mom and Dad, she managed to keep them all at bay. David, however, was more persistent. Besides, he never had to take "No" for an answer because he didn't ask for much. For a long time, he simply crooked his right index finger and motioned for her to come near to him. Then in a soft whisper he would simply say "Hi," after which he would go his way and she hers.

Unusually handsome, David was tall and well built with twinkling, soft brown eyes and a mane of wavy black hair. He was a good student, a good athlete and well liked by his peers, teachers, and coaches. Though he wasn't shy, he was reserved, soft-spoken, and unimposing.

He came from another coal mining community called Dorothy, four or five miles down the river from Ameagle, going toward Whitesville.

When David was born, his parents were having marital difficulties and did not want to face rearing another child, so they gave him over to his paternal grandmother to raise. Afterward, he seldom came into contact with his parents. His father remarried and moved to Charleston where he worked as a policeman. "My mother remained nearby, but she had no interest in me." David said. "She never gave me things for my birthday or for Christmas." David's memories of his family were filled with cold and cruel rejections.

He didn't receive gifts at Christmas time or for his birthday, but he always hoped he would. He said he'd never forget one particular Christmas, when he was six and his mother came to the house. She said to him, "David, you go on up to the post office. I'll bet your present is at the post office. Go on up there now. I ordered you a pretty red truck. Go on up there and see if its there." David said he went to the post office every day for a month looking for the red truck. It never came.

Aside from an uncle who sometimes slipped a candy bar under his pillow late at night, David recalled few acts of kindness shown him during his childhood. Much like an orphan, he was simply given a place to live, which itself was sometimes used as leverage against him. Though he was well behaved, his grandmother would sometimes tell him she was going to send him away, leaving him to feel insecure and wondering what he would do out in the cold.

Given numerous chores, David worked hard to please. He wanted to feel that he earned his keep. He also went out into the community to seek jobs, though jobs were certainly not plentiful as folks had little to pay anyway.

At one of these jobs he met Jacqueline. "I was cutting the grass at the Presbyterian Home School," he said, "cutting with a sickle. They didn't use mowers then. And Jackie and her mother came walking up. I remember speaking to them and giving Jackie a big smile. They both smiled back at me and we had a short conversation of some sort, with me looking mostly at Jackie. Finally, I went back to work. I was so thrilled to have someone around. I couldn't wait to get back to work to show off, like boys do. Jackie and her mother went on about their business, washing windows. I sneaked a look every now and then, trying to catch Jackie's eye. When she'd look my way, I'd give her a big smile and she'd smile back. Then her mother caught on and said something to her. She stopped looking my way. But, that's where I first saw her. After that, I started looking for her around the school and pretty soon, I found out all about her. Every time I'd see her I'd give her a little crook of a finger motion and when she'd look my way, I'd just say "Hi." It was a long time before we dated. Besides, I didn't have any money to date. I thought about her all the time though, and I was plenty jealous if she paid attention to anyone else."

Dating wasn't easy. With no money and no form of transportation other than his two legs, David just had to dream. Besides, he was an athlete, which kept him at school for long hours of practice, after which he still had chores to do.

Once he did start dating Jacqueline, he'd ride the bus up to New Camp, but walk the distance back because he never seemed to want to leave in time to catch the last bus out. Not until he began to hear Mom making "time-to-leave-David" noises from the kitchen did he begin his departure. She'd begin with clearing her throat and shuffling her chair, but it often took more than a little coughing to get David to move. He'd stick around as long as he could. Then, having missed the bus, he'd have to walk the five miles home, sometimes in a cold and biting wind. He declares there's not a colder spot on earth than the bend in the road at Ameagle where the bus used to stop.

David was love-starved, eager to love and to be loved. As he became more familiar with our family, he adopted us, and we adopted him. It was just that simple.

At any rate, David was home on furlough, and we were making a celebration of it. It was no easy task to fry chicken at 2 a.m. in the morning. The chicken wasn't in the icebox, trimmed and ready for frying. It was in the backyard chicken coop. So to have fried chicken, David had to first get the chicken from the coop, wring its neck, scald it and then pluck its feathers. Mom took over from there.

Actually, David dressed more than one chicken, 'cause our chickens weren't that big. Mom would never fry chicken without frying for us all. She knew we'd all get up to see what was going on.

But this time the pickings were slim. "Ethel, do you think you might have a chicken thief?" David suggested since he figured there should have been more chickens big enough to eat.

Mom looked at me, then back at David. "You're lucky to have any," she said with a smile. "Jimmy's in charge of the chickens. He watches them like a hawk. One gets big enough to eat, it's on the table!"

"I'll say one thing for him," David laughed "He keeps that chicken coop clean."

"And my flowers beautiful!" Mom added, giving me a knowing smile.

That I did. It was a continuous process. We ordered our chickens, usually two hundred at a time, from Rhodes Hatchery in Shady Spring. On the day of delivery, I'd have the coop clean and the brooder light working so it would be nice and warm. The biddies were packed together like sardines, with barely enough room to grow. Some would die right away; I quickly removed them. As the others thinned and grew, they made lots of manure which I shoveled from the coop daily and put directly on Mom's flowers. Then I'd take the biddies one by one to pick the accumulation of manure from their feet where it had balled up like marbles making it almost impossible for them to walk—and subsequently unable to get to their food. I valued having the chickens to eat, so I took my job seriously. The more I kept alive, the more we had to eat.

I considered it a feast whenever we had fried chicken. And having a celebration for David was a good time for a feast, even if it was in the wee hours of the morning. While Jacqueline and David sat holding hands on the blue mohair sofa in the front room, the rest of us joined them to give David the love and acceptance he had come to treasure from our family. I got out the sailor hat David had sent to me soon after he joined the Navy, and Dad, who declared it a magic moment, got out one of his beers. We all whooped it up as we ate fried chicken and partied 'til daybreak. David told us war stories about his Atlantic crossings to England, giving us a sense of closeness to the war. We listened to everything he had to say. He was our war hero. Though we kept tabs on what was happening in the war—we listened to the radio, and Dad read the newspaper daily—it was nice to have some first hand information.

David was like a son to my parents and like a brother to us boys. We all liked him a lot. He would be going back to war soon and to wherever he was in the European war-theater. We had our star in the window.

27

Fourth of July

Rosabelle most always planned a big Fourth of July celebration and she made sure that one of her clan came for us. It was a huge gathering of family, to which Grandma also invited her boarders, her neighbors and a few acquaintances from her church as well.

This time, in the year 1943, Uncle Charles came for us. Charles, like Clarence, was dark-haired and handsome, jovial and carefree. Mom was just as skeptical of Charles as she was of Clarence, but she was grateful for the opportunity to get away with the family. It was our vacation.

Charles came rumbling in the evening before, in one of his jolly moods. "Ethel, come here and give me a hug," he said. "I ain't had a hug from a pretty woman in months."

"You don't need any pretty woman. Your drink is your pretty woman!" Mom sniffed for signs of liquor, but gave him a hug anyway.

"Now, I feel a lot better with a hug from a beautiful woman!"

Mom looked at the car with anticipation and at Charles with doubt. "Do you expect us to get in that car and go all the way to Wills Hollow with you, and you drinkin'?"

"Now Ethel, I ain't had a drop. Cross my heart. Mom wouldn't let me leave the farm unless I was sober." Charles looked at Dad and winked. Dad gave Charles a look of understanding and rolled backward a bit in his wheelchair. "At least half of that is right!" he said with a half-grin, his head cocked to one side.

And Charles took that as an okay for him to continue to cajole. "But, Ethel," he said, "I'm gonna have to have me some nourishment of some kind, or I'm not likely to sleep tonight. And if I'm not likely to sleep tonight, then I'm not likely to be able to get that old car back over to the farm."

Mom sighed. "You're hopeless, Charles."

"But you love me anyway, now don't you?" Charles was a first class tease.

"Help yourself to a beer, Charles," Dad said. "I'll have one with you."

Mom looked on with a stern face. "Now Clifford, you know what could come of this," she said.

Billy and I watched and listened, fidgety as Bantam roosters, pacing back and forth, getting in each other's way and teasing and laughing. We loved it when Uncle Charles or Uncle Clarence came. It was a license to be wild. But Mom retained control. "Clifford, I don't think I'm going to be able to stand bein' cooped up with these two in Charles' car all the way to the farm. You need to have a talk with them!"

Dad suggested we get out of Mom's hair, go to the bedroom and listen to the radio. "Save some of that fun for tomorrow, boys," Uncle Charles added in jest as he opened his beer and settled himself down at the kitchen table with Dad nearby.

We went to bed, but we couldn't settle down. We were too jubilant. This day only came once a year, and for us it was better than Christmas. We eventually calmed down some, afraid to take too many chances. Sometimes Mom took a stick to us though she never really hit us, but she did come close once, so we paid attention. Right now she was pretty focused on Charles. She watched him closely, taking no chances.

But Charles surprised her. He didn't get drunk. He slept like a baby on the sofa in the living room and was up at the crack of dawn like he said he would be, helping Mom load her food and our clothes in the trunk. Mom had prepared something for us to eat on the way so no time would be wasted. We had a ways to go.

Jacqueline took time to primp. She put on lipstick and brushed her hair what seemed like forever. Billy and I fussed. "She's going to take all day!"

"Jacqueline wants to be pretty, look nice," Mom said. "You two look liked you just crawled out of bed. Get in here and wash your faces and brush your hair. You think I'd let you go lookin' like that." Jacqueline looked at us and smiled as she passed by us on her way to the car. She did look right pretty.

Then Dad rolled to the doorway, donned his hat and announced he was ready for the trip. "Let 'er roll," he said. Charles carried Dad out to the car. Jacqueline, Billy and I followed. Mom was the last one out. She locked the doors, double-checked them, and then hurried out in her prissy way of walking and slid into the middle of the front seat. The rest of us piled into the back. Charles got behind the wheel and off we went. We waved to everything we saw moving as we left New Camp.

Charles soon had us all in stitches with a steady stream of jokes and funny stories though we were giddy enough as it was. Mom and Dad laughed as hard as the rest of us. Dad put his arm around Mom's shoulder. I thought they looked like sweethearts.

"Now admit it, Ethel," Charles said as we arrived at the farm. "Your brother-in-law is the best on the road, now ain't he!" Mom said she couldn't argue with that. She gave Charles a hug and thanked him for coming to get us.

Clarence called out to us as we wheeled into the driveway. He hurried to the car, greeted us warmly and then carried Dad into the house where Grandma had a rocker waiting for him close by the cook stove where she was busy frying chicken. Clarence's hands were bloody. He held them up for us to see. "Got to get back to my job," he said. "Wringin' chicken's necks!" Dad chuckled and waved Clarence away.

We kids headed out to the chicken-killing area, curious to see how the mass production worked. Clarence began anew, wringing the chickens' necks with one hand and chopping off their heads with the other. Then Corbitt took the headless chickens and hung them by their feet on the clothesline where they hung until they stopped dripping blood. At that time, Charles stepped in to help. He took the chickens from the line and tossed them into a big tub of hot boiling water.

Charles saw my eyes moving back and forth and looked at his brothers and winked. "Jimmy, make yourself useful," he said. "Throw a few pieces of wood on the fire. Gotta keep this water hot!" I hastened to the woodpile, eager to be a part of it all.

Corbitt's boy, Richard, took the chickens from the water and plucked their feathers. Corbitt's other boy, Joe, then cut them into frying size pieces. Billy started right in helping Joe. They were the same age and the best of buddies.

It became my job to cart the chicken pieces off to Grandma, who dipped the pieces in seasoned flour and fried them in great big skillets filled with hot lard. The smell of the chicken frying was enough to make the day, with nothing added.

Jacqueline set off with Corbitt's girl, Mary. Mary was as pretty as an angel and had a voice like a nightingale.

All of Corbitt's kids sang and played musical instruments. They also lived right next door to Grandma and had the advantage of learning to play her pump organ. Grandma, who was schooled to read music and to harmonize, knew how to get the most from her clan. Corbitt's kids all said she was strict. I thought they sure were lucky.

Mom gave assistance to Corbitt's wife, Edith, and to Clarence's wife, Faye, as they set up tables for the food. I was the only one who came back often to check on Dad because by now I was used to it. I had to see if he needed anything, to "write a letter" or needed a drink of water. I was his legs—so to speak.

A friend of Mary's asked for Lee. "Lee isn't with us this time," Mom told her. "He's away in the Navy."

"Oh'" the girl said, visibly disappointed.

Relatives came from all over, but our family lived the farthest away.

Cova, a highly respected seamstress in the Charleston area, and her husband Homer came. Cova and Homer had no children, but they had a model T Ford that made a lot of noise when they arrived. When we kids heard the ooga, ooga horn, we went running. "Uncle Homer's here," we called back and forth. Homer worked for Lewis Hubbard, a food distributor in Charleston. He always brought the unusual food we couldn't wait to see. Bananas, watermelons and cantaloupe, grapes, he brought them all. And this time he brought store-bought "light bread," the first I ever had.

Then came the Morrises. Cora was married to Waitman Morris who had his own filling station and was running the bulk plant for all the other filling stations in the Charleston area. We considered them to be the moneyed ones. They lived in a rented house on Fort Hill, a prestigious location in Charleston overlooking the Kanawha River. Their kids were always dressed better than the rest of us, but when we got together at Grandma's it made not a bit of difference. It was fun for all.

Uncle Connie, who was now a truck driver for Bell Trucking Lines, came with his wife Wava, who was from somewhere over in Tennessee. She spoke in a refined way, using those long *i*'s. They had no children, but Wava had a camera and took lots of pictures. She believed in the occult and was a respectable medium. Everyone seemed to want to talk to her.

Charles's wife Garnett and their two girls, Pat and Jo, were there. Pat and Jo were close to my age.

Uncle Coy wasn't there. He had moved, with his second wife, Edith Wilcox, to California, where he had opened his own barbershop. Dad said he missed him.

The women helped each other spread the food on long, long tables. They socialized. The men socialized, and the kids played. It was a most joyous occasion, just as Grandma wanted. Even Opie made his way back home from his poker travels to be with the family on the Fourth of July.

The men took but a short while to set up a card table in the yard, in the shade of the trees. Dad was carried out so that he could participate. Rosabelle endured the card playing, but frowned on poker. It was gambling, she said. Pure and simple. Gambling. A sin against God. Opie never pressed for poker on her territory. He just played cards. He had made his declaration many years prior, and it had served him well. "As soon as the kids are on their own," he'd said, "I am leaving and I'm going to play as much poker as I want, where I want and when I choose! I'm going to die with my boots on, playin' poker, and that's that!"

For all his talk, Opie never totally relinquished his responsibility to his family. He came home occasionally to see Rosabelle, and mended and repaired—just as he did when he visited us about once a year. He was a good carpenter. And he always sent Rosabelle money from wherever he was. *She never refused the money!*

Opie loved Rosabelle's fried chicken. He'd come all the way from California for her fried chicken, he said. Rosabelle just shook her head. The scent of chicken frying wafted all over the farm, and when it was ready Rosabelle called loudly from the porch for all to come. With her high resonant voice, she didn't need a bell. The adults ate first. Always. This was tradition, but they always left plenty for us kids. I liked the watermelon and fruit the best, anyway. It was something we didn't get often.

At some point, a hush sort of fell over the place. One by one, everyone became quiet, cocked their heads, and turned to look in the direction of the barn, from which melodious singing could be heard wafting through the air. It was enchanting, attention getting.

When it got unusually quiet and everyone was looking in the direction of the barn, Jacqueline and Mary leaned out of the big hayloft window and began to yodel, just like the yodeling you might hear in the Alps. Knowing this time they had an audience, they put on quite a show. Mary had taught Jacqueline to yodel and together they really sounded good. They were praised the rest of the day!

Some of the neighborhood boys were hanging around, too, I noticed. Jacqueline and Mary blushed and smiled a lot.

The yodeling so inspired Grandma that she called for all the adults to come together on the porch. "After Wava takes a few pictures, we will commence with the singing," she announced. Clarence carried Dad over and placed him on the edge of the porch where he could brace himself between his brothers for the pictures. Afterwards, they helped him into his rocker where he sat on the porch with the crowd. Grandma handed hymnals to the adults and then began selecting the songs. Before long the music portion of the day was underway.

One or more of Corbitt's kids accompanied the singing by playing the organ, guitar, or mandolin. Uncle Waitman joined in with his fiddle. Together, they were a terrific group of musicians. We all listened and sang, but only the adults got to sit on the porch.

As the day wore on, Grandma and Edith, Corbitt's wife, and some of the older girls went off to milk the cows. We kids followed; we liked listening to the sound of the milk as it squirted from the cow's teats into the tin pail. The milk was carried off to the cellar to replace the already chilled milk, which would now be used to make milkshakes. I was about to get my very first milkshake.

Next to the cellar was the barn. "Go on over to the barn, kids," Grandma told us. "Play around in the hay and up in the loft. Corbitt's kids will make you a nice malted shake." Using a special tin container, Joe and Richard shook the cool milk, to which some malt and a little cocoa had been added, and we had chocolate-malted milkshakes. *Hmmmmm, hmmmm good.* I took one to Dad. He said it reminded him of when he was a boy.

At day's end, most everyone would leave. It was hard, saying goodbye to all my cousins, aunts and uncles. We had such a good, good time together. Jacqueline left with Aunt Cova who wanted Jacqueline to come to work for her, in exchange for which she would make Jacqueline some dresses for school. Jacqueline was excited about the dresses, but she was anxious about working for Cova. Cova was a taskmaster somewhat like Grandma Smars, she said. At Aunt Cova's, Jacqueline had to "bite her tongue."

Aunt Orphie came and got Mom so they could have a few days together. Billy and I stayed with Dad at Grandma's, though Billy went to stay with Corbitt's boy, Joe. They lived next door to Grandma. We often did this for a week or so before returning home. It was our vacation.

Grandma's was a bustling place. She was a busy, busy, woman and she kept those around her busy too. Billy and I and all of Corbitt's kids helped with the livestock and with the gardening. And then we played. We would be completely exhausted after a day of hard work, raucous play, fresh air and a sumptuous big dinner. Grandma had a big long table, which seated twelve or more. Corbitt's family and the boarders ate there as well.

Staying at Grandma's was a delightful time. I was so happy that Dad could sit in the rocker and be a part of it. I could see that it pleased Rosabelle to have him there, too. She kept him near to her as she went from chore to chore, carrying on a continuous conversation, though I noticed that Dad mostly listened. They reminisced about past socials and events and who was now doing what. She'd say something like, "Clifford, do you remember so and so," and so it would go. She talked all the while she worked, not missing a stroke as she churned butter, swept the floor, washed the dishes or whatever needed doing. Sometimes Grandma would be talking when suddenly her head would nod and she'd begin to doze. After a bit, she would awaken and take up where she had left off as if nothing had happened. I thought it was phenomenal!

Something was always happening around Grandma's. One night as I lay sleeping on the soft feather tick next to Dad's bed, someone came knocking on the door. "Aunt Rosie, you need to come. Bessie's ready for her baby. She needs you, now!"

Grandma, called Aunt Rosie by those in the community, quickly got dressed, grabbed her medical kit and headed out to the barn for her horse. She then took off somewhere to deliver a baby. The details we heard all about the next morning at breakfast.

Rosabelle was a midwife and in her lifetime delivered more than 500 babies, using whatever form of transportation was available to her. Sometimes she rode her horse, other times the train, and sometimes she walked. She only went by automobile if someone came for her in an automobile. She never owned a car. Only on occasion was there a problem she couldn't handle, a stillborn or a breech. These were the sad occasions, which she also told about.

But there was no doubt that Grandma was a well-respected and loved person who served her community well. Kids flocked to her door where she often handed out cookies or candy. No one was ever turned away from Aunt Rosie's.

It was always fun at Wills Hollow. We were never really ready to go home, though we missed Mom, but the day did come when we headed back to New Camp where there would be plenty of work to do. The garden would need attention. Grandma Smars would come to help Mom with the canning and preserving of fruits and vegetables, though she wasn't as energetic as she used to be.

*   *   *

Jacqueline came home with the dresses Aunt Cova had made for her and handed them over to Mom with tears in her eyes. Cova was an excellent seamstress and sewed for the finest in the Charleston area, but she failed to keep up-to-date with Jacqueline's age group. Mom looked the dresses over carefully, deciding how she would alter them to make them stylish to look like the dresses Jacqueline's friends would be wearing. "They'll be fine, Jacqueline. I can fix them," she said, giving Jacqueline a hug.

Billy went back to work at Roy Flint's grocery store. Roy had admired Billy's energy and drive as a newspaper boy and had asked him to come to work for him as a stock boy. Each day he gave Billy a quart of milk to bring home. Mom said she appreciated it.

Mom heard from Lee. He had completed his basic training, but would not be sent to war. The stress from the training had brought on several seizures, and he was given an honorable discharge and was sent to the Veteran's Hospital in Roanoke, Virginia. Mom was saddened again.

"Ethel, when Connie comes through here, he can take you down to see Lee," Dad told her. Uncle Connie was a truck driver and his route took him through our area on his way to Roanoke.

"Oh, Clifford, maybe we ought to just bring him home."

"Give it some time, Ethel. You'll want to go see him there at the hospital, first." Dad wasn't' sure just what Lee's treatment would entail, but he thought it best not to be too hasty about bringing him home.

We heard from David. He was on one of the Liberty Ships taking supplies across the Atlantic Ocean to the war zones. We still had our star in the window.

I went back to playing with my buddies in the community. We wore our black armbands and took our jobs seriously as Junior Commandos out looking for warplanes that might fly over Ameagle!

Dad would say, "Jim, you had better get your group together. I hear planes overhead." I'd go gather my buddies: Bobby Toney, Charlie Martin, Jim Eddie Fowler and Jimmy G. Stewart. We gathered at the empty garages where we studied pictures of all the enemy planes, the Japanese zero, dive-bombers and German bombers and fighter planes. We discussed what we, as soldiers, were to do if we saw one of the enemy planes go over Ameagle.

It was wartime. We did what we could to help the war effort. We gathered scrap iron, saved string and tin cans and other items which had suddenly become scarce. Dad listened to the radio and read the newspaper everyday to keep us all informed as to what was happening.

We kids enjoyed looking at the new pennies, which in the years, 1942 and 1943 were made from zinc. They were shiny and looked like dimes. You could almost pass them off for dimes.

Dad settled back into his routines. He now had a larger wheelchair, one of those big wooden ones, another gift from the Presbyterian Church. He said it was very comfortable, but he couldn't *turn it on a dime!*

Grandma Smars came to help Mom can and preserve foods for the winter. We kids helped, too. Our job was to scrub the jars and lids and place them in boiling water until they were sterilized. Billy kept the fire going under the tub of water in the backyard. We all carried water from the neighborhood pump. We peeled peaches and apples and strung and snapped green beans. We were busy for days on end. Our kitchen was like a steam bath, but not one of us complained because we knew the canning and preserving meant we had food. The canned goods were housed on shelves on the back porch. When all was completed, Mom liked to stand back and admire her colorful and artistic arrangement.

"They are quite beautiful," Dad would always tell her. She would smile and give him a hug.

After the canning days were over, Grandma Smars had us all on the porch stringing beans to dry for "leather britches" as she called them. We took pride in making our strings all about the same length so they looked neat enough to complement the canned goods.

One day, as we sat stringing green beans, Jacqueline came running in with the mail. She waved a letter in her hand. "It's from Aunt Orphie," she said. Mom dropped everything. She loved getting letters from Aunt Orphie.

Quickly opening the letter, she began reading with a smile but suddenly gasped. "Oh, lordy," she said, "Orphie's boys are missing in action. Russell and Vernon, both. Both are down behind the enemy lines in Germany. Eugene's okay. They're sending him home." All three of Orphie's sons were in the war.

"Oh, Ethel, we'll have to go to her," Evaline said. "She'll need us."

Dad said, "There's no question. You must go.'

28

Give Me a Hand

Late in the spring of 1944, on her way home from her job at the grade school at Long Branch, Mom made her daily stop at the post office. She looked each day for a letter from Orphie, eager to hear whether Vernon had been found. Russell had been located and was on his way home. We talked about it often.

"No letter today, Ethel," the postmaster said. "But you do have three big packages. Too big for you to carry, though. Addressed to Clifford."

She hurried home. "Clifford, we have packages at the post office. Big packages. I couldn't carry them. They're addressed to you," she said, out of breath. "What on earth have you ordered?"

"Not for you to know, Ethel. Just send the boys on down to get them."

"Hurry on, boys," she told us. "Must be something for you. I have no idea! Clifford, what have you ordered?"

"Not telling, Ethel," Dad said with a mischievous grin.

Excited and curious, Billy and I hightailed it to the post office, where we got the packages and scurried out.

"These things sure are heavy."

"I know. Feel like rocks! Can't be rocks, though!"

"It's not even Christmas!"

"Not even a birthday!"

We hurried home and stood nearby, eagerly waiting for Dad to instruct us to open *our gifts.* But he only said, "Put the boxes in the corner in my bedroom, boys." Billy and I looked at each other, raised our eyebrows, grinned and did as we were directed.

"What's in the boxes, Clifford? You can't make these boys wait like this. *We* need to know."

"*We'll* know shortly what is in them," Dad said, but he didn't make shortly come too soon. For days the boxes sat in the corner and no amount of coaxing could get him to tell any of us, including Mom, what the boxes contained.

And then one bright and sunny day while we were away at school and Mom was away working, Dad asked our neighbor, Harry Kinder, to give him an assist with opening the boxes. Harry was a slender, wiry, dark-haired, good-looking man whose main aim in life it seemed was to have a good time. When he wasn't working, he was out and about, socializing, as was his thin and wiry, light-haired, pretty wife, Nellie. They were good, fun-loving people, and Dad enjoyed their company.

"Harry, I've got a surprise for the family. I need your help with a little assembly here," Dad said.

"Hey, I'm here to do your bidding," Harry said, throwing out his hands with a broad grin. "Anything you say!"

Dad showed Harry to the boxes. Harry split them open and brought out the contents. "Hells bells, Clifford, what in tarnation *are* these things?" he said.

"You'll see, after we put them together. They're my leg braces and crutches!"

"Braces and crutches! You mean you're gonna try to walk, Clifford!"

"You got it!"

"Holy shit!" Harry gave Dad a look of stupefaction and scratched his head in amazement. "Damn and double-damn!"

Grinning with anticipation, Dad urged Harry on. "Well, don't just stand there Harry. Let's put these things together."

Harry took the crutches from the package, then began to study the braces. "God almighty, Clifford, look at all these pieces. How are we supposed to figure this out?"

"Can't be much to them, Harry. This piece is a harness," Dad said, fitting the harness around his waist. "And the braces attach to the harness. It would help if they were put together first."

"We'll get these things together," Harry said, not letting Dad get the best of him. "These things are stainless steel, Clifford," he said as he finished assembling them, "they'll last you a lifetime." Then he gave Dad a quizzical look. "How you gonna manage this, anyways?"

"Just get me going, Harry."

"Will do!"

With a few personal adjustments of the leather harness and leather straps, Dad was ready for fitting the braces onto his legs. It took all the strength he could muster at first. "I can't believe my abdominal muscles are so weak, Harry. Feels like I'm pulling my gut out."

"Lord, Clifford, the way you work out, you got to be strong. I mean, everwhere except your legs."

"These muscles through here are hard to exercise, Harry," Dad explained, rubbing his abdominal area. "But it looks like I'm going to get my chance right now. Here, give me a hand. Let's give it a try."

Dad's energy dwindled quickly. He huffed and puffed, as he rested between the upward thrusts it took to pull himself up into an upright position. After several trials he found it a little easier and finally, after lots of effort and determination, he made his first trip up all by himself.

"Clifford, I'd a never believed it. You up here movin' around like you're walkin'!"

Dad smiled, proud of his accomplishment, but what he was doing was no easy task. Getting up and staying up was difficult. He needed something to hold on to, to pull himself upward, and once up he needed to have something to hold on to for support while he adjusted the crutches and locked the braces in place where they were hinged at the knee.

The whole process took several minutes and it made him light headed. His abdominal muscles burned with pain and he was certain that he had definitely overdone it. He had been too ambitious. But he figured the surprise for the family in the end would be worth the extra effort on his first day.

Harry only helped when needed because Dad said, "No, Harry, you won't be around the next time. I'll do it myself." Once he felt comfortable with the outfit and the process, he settled back into his wheelchair and rested. His brow wet with sweat, he said he felt like he had pulled double time in the mines. "I'm going to take a rest now, Harry. I'll need all my energy for the big show."

"What show, Clifford? You mean you got something else planned here?"

"Tell you later. I've got to rest up a bit."

"No problem," Harry said. "We'll take us a rest."

*   *   *

Several minutes before time for Mom to arrive home, Dad announced his plan. "Put my crutches down by the fence, Harry," he said. "I'll roll down the ramp and meet you at the gate."

"Clifford, you don't mean to say you're going to get up out there in the yard, now, do you?"

"Yup, that's what I'm going to do. But I need you to help me." Not a problem. Harry was there for the duration.

Down at the fence, Dad worked himself up into a standing position and with Harry behind him for support, he managed to hold on to the fence while he made his adjustments with the crutches. Had it not been for the flow of adrenaline, he would never have made it over the yard's uneven surface. Little patches of slippery grass or an occasional soft spot in the soil made for a good many little adjustments. It was so tiring; every part of his body that had feeling ached from the effort, tempting him to just give up and try again another day. But, his eagerness to have his surprise work kept him going. He needed to grab hold of the fence a lot, and he had to keep the crutches in balance. His armpits ached from the effort. But he eventually got the hang of it and walked, well, not really walked, but swung his lower body forward a few inches at a time until he made his way a few feet along the fence, all by himself!

Harry was astounded. "By damn, Clifford, look at you! Walkin'! In the yard of all places! I'll be damned!"

Harry brought the wheelchair closer so Dad could sit a spell and as he did so, he called to Nellie. "God almighty, Nellie, you got to come see this! Cliff's out here walkin' in the yard!"

Nellie came flyin' out. She was flabbergasted as she hugged and embraced Dad. Before long, the Coots' came to the fence, and Bummy Bumgardner stopped on his way home from work.

Dad always thoroughly enjoyed visiting and talking with those who came to see him. He was known to talk about anything and everything. But this he had kept to himself. This event he had planned over a long period of time—since he had begun putting aside a little money here and there, long, long ago, and he'd kept it a secret, for he intended it to be a big, big surprise.

"Now, Ethel will be coming down the lane in just a few minutes," Dad said to those gathered. "She's not seen this yet."

Nellie couldn't believe it. "You mean to tell us Ethel ain't seen you in these things. God almighty, Clifford, she'll have a heart attack! I almost did myself!" Others echoed Nellie's sentiment, astounded that Mom had not been a part of Dad's scheme. But, there's nothing like a surprise party. All joined in and played along with Dad.

Mom saw the crowd near the fence and her heart jumped to her throat. *What is wrong?* Her first intuitive feeling was that something had happened to one of her kids. She began to run, but coming closer she recognized the group as her neighbors and saw that they were gleeful, so she slowed her pace and peered at them in wonder.

Not expecting to see Dad among the group, and since Harry stood directly behind him, she actually did not see him at first. "What's going on?" she asked. No one said a word, just looked at her and smiled. Then she saw the empty wheelchair. "Where's Clifford?" she gasped, afraid that something had happened to Dad, yet, wondering why her neighbors were still all smiles. Then she saw him, standing against the fence, grinning broadly, his hat falling off to one side of his head. She nearly fainted. She did swoon, and the bag of groceries she was carrying slid from her hands and spilled out onto the grass around her. Bummy grabbed onto her to keep her from falling. "Clif...ford!" was all she could say. She looked at him in disbelief, completely stunned.

Then hurriedly, she opened the gate and ran inside where she could get to him. Placing her hands affectionately on his shoulders, she gave him a kiss, then leaned back to look at him with a broad grin breaking into an open smile. "Oh, Clifford, why didn't you tell me?" she uttered as she adjusted his hat. "You scoundrel. You didn't let anyone know."

"I wanted to surprise you." Dad's eyes glistened as he looked into her eyes, and suddenly an emotional shift caused Mom to begin to cry. Then Dad's eyes teared up and soon Nellie began to cry too. Before long, tears dribbled from Harry's eyes. "Clifford, this is truly a magic moment!" Mom said, wiping the tears from her cheeks with the back of her hand. She laid her head lightly on his shoulder before suggesting that he sit again.

Beyond tired, Dad readily agreed to sit, but he insisted on remaining in the yard until "all the kids come in." He sat back in his wheelchair and bathed in the excitement around him and waited until he saw the big yellow school bus come to a halt and begin to disgorge its cargo of boisterous, jubilant kids. Then he began his ascent once more, even allowing an assist from Harry this time, saying he hadn't the strength to do it again on his own.

Dad and his assemblage of well wishers watched in anticipation as we kids tumbled from the bus and ambled down the lane, wondering, too, why there was a crowd gathered at the fence. When we saw Dad, we were astonished. None of us had thought about Dad ever standing, much less moving about in an erect position. He stood beaming as we gathered around him and joined in the joy of his accomplishment. It was exhilarating! I was amazed at how the braces and crutches worked. It was like a miracle had happened.

We had not seen Mom so happy in quite some time. We all were happy. We couldn't wait for Lee and David to hear about it, and Uncle Coy and Opie and all Dad's family and Mom's family and Dr. Williams, and Dr. Battalion and Reverend Pindar and Reverend Myers, and just about everybody we could think of. "Just wait 'til so and so hears about this," we said again and again. Billy set off on his bike. Jacqueline went to tell her friends, and I went to tell mine. In all of my life, I had never seen Dad stand. It was shocking.

"Hell's bells! Clifford," Harry declared, "we're steppin' out tonight. You and me, we're going down to Whitesville and hit all the high spots!" Harry and Nellie cackled. They would have their own celebration, for sure.

And Dad was thrilled beyond belief. It had been eleven years since his accident. He had only dreamed that this day would come.

*   *   *

Opie came to visit just as soon as he found out that Dad was walking with braces and crutches. He, too, was astounded. "I wish old Coy could see you now," he said to Dad. (Coy was in California and hadn't been to visit for a long time.) "Coy would for sure want to take you out, over to see your mom and show you off a bit. Me, I can't take you anywhere, not havin' a car."

"Well," Dad said, "now that you've seen me up and about, you can tell the others in the family. Tell them to come see for themselves. I could use a little company." Opie promised that he would. He stared in wonder as he watched Dad shuffle along the fence.

Mom gave Opie a list of little things to be done. "I declare, Ethel, I believe you just make up some of this stuff for me to do," Opie said as he perused the list. "This list gets longer every time I come."

"Now, Pop," Mom said while stifling a snigger, "you wouldn't stay any time if we didn't have things for you to do. You'd be flyin' off right after you said your hellos. We like your company."

"Well, that explains it. You're deliberately tearin' this place apart, so's I'll be here for awhile. I need to be out earnin' some money, sittin' in a good poker game somewhere." Opie smiled as he drew on his pipe and set off to begin his repair work.

The list was long, but Opie seemed in no big hurry to complete his tasks. He sat around with Dad a lot, played cards, shared a beer, and shot the bull. He was an incessant talker. "Cliff," he said, "where'd you get all this knowledge? Can't talk about anything you don't know a little something about."

Dad, proud that Opie was cognizant of his academic accomplishments, just smiled. Opie took out his list and looking it over said he'd best get back to business. "If I don't get some of this done in a hurry, Ethel will be here with another list and I'll never get away," he said. "I've already been here a week, and I'm only halfway down this list. I'll never get done at this rate"

I figured Opie was beginning to get "itchy feet" so I wasn't surprised when he called to me, "Come here, Jimmy, I figure I'd better start teaching you how to do some of these things. I may not be around the next time it needs to be done." Dad gave Opie a smile of gratitude.

"I'll have dinner ready directly," Mom said, giving me a smile. "There'll be something special for you fellas."

Mom's words of inclusion made me feel like a big man in demand. I eagerly accompanied Grandpa and proved myself to be a quick learner. "Jimmy, if you keep this up, there'll be no need for me to come again," Opie said jokingly. "I don't want you to put me out of a job!"

"But, we want you to come," I said.

"Well, then, I'll come, Jimmy, but the next time, I'll just sit back, smoke my pipe like a gentleman and make up a list for you like your mom does for me." It seemed I grew a foot in that hour of work. I figured that the next time Mom needed something done, I'd be the one she'd call upon.

A few days later, just as Opie was preparing to leave, saying it was time for him to hit the road, news of President Franklin Delano Roosevelt's death came over the radio. Opie sat down, stunned, as he listened intently along with Dad and Mom and the whole household to the details of the President's death as they poured forth from the radio. A feeling of sadness overcame us all as we talked about the loss of a respected president—a president especially revered among coal miners in general. Everything seemed to shut down as a mantle of mourning overtook the camp.

Opie behaved predictably. "I'm goin'," he said. "I'm goin' to Washington for the funeral. Takin' the first train out of here. I'll go to my brother John's in Silver Springs, Maryland. Stay with him and go to see the funeral procession of the President. "Jacqueline," he said as he looked around the room, "you pack up a few things. I'll take you with me. You're in high school now. Be good for you. You'll see a little history in the making. See the funeral procession of the best president this country has ever had."

Jacqueline looked shocked. "I can't go," she said hesitantly, looking at Mom and then at Dad. Jacqueline never wanted to venture far from Mom. But Mom said, "Oh, go Jacqueline. Pop will take good care of you." So Jacqueline went with Grandpa to Washington, DC and stood among the thousands who came to honor the loss of a beloved president. Her most vivid memory would be of the casket being pulled by beautiful white horses. She had several little photos of her and Opie, taken in a photo booth. It would be her only memento of the trip.

29

Right Thing to Do

In December of 1944, Mom finally heard from Orphie. "Oh, thank God," she said, as she opened the letter and read aloud. "Vernon's been found. He's on his way home, right now! Oh, thank God!"

"It's a time to rejoice," Dad said with a sigh of relief. "Ethel, write Orphie right back. Tell her how happy we are. Let her know we've been with her and Johnny throughout."

But as we rejoiced on the one hand a terrible tragedy beset us on the other. A neighbor, Pete Toney, was killed. He is the first dead person I ever saw, and it had a tremendous effect on me. It was perhaps the one and only time Dad was unable to get me to feel better about something.

Pete was young, only thirty-two, and he had a nice family. His son Bobby was one of my playmates, and it was horrible to think of his dad as being dead.

Pete was the only person in New Camp who owned a riding horse. He kept it housed in one of the garages provided by the coal company—for cars, that no one had.

In my mind I kept seeing Pete riding his horse up and down the lane between our houses. I always marveled at his horsemanship as he came riding down the lane with the dust flying up around him and his flock of coal black hair blowing in the wind. I was so impressed. His real pleasure was riding that horse. I'd watch in awe as he rode by my house, fantasizing that someday he might take me for a ride too, like he did with his own kids. I'd see him putting Bobby and his sister, Violet Louise, up on the seat in front of him. They'd laugh so joyfully as they rode by, having so much fun.

And now Pete was dead, killed in the coal mines, and people were going into his house with food and flowers, crying and offering condolences to his family. I could hear them. Our whole family was shocked by it. I heard Dad say to Mom, "Ethel, he was so young. They're going to have a hard time of it. See if there is anything we can do." And Mom stood shaking her head and looking across the way toward their house. She talked about what she could do to help, and I just felt this sadness come over our house too.

It was frightening. I didn't know what to say or do. I was thinking about Bobby. Identifying strongly. It was the first time I actually thought about my own parents dying. It was too close. I knew now that someday I would have a similar experience with death, and I began thinking about it. It wasn't just a heaven or hell thing anymore. The questions were forming: *What is out there? What really happens to people when they die? Is there really a heaven and hell? What determines who goes where?* It all lay heavy on my heart.

I felt I was supposed to say something to my playmate, go visit with him, console him, yet I knew not what to do. Dad sensed my predicament. "Jim," he said, "Bobby's suffering a great loss right now. His whole family is. This has been a great shock to them. They will be a long time healing." *Healing?* "There will be a wake for Pete tonight."

"A wake! What's a wake?" Dad went on to explain what a wake was for and what I could expect to see. What people would be doing. The more he talked, the more anxious I became.

"I don't have to go to that, do I?"

"No, Jim, you don't have to go. But it's the right thing to do. It's the way you show respect. Your Mom will go with you. She'll take some food."

"Well, what am I supposed to do?" I was dreading what lay ahead when guilt overtook me, and I found myself thinking about the times I had sneaked into the garage and ridden Pete's horse without his permission. Buddy Griffin and I often played down around the garages. We climbed around in the rafters and when no one was around, we dropped from the rafters down onto the horse. One of us would sit on the horse as the other led it back and forth by the reins. Now, Pete was dead and I was filled with remorse. Worse, I wondered if Pete could somehow see me now, and whether he now knew what I had done.

Wisely, I kept my feelings of contrition to myself and instead made plans to go to the wake. Mom made me freshen up a bit and wear my better clothes, though my pants were still too long and had to be held up with suspenders, high above my waist. The white shirt was fine. The shoes were the same for any occasion since I had but one pair.

We set off with the macaroni and cheese casserole Mom had made and walked across the road slowly, me with my hands in my pockets and my eyebrows knit into a permanent look of anxiety. We did not immediately go inside. There were so many people, and Mom took time to speak with many of them. I didn't remove my hands from my pockets, nor change the pained expression on my face.

The whole place smelled of flowers. A sweet musk smell I have never forgotten. Flowers were everywhere, all the way up to the ceiling, in the house and on the porch. Flowers were an open expression from the community of the love and respect they felt for the deceased and his family.

When we did go inside, Mom had me sign the register as she had done, after which she proceeded to give Mrs. Toney a big hug and then expressed her sorrow—which brought a new round of tears and sadness. Mrs. Toney thanked us for coming and even gave me a hug. I found myself looking over her shoulder at Bobby. I saw the pain on his face, and I longed for the courage to say or do something that would be appropriate, but I could not. I was too traumatized.

The family stood all together in a line. I could see from their red and swollen eyes that they had been crying. I felt a tremendous feeling of sadness for them. They would be a family without a husband and father.

Overwhelmed by the number of flowers and the smell of the flowers and the funereal atmosphere, I couldn't move. I just stood there, frozen in place until Mom directed me to go with her to look at Pete and pay our respects. When finally I dared to look at the casket, I took my hands from my pockets and began twisting them nervously.

The casket was on a raised platform, and along with all the flowers it took up a full half of the living room. I quickly took a cursory look, taking in the slate-blue casket, the body and the flowers all at once. Pete's face was waxy white. His long straight black hair, swept back and away from his face, presented a sharp, sharp contrast to the puffy white lining surrounding his head. Everything seemed so unnatural, almost surreal. The sights, smells, and the feelings of sadness etched in my memory. I turned and looked toward an open window for the remainder of the time I was there. I was only pretending to pay attention to what was happening outside.

Mom sensed my misery and at an appropriate moment, said, "Come on, Jimmy. It's time we go." We only had to cross the road because our house was directly across the lane from the Toneys', so in a way, it was like we were still there. Dad wanted to know how it went, what was said, who was there. He said that he really regretted that he couldn't go over. Mom said the family understood.

For the remainder of the night, I thought of nothing else. It was a time of learning for me and for my family. We talked about it a lot. Dad said, "Dying happens to all of us sooner or later, something we have to face. Though not usually so young. Accidents are a terrible thing. There will be lots of pain and suffering for their family." I began to feel just how vulnerable we all were, and I clearly knew I was not ready to have anyone in my family die.

"What happens when you die?" I asked. Mom took that one. She liked the idea of heaven and a better life in the hereafter. Not something to be feared. "Live a good life, do right and make the best of what comes your way. God will reward you in the end," she said. Not comforting enough for me. I was carrying the sins of riding Pete's horse on my conscience at that very moment.

Though Dad tried to offer reasonable explanations, he was not successful either. Nothing really helped that much. I couldn't get some things out of my mind. My dog Sparky howled all night. Somebody had told me that dogs do that when someone dies. The night dragged on and I slept fitfully, often awakening and noticing that there were still lights on and that people were still milling around over at the Toney's. I wished I'd had the courage to tell my parents about the horse.

Pete was buried the next day. I saw the funeral directors take him from the house and put him into the hearse and then load up all the flowers, which they took as well. I watched as Mrs. Toney and all the kids, all dressed in dark clothing, got into cars and followed along slowly behind the hearse. It was a sorrowful event. No one in my family went to the graveside funeral and burial. We had no way to go.

All the Toney kids were back in school within two days. I still did not know what to say, so I acted as if nothing had happened. But others didn't. I heard one of the girls in class say to Bobby, "Who's going to make money for your family now?" When I saw Bobby tear up, I realized that asking questions was not the right thing to do. Bobby was now the man of the house. He had a lot on his shoulders.

Not long afterwards, the Toney family moved to another location, and eventually Mrs. Toney remarried. I didn't see Bobby much again until high school.

30

Toby

Toby was the son of Harry and Nellie Kinder, who lived next door to us. Dad called Toby my shadow because he hung so close to me, always wanting to tag along no matter where I might be going. Being younger didn't seem to bother him; he just liked being a part of the adventure in my life. If he had free time, he was looking for me.

In his younger days, Toby had this impish look about him, a small frame, huge blue eyes, and tightly twisted black curls that defied combing. It would have been hard for me not to like Toby. He worshipped me. We became regular sidekicks as he followed me from place to place, always ready for a piece of the action.

*　　　　　*　　　　　*

One fine summer day in August of 1945 as I was preparing to go fishing I heard Dad say, "Jim, here comes your shadow." I looked to the screen door and there was *the shadow*, peeking through the screen. As soon as he saw me, he jumped backward with a beaming, happy face.

"Whatcha doin', Jimmy?"

"Gettin' ready to go fishin'."

"I go with you?" Toby asked enthusiastically—through the screen.

"Go get your pole," I said as Dad and I exchanged grins.

Toby was off the porch and back on again in a flash. "I already got the worms, Jimmy," he called from the porch. "Dug them out this morning."

Dad smiled as he eyed my pole. "The string isn't long enough, Jim" he said. "Bring it to me, I'll fix it for you."

"Mine too, Clifford?" Toby's nose was pressed to the screen door again.

"Bring it on in, Toby." Dad said with a chuckle. Dad took delight in watching Toby hang around with me. I think he figured we were good for one another in some sort of way. "Did you ask your mother if you could go, Toby?" Dad wanted to know.

"Yep," Toby answered. "She said anywhere Jimmy goes you can go with him. Just be back before dinner."

Dad watched us out the door. "You boys catch us a mess of fish, now. I'll have the skillet ready when you get back." No matter the size, Mom or Dad always fried the fish I caught. So, I made it a point not to come home empty-handed. When Toby and I both fished, we usually caught enough for both families to have a fish fry.

We took off in the direction of Walter Griffin's place where there was a good-sized fishing hole with lots of big rocks to sit on. If any fish were to be caught, the fishing hole at the Griffin place was the place to catch them.

Barefoot, carrying our poles in one hand and a tin can of worms for bait in the other, we splashed and played along the way as we waded in the creek looking under rocks for "crawdads" and grampus to add variety to the bait.

Dad watched us out of sight. I knew he longed in his heart to be able to go along with us. He'd told me that he'd been a top-notch fisherman in his day, when he'd bring home a dozen fish at a time. Nothing would make his mom happier, he'd said. "Lord," she would say at the dinner table as she offered up a blessing for the food, "Clifford has put food on our table today, and we thank you Lord for making him the good fisherman that he is. Amen."

We fished for probably a good hour before hunger pangs began to sting our bellies. Fishing had been good. We already had two good-sized bass and a few red-eyes on a stringer in the creek. We secured the fish and set off to satisfy our hunger by talking ourselves into taking "only a few" of Walter Griffin's peaches. The tree was full of ripe peaches just waiting to be picked. We helped ourselves to a few of the biggest and best, tucked them under our shirts and scampered back to the creek where we laid the peaches out on a flat rock, just as we had done numerous times before. We threw our poles back into the water and began eating the peaches. I had just finished eating one and had my arm raised to throw the pit away when we heard a gunshot. KA-POOM! Both of us jumped nearly straight up off the rock. Our feet hit the water on the run as we headed up the creek, away from the Griffin place. When we heard the next KA-POOM, accompanied by Walter's voice "I told you boys to stay out of my peaches, now I'm going to teach you a lesson!" our feet were moving so fast it appeared that we truly *walked* on water.

We crossed the creek so fast that even when we stumbled we were still on our feet running. Straight up the creek we went until we were out of sight of the Griffin place, and then we hid on the hillside above the creek just to be sure we were safe. We expected Walter to trail us with his dog, hunting us down like we were jackrabbits. Huffing and puffing, we spoke not a word until we were sure we were very well camouflaged. We looked about in every direction, trying to locate Mr. Griffin, but could not see him. We assumed he was doing the same thing we were doing, *hiding from us*, so that he could get a better shot at us next time.

After a while, when we heard no movement, we moved as quietly as we could and went farther up the hillside, where we had a better view, but we still could not see Mr. Griffin. We lay low for what seemed forever before Toby got worried that he'd be in a heap of trouble if he stayed any longer. "Besides, Jimmy," he said, "I'm so hungry I can't stand it." He whispered that he was going to make a run for it, cross the creek, and take the highway home. I refused to go, saying that I was stayin' 'til dark. I was not willing to take the risk of getting shot at again.

As the day wore on, Dad said to Mom, "Jim and Toby have been gone a long time. Don't you think they ought to be home by now?"

Toby's mom, Nellie, was sitting on her porch having a cigarette. Mom called to her, "Nellie, have you seen Toby and Jimmy?"

Nellie gave Mom a look of concern. "Ain't Jimmy home yet? Toby's in the house. Been here for a while. He's being punished. Come crawling in here past dinnertime." Nellie turned to call through the screen door. "Hey, Toby, where'd you leave Jimmy? Ethel's lookin' for him." Toby came creeping out the door, head hung low. "He stayed up at the fishing hole," he said. "Said he was stayin' 'til dark."

Mom was confused. "Well, why would he stay 'til dark?" she quizzed. "He knows he's supposed to be home, just like you."

Toby began fidgeting. He saw that it was almost dark. He began to worry. He thought maybe Walter had shot at me, maybe killed me, and he thought maybe he had best own up to stealing the peaches and take his punishment. "Jimmy's hidin' out," he said.

"Hidin' out? Why would he be hidin' out Toby?" Mom said, with urgency in her voice.

"Well, we was fishin' up at Walter Griffin's place cause Jimmy says that's the best place to fish, and we got hungry and we stole some of Walter's peaches and he got out his gun and shot at us. Twice! We run as fast as we could up the creek. Left all our fish and the poles and everthing. We hid in the bushes so's Walter couldn't see us. We was afraid to come out, 'cept I knowed I'd better get home before dinner, so I took my chances and ran across the creek and down the road to home. I tried to get Jimmy to come with me, but he said 'No, he was waitin' 'til dark. He wasn't takin' no chances.' He might be dead!"

With one hand, Nellie jerked Toby off the ground by the straps of his overalls. "Well, you're in big trouble now, all right. Now it's almost dark and Jimmy's not here, and we'll have to go lookin' for him. You been home for a hour or more and you ain't said a word about Jimmy."

Mom and Nellie started out on the run in the direction of the Griffin place, both fuming at the very idea of Walter shooting at their kids. Nellie was steaming mad. She huffed and puffed as she dragged Toby along the highway. Mom was livid. Her face was flushed with anger, yet splotches of white revealed her fear that something had happened to me.

I saw them coming. It was a comical scene, with Nellie dragging Toby like that, but I didn't feel like laughing. I knew it would be safe for me to come out now so I edged along the creek bank until I had a clear path and then I darted across the creek and straight to the safety of my rescue team. Mom saw me coming, and seeing that I was okay and no longer fearing for my life, she balled all of her emotion into a one big fit of rage and started for Walter's door, with Nellie on her heels. Walter saw them coming and met them at the door with his hands held high, ready to explain.

"Walter Griffin, what do you mean, shootin' at these boys! They're just kids. Have you lost your senses?" Mom was going at him. "I've a good mind to turn you in to the sheriff."

"Now, Ethel, I didn't shoot *at* those boys, I shot up in the air. I just wanted to scare them. They've been stealin' my peaches every time they come around here, and I wanted to teach them a lesson. I never intended to hurt them. Just wanted to scare them off, which I *thought* I did."

"Oh, you scared 'em all right," Mom bellowed. "Jimmy's been hidin' on the hillside here for hours, afraid to come out 'til it was dark so you wouldn't see him. What kind of scare is that? Why didn't you check to see where they went and then bring them on home yourself to get their lesson from home for stealin'?"

"Right," Nellie chimed in. "Don't neither of our families cotton to stealin'. We'd a took good care of both of 'em if you'd a told us. These boys'll be ruined for life. Toby was a scared to tell 'til he thought maybe you'd done shot Jimmy and killed him."

"Now you ladies know I wouldn't be about shootin' any kids."

"Well, shootin' in the air is just as bad!" Mom ranted. "They're both scared to death! This is no way to treat kids in the neighborhood, Walter."

"Yeah," Nellie said. "What if it had been one of your kids stealin' my peaches, and I'd a shot at *them*. Now you know I ain't a good shot, so I'da probably killed 'em."

"Ladies, I'm sorry for shootin' the gun. I know it was wrong. Like I said, I shot up in the air just to scare them off. I just got dang tired of them stealin' my peaches."

We all turned at the same time. Nellie took me by the arm and wedged me between her and Mom. She still had a strong grasp on Toby. We all trotted off to home with Toby and me saying very little. I knew Walter Griffin would have a hard time living this one down. The mothers in the neighborhood could be hard to deal with when it came to protecting their children.

When we got to the house, Nellie came inside to help Mom and me and Toby recount the story to Dad, who had been nervously awaiting our arrival—especially since he'd heard Toby say that since I wasn't back by dark that most likely I'd been shot!

Dad listened as we all talked at once. His face paled and his skin grew taut. His hands gripped the arms of his wheelchair. Then he squared his jaws and said determinedly, "If I could get out of this chair, I'd teach Walter a lesson!" With those words, Toby and I began to feel like neighborhood heroes. But that feeling soon diminished as Jacqueline unexpectedly surprised us all by coming to the defense of Mr. Griffin. She was a friend of the Griffin's daughter Katherine. "Oh," she said, "Mr. Griffin wouldn't shoot at those boys. He just wanted to teach them a lesson. They've no business up there stealin' his peaches anyway. Jimmy, you ought to be ashamed of yourself."

Bug-eyed, I looked at Jacqueline in disbelief. I think she was afraid that Mom and Dad wouldn't allow her to visit her friend anymore. Dad looked at her in shock as well, but he seemed to understand. He turned his chair toward us boys and closed it out with a, "Well, I guess you boys have learned something today."

I watched as Nellie dragged Toby out the door and across the yard to home, all the while scolding him for being late and for stealing peaches. He looked back over his shoulder at me as if to say, "How did it ever get to this?"

*   *   *

A few days later, Dad saw Toby's face again, pressed against the screen door. "Toby, what is it?" he said.

"Where's Jimmy?"

"Jimmy's out playing with his Junior Commando group," Dad told him. "They're probably down by the garages."

Toby was off the porch and running before Dad could say anything else. He wanted to be in the thick of things. Life was exciting for him when he hung around me. Toby found me with my buddies down at the garages and hung around pretending to know what we were doing.

When the Junior Commando group disbanded, Toby, still talking about the enemy planes he thought he heard fly over Ameagle, headed home with me. I tolerated his hero worship, often using him as a sounding board for my ideas. He mostly just played my tape back again which is about all I needed to hear.

I had been toying with this idea that a paralyzed man could be made to walk if he was scared bad enough. I'd heard it said and I'd heard about a woman who'd been scared into walking again, but I didn't know why it worked. Toby said he'd *heard* about it too. Said he'd heard that if you threw a snake on someone who was paralyzed they'd for sure get up and walk. I told Toby that I was giving it some thought—to think of some way to scare Dad out of that chair—and a snake didn't sound like too bad an idea, but he was not to tell anyone. He swore, "I won't tell a soul, you can break my arm if I do."

I told Billy about my idea, thinking he might have heard about such things before and if he had that maybe he'd join me in scaring Dad into walking. But Billy was nonchalant. "Oh, Jimmy, where'd you hear such stuff? It might've happened to someone but I don't think it will happen with Dad. Besides, I ain't gonna handle any snake."

"You don't have to," I said. "But you don't need to be afraid of snakes. Toby and me see snakes all the time. We catch 'em and play with 'em. Ain't nothin' to be afraid of."

"Well, what makes you think Dad will be afraid then?"

"Well, if I surprise him with it, he won't know what to expect, and he'll jump up from the chair and come after me."

"He'll for sure come at you," Billy said, dismissing me as he took a bite out of an apple and rode off on his bike. I still thought the idea was a good one, so I took it up with the only one who stood by me no matter what—Toby. I went off to find him. Amazingly, he was never too hard to find. "Toby," I said, "let's go snake hunting. When we find one we'll put it in a sack and hide it some place." Toby looked up at me with bright blue eyes that said he thought he was going on the biggest adventure of his life. We searched and searched, giving up around dusk, because we sure didn't want anyone looking for us again. "See ya tomorrow, Jimmy." Toby waved goodbye at the fence, with a look of idolization on his face. I knew I had a comrade here.

Every day for a week we searched for a snake. "Seems like if you ain't lookin' for somethin' it'll rise up and bite you," I said, getting discouraged. "Yeah," Toby consoled, "them things is everwhere 'til you want one. I seen one just t'other day, comin' down from the hog pens, crawled right across the road in front of me, long as a broomstick, took off in the weeds."

"What kind was it?"

"Heck if I know, looked liked a black snake, 'cept it was kinda fat and wuzn't goin' very fast. Them racers usually fly!"

"I know," I said, 'cause they're racers. Them's the best kind to catch, cause they won't hurt you none, maybe just knick you. Dad told me that. But they ain't poisonous, I do know that. Anyways, if it wasn't moving fast and was big and fat, it was probably a she snake and was goin' off to have babies. Right about where you saw it. That's where we should go looking." So we took our sacks and went in the direction of the hog pens. It was smelly down there, but the trees were sure fun to play in. We climbed around a bit, looking down at the ground below, hoping to see a snake.

Toby found the location where he'd seen the snake, and we climbed down from the trees and went looking. The whole area was covered with weeds. We took a stick and parted the weeds, but it was actually in a clearing where there were no weeds that we saw the snakes, several of them.

"I found one Jimmy! Over here!"

"Well, good, Toby," I said sarcastically. "I'm sure the snake is gonna stay right there and crawl up into your sack! You done scared him off."

"Nuh, uhh. They're still right here, a whole bunch of 'em, just crawlin' off in ever direction."

"Well, grab one, or maybe two. That way we'll have a back-up."

"Got one," Toby said as he tossed it into his sack and twisted the sack at the top to keep the snake inside. I reached for one but it got loose and slithered away. At about the same time, a larger snake came from somewhere and was coming right at me. I thought to myself, "Jees, if I was in a wheelchair, I'd sure walk. It scared me silly." But I intuitively reached out and grabbed the snake and fought with it briefly 'til I had it under control and tossed it into my bag. The bag was hard to close off because the snake was so big, but I did it and I felt really proud. "Now we have two, Toby," I said. "If one won't do it, I bet two will!" We made plans on our way home as to when and how we would execute the *cure*. Toby said he'd just as soon not be a part of it, but he'd like to watch, especially the part when Dad would jump up from his wheelchair and come after me.

We hid the snakes under the house and planned to look in on them regularly until we were ready to use them. Actually, the snakes stayed rather calm, which surprised me.

The very next day turned out to be a good day for the event. It was sunny and warm, so Dad came out onto the porch. I watched as he turned on his radio, and then sat back in his chair as he prepared to listen to a baseball game. I went next door to get Toby. We fiddled around under the house for a few minutes. Then, I reached inside the bag for the big one, took it out, and without hesitation, rushed up onto the porch directly toward Dad. He was totally startled. "What is it, Jim. What? It's a snake. Wh....?" He didn't get more than a few words out of his mouth before I threw the snake directly at him. He actually moved upwards as his hands instinctively covered his face. He screamed as he dodged the snake coming at him; his chair nearly toppled over. The snake slithered over him and off the porch in no time—probably as scared as Dad was. I stood frozen in time like I was watching everything in slow motion. I watched to see if Dad was sufficiently scared enough to rise and come after me. He was scared all right, and mad as a whole nest of disturbed hornets. "Jim, if I could get out of this chair, I'd beat you to death!" he said in short gasps as he steadied himself. I ran off, not knowing what to say or do. Toby was around the corner of the house. He had seen it all. "Didn't work, huh, Jimmy. Want to try the little one?" I shook my head. I was totally deflated, feeling really empty inside. I knew of no way to explain what I had done.

Having heard Dad's scream, Mom had come running to the porch and after hearing from Dad what had happened, was coming after me in a huff. I was really in big trouble. But Toby saved the day. "It wasn't a bad thing, Mrs. White," Toby told Mom as she cornered the house. "Jimmy was just tryin' to make his dad walk. Said he'd heard that if you scared a crippled man enough he'd walk." Toby looked off in the direction I had run and gave Mom the clue as to where I was.

By the time she reached me, I was as high up in the pear tree as I could get. I must've looked forlorn, because she just said, "Jimmy, come on down from there," in a tone of voice that let me know that it would be safe to do so. I tumbled down slowly, watching to see her reaction and practically fell into her arms. "Mom, I didn't mean to hurt him," I said. "I really thought it would work."

She just shook her head and put her arms around me. "Well, you'll have to tell that to your Dad. He needs to know you didn't mean to hurt him." So we walked back around to the porch. I hung my head in shame. Dad was still out of breath, still very frightened, but he made it easy. He didn't say anything 'til Mom explained why I had thrown the snake at him. Then he said he'd heard about such happenings himself. "Jim," he told me, "your heart is in the right place, but right now, *mine* is not." His face relaxed somewhat but he could not bring himself to smile.

*   *   *

So now I knew. Dad hadn't been able to get to Lee when he'd had the "fit." He hadn't been able to get to his feet to go after Walter Griffin. And he wasn't able to come after me when I threw the snake at him. He would never walk! That ended it. I saw Toby sneaking along the fence, going home. He was glad it was over, I guess.

31

You Drive, I'll Ride

The year 1946 rolled around. The war was over and David was home from the Navy. He worked in the coal mines and still courted Jacqueline, who had graduated high school and was now in charge of the dry goods department at the company store at Ameagle. She made $80 a month, $10 of which was deducted for our rent. We had not paid rent for twelve years.

Jacqueline spent most of her paycheck on the family, though she first bought herself a bicycle, which she used as transportation to get to and from work. And she put some clothes on layaway as she said it was important to "look nice on the job." She even bought me some new pants for the first day of school. Having new clothes on the first day of school was like moving uptown. No more patched overalls for me, though admittedly, the patches had been fewer in recent years.

Billy bought his own clothes. He still worked at Roy Flint's store, but he now drove the delivery truck. Since most folks in our area still had no cars, they bought their groceries in large quantities and had them delivered. Billy worked as hard at this job as he had at any of his other jobs, which is why he had the job in the first place. He was a proven hard worker. But now he was more intent than ever, socking away as much of his earnings as he could possibly spare, for he wanted a car of his own for his senior year in high school. The only time he took time off from work was to play football, his one sport. He was one busy guy. When he wasn't working he was out with some girl. I only saw him at night; we still slept in the room with Dad.

Lee continued to go back and forth between home and the Veteran's Hospital in Roanoke, Virginia. He liked it at the hospital, but Mom said she didn't like some of the shenanigans that took place there. What really upset her was that an older lady, an employee of the Veteran's Hospital, wanted to marry Lee, and Mom just wouldn't have it. So, she brought Lee home more often and kept him home for longer periods of time. Lee said he missed being at the hospital. There, he had lots of activities and social life. At home, he mostly just helped out around the house. But, Mom finally had her way and brought Lee home for good, though he resided for a short while in Beckley while he took a short course in auto mechanics at Beckley College as part of a retraining pro-gram for Navy veterans.

Dad was still the neighborhood man of all trades. His life was much the same, but Mom's was changing. She was active once again in the community, resuming her interest in helping others in need through the church group, the Willing Workers. She had joined the Women's Moose Club in Whitesville. She had both Bessie and Orphie teaching her how to drive as she anticipated the day she would have her own car. Just like Dad, she wanted to know what she had missed all these years.

I was in junior high school and already lived and breathed sports. I had more background than most of my coaches because Dad and I still had sports conversations all the time. My athletic *skills,* though, needed a great deal of honing.

Dad gave me pointers. "Jim," he'd say, "the way to be the best on the team is to put more of yourself into whatever you're doing. Practice just a little harder than the rest. Run just one more lap, do just one more pushup." I knew what he meant. I remembered how he had managed to strengthen his upper body by pushing himself beyond his limits just about every day. And how, when he'd had setbacks, like attacks of malaria, he never gave up, but worked his way back up again. Dad was my mentor. How could I do anything less?

My days were full because I had also assumed Lee's chores as well as taking on a small newspaper route, though never as ambitious as Billy. But, I was a hard worker and often took odd jobs in the community. Cutting grass was my least favorite thing to do because it had to be done with a hand sickle. But, it was a way to earn a little spending money.

Dad stood in the yard as often as he felt up to it and the weather conditions were right. He moved along the fence and talked to people as they passed by. During the past winter he had suffered an unusual number of bouts with the malarial fever that he still considered one of his demons. He relished the outdoors where he could be close to the birds, the sunshine and the wind. He was the first to notice the scent of the flowers in the yard, the freshness of the air after a warm spring rain, the new growth on the pear tree and the redbuds and dogwoods blooming on the hillside above the creek. He said being outdoors reminded him of when he was younger and was a nature boy at heart—when he hunted, fished and trapped. He liked reminiscing. "When the stickwood is in bloom, look in the hickory trees, Jim. That's where the squirrels will be," he would say, recalling his hunting days.

It tore at my heart to hear him talk like this, knowing that he ached to be able to get out into the woods and on the road. "As soon as I get a car of some kind, I'm going to take you hunting, Dad," I told him.

"Jim, I don't believe anything would pleasure me more," he said. "We'll get us a big buck."

*   *   *

For Christmas the year I turned thirteen, I got a BB gun. I took it out in the yard one summer day at a time Dad was out walking the fence. I sat down with the gun and proceeded to practice a bit. I saw a bluebird high in a tree across the road and shot at it, not really intending to hit it.

I didn't think my aim was that good, but to my dismay the bird fell from the tree and onto the grass. Dad saw the whole thing and turned to me in astonishment.

"Jim, you've killed a blue-bird!"

"I didn't think I'd hit it," I said. "I was trying to scare it, make it fly."

Dad was not appeased. "Go bury the bird and don't tell your mom you shot a bluebird." He was ashamed of me. I felt terrible. It was something I would never do again.

*   *   *

David joined us in the yard one day as Dad and I talked about the hunting trip we would take once I had wheels. "Cliff," he said, "the first chance I get I'm going to take you out someplace, too. I've about saved enough to get a car. When I get one, we'll hit the road." Dad smiled broadly. Now he had two people interested in taking him places. He was *ready to go*!

A few months later, David came to the house one day sporting a blue '41 Chrysler, fluid drive. Dad, Mom and Jacqueline were sitting on the front porch stringing beans when he arrived. David was all spiffed up 'cause he was coming to see Jacqueline anyway. She was as surprised as the rest of us. Her face beaming, she jumped from her chair knocking it backward as she ran to see the car. "Oh, David, it's so pretty!" she said.

"Thought you'd like the color, blue, just like your eyes."

"Oh, I do. I do."

"Well, come on, let's try her out." David opened the car door and motioned for Jacqueline to get inside. She piled into the front seat, all smiles, hands and knees together, like a pretty little schoolgirl. Mom put her beans aside and dashed out to take a look, too. She oohed and ahhed, the way people do over new things, inspecting the car thoroughly with a longing in her eye. She was *going* to have a car. As he opened the door on

· 231 ·

the driver's side, David called to Dad, "Cliff," he said. "After Jacqueline, you're going to be the first to get a ride in this old tub."

Dad was delighted. "Well, hurry up and take her on out."

After that day, Dad got lots of rides because whenever David wasn't working and had nothing pressing to do, he came to our house. He'd walk in and say, "Where'd you like to go today, Cliff?" and Dad would give him the "Let her roll" sign with a flip of his hand and a roll toward the door where he would don his hat and wait to be carried to the car.

On the way to the car, David would ask, "Where to, Cliff?"

And Dad would reply, "Anywhere wheels roll, Dave." Dad was like a prisoner who after fourteen years of confinement had been released to rejoin the world. He'd done his time but he wasn't sure what was out there. It was hard to make choices. Anywhere they went would be a pleasure.

From somewhere Dad had obtained a collapsible wheelchair. "This thing will be necessary now that I'm out running around," he said. "You never know when I'll need to get out and roll in to see someone."

Oft-times I went along. I jumped in the back seat and gloried in the feeling of power that having a car did for a person. Mom would stand on the porch and wave us off with a smile. She had a strong suspicion that David frequently took Dad up Sandlick Hollow, or down to the whiskey store in Whitesville, but she never said anything. She trusted David to do whatever he thought best, though she couldn't resist an occasional warning. "Now, Clifford, I don't want to have to decide whether your hide is worth getting out of jail or not," she'd chide. *It was a possibility.*

David was good to us. He even used his paycheck to help our family out. And what he could get for us in the way of a discount through the mines, like coal, he got, too. Even had it delivered to our house—a generous and kind thing to do. He said we were his family now, even though he and Jacqueline were still only courting.

*   *   *

Through his bartering, Dad had acquired a shotgun and a high powered rifle which I was now allowed to use. In the hills around our house I hunted squirrels, grouse and rabbit and became quite good at it. Dad liked to talk about my hunting. He'd appear so proud as he watched me come in with my wild game. "Jim, you remind me of myself when I was a boy. I sure did love to hunt," he'd say. I always told him that as soon as I had a car I'd take him hunting though I knew not how or where. He'd smile and say, "We'll get us a car one of these days Jim, and then we'll go."

I hadn't as yet been deer hunting because there were no deer in our neck of the woods. Just the same, I'd heard others talk about going to the places where you could hunt deer and I ached to go. Since David had a car, I began bugging him about taking a hunting trip. Dad heard us talking and began telling us hunters where we would most likely find the deer. But David said, "Cliff, you just hang on to that info, 'cause now that I've got a car, you're goin' deer hunting yourself." Dad's eyes lit up. "How 'bout this weekend?" he asked with a boyish grin. He already had a place in mind, which made it easy because to go deer hunting we needed a place to stay. The weekend was good for David and me, but Billy had to work. Dad said he was sorry about that, but we didn't cancel the trip.

We went to Marlinton, in Pocahontas County, where a friend of Dad's had given us the use of his cabin for the weekend. I suspected that Dad bartered to get it. The cabin was located in a rather isolated area, deep in the woods, but had a decent road, so getting to the cabin was not too difficult. I carried in the food supplies, the guns, and Dad's wheelchair. David carried Dad, for which I was grateful. David was strong. He carried Dad all the way up the hill and up the steps into the cabin, making it seem like it was no big deal.

"First things first, now," Dad said, as soon as he was situated—meaning he wanted a shot of whiskey. Every moment counted for him.

"No problem," David said, fishing the bottle from under the front seat of the car. Dad said the whiskey warmed his bones and cured his chills.

We put all the food supplies and bedding inside the cabin and then organized our hunting gear. The plan was for Dad to hunt from the porch, so we situated him in a corner of the porch where he had a nice radial view. He was already taking aim when David and I set off, careful to go in an opposite direction.

We hadn't gone far before we heard a shot. KA POOM! Hurrying back, we saw Dad take aim again and get off another shot.

"Goodness, Cliff," David said. "Did you get one already?"

"No, but I think I nicked him."

"Whew!" David and I figured we'd better stay close by. We looked in the general area of Dad's shot but saw no blood, so we figured he'd missed.

Dad stopped hunting early. "Wheel me on in, boys," he said, on one of our trips back to check on him. "I'll see if I can cook us up some cowboy stew." *Good news to us.* The air had a nip to it that Dad had trouble tolerating, anyway. He never seemed to be completely warm. He wore flannel and wool indoors and out.

David built a fire in the stove and made sure everything Dad would need was within his reach. I threw some blankets on the beds. Then David and I headed back out to hunt. We hadn't been gone more than thirty minutes when we heard Dad yelping. "Help, Jim. David. Get in here. Quick! Help! Jim! Help!"

We came on the run, grateful we had not gone far. Running through the open door, we found Dad near the cookstove, *covered* with wasps. Fortunately, none had yet stung him. He sat frozen, afraid to move, and rightfully so. David and I swatted for what seemed like ten minutes, but we eventually killed all of the wasps and then removed the nest from the cabin. The wasps had been nesting in a rafter and the heat from the stove had caused them to come out of their hive, but they were disoriented and not one of them stung us. We considered ourselves lucky. Dad said the angels were watching out for us.

Dad enjoyed his little trips out, ready to go in a cat's breath. He'd often give Mom teasing looks, as he headed out on an adventure. "Your mom wants a car too, but she won't take me hunting," he'd say, as we headed out the door.

"With your aim, you'd probably shoot me," she retorted.

Dad grinned. "I take care never to injure my drivers," he said with a laugh. He turned to me. "When she gets a car, your mom and I will run around everywhere. Up and down all these hollers, Toney's Fork, Sycamore, Workman's Creek, Dorothy, White Oak. I've got a lot of people to meet around here."

I could see Dad's thinking. The more drivers the better. He wanted all of us to have access to cars. He was making up for lost time. Dad wanted to make *his* "tracks".

He liked his hunting trips. He forever talked about the deer-hunting trip we took with my friend, Jackie Boling, and his grandpa, Burns Osborne. I had been invited to go along with Jackie, and Burns said to Dad, "Cliff, why don't you and Dave come along too. Old Dave can drive."

The weather was perfect as we set off to go. The air was cool and crisp and the sky was a clear, deep blue color. On the way we discussed how Dad would do his hunting from the porch while the rest of us would go elsewhere *far beyond his line of fire*, and while we were gone, Dad would fix us some dinner. I was feeling right proud.

The cabin was old and rustic, but accommodating. We quickly settled in, putting our things in place. Jackie and I, eager to hunt, got our guns and sat across from each other in the middle of the room and began to discuss how the guns differed. I had my gun pointed down between my legs and was showing Jackie that the gun wouldn't go off with the safety on. Certain that it would not go off, I pulled the trigger to show him and KA-POOM, the gun went off, sounding like a huge firecracker. A deafening echo resounded in the cabin and smoke from the gunpowder filled the area as it smoldered up between my legs. I had shot a hole straight through the floor. Mortified and so scared I almost wet my pants, I looked around. It was like looking at a movie scene in slow motion. Jackie looked as if he had been shot at and missed. Dad's face was frozen in shock, and David's mouth was on his chin. Burns, who had been taking a sip of coffee at the time the gun went off, had thrown the cup, just missing Dad's head. When Burns got over the shock and realized what had happened, he rose and came at me. Visibly upset and shaking all over, he lit into me, using a few choice expletives, which I accepted humbly, ashamed as I was of what had happened. "Damn it boy," Burns sputtered, his face red. "Don't you know better than to pull a trigger in a house with a loaded gun? That was a stupid dumb trick! Look what you've done!" I stammered for a second and then tried to explain to Burns that the safety was on and I didn't know what caused the gun to go off. Burns grabbed the gun from me. "You didn't have the safety on. God damn it, this is what a gun looks like when the safety is on and when the safety is on, the gun will not go off!" Burns pointed the gun toward the ceiling and proceeded to pull the trigger to show me. The gun fired again, KA-POOM, this time leaving a gaping hole in the ceiling just above where I had shot a hole in the floor. Now, Burns was mortified. I caught a slight wisp of a smile cross Dad's lips, before he offered to make amends. "That gun has got to be defective," Dad said. "We'll make it up to you, Burns. We'll repair the damage before we leave." And, for what seemed forever to me, we all sat quietly with only an occasional word of conversation.

Almost an hour went by as we sat in this obvious state of discomfort before Burns finally said, "Fellows, there's no sense in us just sitting here, we'd best go on and make the most of this hunting trip. We'll go on out and hunt, but Jimmy you'd best use your Dad's gun and let him use yours. Don't reckon he'll do as much damage from the porch." Still nervous from the incident, we could only titter as we nervously began to resume some ordinariness to our setting. We left Dad situated on the porch where he had a good view. I told him I'd be back to check on him. "I won't need much time hunting," he said. "I'll get in here and cook us up a good dinner."

None of us had any luck hunting though we saw deer. But we did have a good time. Everyone said they liked Dad's cooking. Jackie and I had KP duty while the men drank coffee and shared a few jokes.

As we prepared to leave the next day, Dad and David wanted to see that the boards were replaced in the cabin, but Burns said no. "The cabin's old anyway," he said. "I'll get it fixed." He just never invited us to go with him again.

*   *   *

It was my 14th birthday, September 28, 1946. We were seated around the table having cake when Grandpa Opie popped in out of nowhere, carrying his little black leather satchel. He still had the pocket watch that had chimed at the time of my birth. He brought it out and it chimed again. Opie sure had a way of adding a little spice to any situation. Dad was glad to see him, ready as ever to hear about all of Opie's adventures.

This time Opie had come on the train. Sometimes, he came by bus. He never came by car, and he never stayed long. Usually, he'd have a nice visit with Dad and check with Mom to see what he could do to help. He mended and repaired what needed fixing, and then he'd just up and leave one day, as quickly as he'd come.

Opie lit his pipe, straddled a chair and leaned back to smoke and talk in Opie fashion, telling Dad about his travels in New York, Los Angeles, and Las Vegas. When Dad told Opie about the hunting trip, Opie laughed heartily, then said, "Cliff, if you can stand a hunting trip, I reckon you can go just about anywhere. How would you like to go with me over to Lashmeet to visit your Uncle Walter? Take you back to see your old homeplace. Back over where your cousins Joe and Rose lived. You reckon old Dave would take us?"

Dad was immediately excited. "Do no harm to ask," he said. And so, as soon as David came for his daily visit, Opie promptly asked if he would take them to Lashmeet, and David did not disappoint. "You want to visit your brother, Opie," Dave said, "we'll visit your brother. As long as the weather holds up and I don't have to work overtime. You might have to help me fix flat tires along the way, though. My tires are thread bare."

Grandpa quickly looked around for a warm body. He didn't know a thing about cars and wasn't planning to learn. Spying me, he said "We'll take Jimmy for that."

The possibility of having flat tires on the trip did not deter Dad either. He was not easily discouraged when it came to adventure. He'd told enough *Charlie* tales to believe he had the resources to get him out of anything. He said he thought taking me along was a good idea, too. "And take plenty of spare parts," he added. Tires, still scarce from the war, were hard to come by. So folks used a lot of patches and boots, which were pieces of rubber to plug holes when you had blowouts.

Our trip took us over Spruce Mountain—a wretched mountain to cross at any time—and then on Route 19 from Beckley to Shady Spring and from Flat Top Mountain to Spanishburg where we picked up Route 10 going toward Lashmeet. Past Spanishburg, at Lake Shawnee, is where we turned to go to Lashmeet, and that is where we had our first flat.

No problem, we figured, grateful as we were to have gotten that far. David and I worked together as we cranked up the car, took off the tire, blew up the inner tube to see where the hole was, patched the hole, and put the tire back on. Meanwhile, Grandpa sat by the side of the road, smoked his pipe, shot the bull with Dad and occasionally sent a chiding remark our way: "You fellers need any help? I'm just sittin' here, nothin' to do. Just takin' in the sites. The leaves sure are pretty this year." David and I just grinned at each other.

We got back into the car and we set off again, hoping we'd have no more flats, but such was not our luck. Just beyond Lake Shawnee, almost to Lashmeet we had our next one. "Oops," Opie said. "Sounds like trouble." David and I groaned as we piled out. Opie reached under the front seat for the bottle of liquor; then he and Dad pleasured themselves while David and I repaired the tire. As we drove on, Dave and I had little to say as we were listening carefully for signs of trouble, but Dad and Opie chattered away like two carefree boys with not a care in the world.

Luckily, the next leg of our journey was without mishap and we wheeled on into Lashmeet and up to Uncle Walter's little country store, which was in the crook of the road just as we started up the hill to Lashmeet, toward the Mount Olive Baptist Church.

Uncle Walter was greatly surprised. "Well, if it's not Opie," he exclaimed, moving quickly in our direction. "Look here, Josie, old Opie's come to visit," he called to his wife, as he fairly dragged his brother from the car. I could see he looked an awful lot like Grandpa, maybe two inches taller, but balding, and had the same blue eyes and the same horn-rimmed glasses.

"Who's this you got with you?" he said, giving us the once-over.

"This here's my son Cliff," Opie said, pointing to Dad as he shook himself out and readjusted his hat. "Cliff's the one had his back broke in the mines. Uses a wheelchair."

"Oh, yes, I believe I recollect you writing me about that. Some time back, wasn't it Cliff?"

"Sixteen years, four months to be exact," Dad said, recalling vividly the accident that had cost him the feeling in his lower body forever after.

"And this here's Dave, Jacqueline's beau, and this here young feller's Cliff's son, Jimmy," Opie continued

"Glad to meet you boys." Walter gave us all a big handshake, then turned and introduced his wife Josie, who had made her way to the car. "It's been a long time no see, Opie," she said as she shook hands all around. "You've made us happy today, payin' us a visit." After introducing her daughter Ruby, who had also joined us, she said, "Ruby, get these fellers a Coca-Cola from the cooler, they must be mighty thirsty."

Ruby was the spitting image of her mother, average build, quick agile movements and not a drop of fat. Both had twinkling blue eyes and a perpetual smile, exposing strong even teeth. Josie wore her wispy gray hair in a bun atop her head, and Ruby, a brunette, wore her hair curled loosely about her shoulders. I thought she sure was pretty though she was a full-grown woman and already married. She had just stopped by for a short visit with her parents and to give them a hand at the store. Her husband Berwin, she said, had not come with her because he was putting up some hay.

David helped Dad into his collapsible wheelchair and wheeled him into the store where Opie had already plopped himself up onto the counter, his legs dangling and his hands clasping the edges, as men were wont to do in country stores.

I opened all the Coca-Colas, little six ounce bottles, using the opener on the side of the cooler and handed them all around. As I sipped my cola, Aunt Josie noticed my look of awe at all the candy inside the candy case. "Jimmy, how about you get you one or two of these chocolates here," she said, sliding the case open and allowing me to pick my own. I thought I could get used to this kind of treatment in a hurry.

"Now, fellers," Uncle Walter said, after showing us all around, "let's us all go up to the house and set a spell on the front porch. Ruby, here, will mind the store. Ain't that much to do anyways." Looking around and noticing that I just sort of stood there, lost amid the grown-ups, Walter put his hand on my shoulder and looked at Ruby as she stood behind the counter smiling at me. "Jimmy can give Ruby a hand," he said, giving me a wink.

"And, I'll fix up a dinner," Josie said. "I know you're hungry. Won't take me no time." She headed out toward the house, which was up a little hill to the right of the store.

David carried Dad up the hill as Uncle Walter brought along his chair. They'd no sooner set up on the porch and begun conversing, when a whole hoard of kids descended on them. "Lord have mercy," Uncle Walter said, "ain't you kids ever seen company before?" He apologized for all his youngin's kids swarming in on them and shooed them all over toward the store, where they swooped down like a flock of crows, all ogle eyed. On that day, I met a host of my cousins.

Uncle Walter had eleven kids of his own and these were his grandchildren, filing in to take a gander at me. "You want to go up to the cemetery?" one said. "Show you where all the Whites is buried." I looked surprised, but Ruby said that's what everybody did when they visited. So I headed off with the gang of all ages and listened with interest as they plied me with conversation.

"This here's where I live," one said. "And this here's where I live," said another. I never did get their names straight. And, they all looked a lot alike.

When we returned from the cemetery, Aunt Josie was calling for me to come to dinner. "Come on, Jimmy," she said. "You come on and eat with the big folks. You're a guest. I've got fried chicken and apple pie. Now, I know you're gonna like that." I sat down with the grown-ups, feeling mighty proud, while my cousins hung around and gawked, waiting for their turn.

After dinner, the adults talked for a respectable amount of time before David signaled to Opie that he thought we should be on our way. Then, Opie and David and Dad went on about how good Aunt Josie's cooking was. All the while I was conspicuously quiet, listening and watching, taking care to see that Dad's needs were taken care of.

Opie was the first to rise from the table. "Hate to eat and run," he said, "but Dave here says he and Jimmy don't want to be fixin' flat tires in the dark when we go over Spruce Mountain."

And so we started for the car, with Uncle Walter and Aunt Josie and all the clan right behind us, saying how they enjoyed having us and imploring us not to wait so long to come back. Every last one of them gave us hugs. I felt like a warm fuzzy. As we got into the car, I noticed that Dad and Opie were all smiles, too. They were feeling good. I knew why. I'd seen Uncle Walter sneak them a shot of moonshine just before dinner. Not David though, he didn't drink the stuff.

We started out, with arms waving everywhere as we said our final good-byes. Then, as we made our way back to the main highway, Opie just up and spontaneously said, "Dave, while we're here, how 'bout you run us by the old farm where Cliff was born. Land used to belong to Rosabelle's family." And David, always obliging, said, "Fine with me." So we turned in the direction of Princeton and drove for a couple of miles before Grandpa said, "Whoa, turn right here."

David eyed the road questionably, but turned onto it anyway. Driving over what was truly a country road, Dave and I held our breath as the old car felt every pothole and rough spot on the road while Dad and Opie beamed, seeming only to notice the scenery. Finally, we came to a nice piece of land that was grown over for the most part, since it was not in use as farmland anymore. Opie got out and looked around. He spotted a fallen-down chimney, which he said was where the old homeplace used to be. He pointed out a huge maple tree, which he recalled was in the yard. "Rosabelle used to love to sit under that tree and peel peaches or whatever the heck she was always doing. That tree had a swing off that lower branch there that the kids sure did love. Do you remember that, Cliff?"

Opie's comment brought a smile to Dad's face. "Don't reckon I do. I had just turned three when we left here, as I've been told." But I noticed that Dad took it all in. It was where he had been born, a place he had never been back to. It kind of made him choke up a bit. He did ask where cousins Joe and Rose had lived. Opie couldn't quite recollect, but said it was in the general area.

After this little departure, we all heaved a sigh as we came back onto the highway once again. Dave said, "We'd best get this old car headed back to Ameagle. You fellers know that I've got to work tomorrow, now don't you."

"Take it away, boys!" Opie remained light-humored. But luck was not riding with us on the way back. We had a flat tire on the half-hour almost predictably all the way to Beckley. The car went down the highway, plunkety-plunk, plunkety-plunk. The tires were filled with so many boots—some of them had two or three by now—that we were beginning to make emergency plans.

During the times Dave and I repaired tires, Opie sat by the side of the road on his haunches, the coalminers crouch position, he called it. "You fellows need any help?" he'd say. "I'm not the best at this sort of thing. Never had a car. Too much trouble. Dang flat tires, engines blowing out, radiators heatin' up. Give me a train any day." By the time we reached Beckley, David and I were about ready to put him back on a train, but we knew he only jested.

The trip back was like one of *Charlie's* adventures from beginning to end. It was raucous fun and adventure for Opie and Dad, who kept a boyish grin on his face throughout, and tortuous pain for David and me. We had eleven flat tires before it was over with, the last one happening right in front of the Café Eatery in Beckley. The café became a landmark in my mind because unbelievably we would have no more flats after that one though we expected to have several more. It was almost dark and we still had Spruce Mountain to go over. I fig-ured it would take a miracle for us to make it over that mountain without trouble, what with all its hairpin curves and ups and down. It was so unlikely that we would have no more flats that I truly believe angels carried us that last leg of the journey.

It was dark by the time we got home. Mom and Jacqueline hurried out to greet us. "I've worried myself sick," Mom said.

"Just a good little adventure," Dad said. He was worn out, but still all smiles.

Opie jumped from the car and shook David's hand. "You're a hellava guy," he said, which was Opie's way of saying thanks. David carried Dad inside, and I trailed behind with my arm around Mom's waist and her arm around mine. "I feel like Moses coming in out of the desert," I told her. She just smiled and told me she was sure glad we were back safe and sound.

Dad started right in telling anyone who would listen about the adventures. I thought it sounded like another *Charlie* tale, but this time I wanted no part of it. I found me a nice soft bed and delighted in the pleasures of home.

After this trip, David had to put the car on hold for a while until he could get some decent tires. But, once he was able to get them, he and Dad were out and about again, this time scheming with plans the rest of us knew nothing about.

32

Mink's On the Air

During the summer months, we often gathered on the front porch where we listened to the crickets, watched the fireflies flit in and out of the yard, and talked about things. Dad usually instigated the conversations since he was the most up-to-date on what was happening in the world. He read all the time, listened to the radio, and talked with all the neighbors, so he always had something to talk about. But, sometimes we didn't talk; sometimes we sang.

On one such midsummer evening, somewhere around the mid-forties, as we all sat on the porch Mom said she felt like singing, "What about it, Clifford?" she asked.

Dad was always ready to sing. "Pass the hymnals!" he said. "Let's start with *Glory, Glory Hallelujah.*" Rosabelle had taught Dad how to harmonize when he was a lad. He'd taught Mom and together they'd taught all of us, so we had a little chorus of our own, so to speak.

Folks around us had no choice but to listen; they never complained. Some had their own singings. Anyway, I never saw anyone close a window. The Coots and the Kinders were the neighbors on either side. On this occasion, Harry teased as he let us know where he stood.

"By dang," he called from his porch, "I can't sing them songs, but it looks like I'm gonna' be listenin', like it or not."

"He needs some religion anyway," Nellie chimed in. "He ain't never had any."

"Now, confound it Nellie, if they're gonna force me to listen, at least I'm gonna make a request."

"A re-quest?" Nellie emphasized the *re* in request. "Since when do you know the name of a religious song?"

"Everbody knows *The Old Rugged Cross*. Take it away folks! I'll come in on the chorus, help you out a bit."

"It's on page twenty-one," Lee said, smiling. The song was one we sang quite well, especially with the harmony. Dad had a high tenor voice. Lee sang the bass. Billy and I sang the melody and Mom and Jacqueline sang alto.

Dad began the singing with a humm-m and the rest of us found our note and blended in. Then we commenced to sing. We knew all the verses by heart. But we still used our hymnals, the ones the Presbyterian Church had given us years earlier when they switched to new ones. It added a bit of formality to the singing.

We gave a fine performance, and Harry said we did right well. I never heard him join in though.

Jacqueline suggested her favorite, *The Church in the Wildwood*. Billy, Lee and I liked that one too, mostly because we got to do the *Come, come, come, come* backup while the rest sang the chorus.

Harry laughed. "Hells Bells, fellows. I could do that!"

"Well I'd sure like to hear it." Nellie never let it end.

David appeared out of nowhere. "No sense in you guys having all the fun," he said as he sidled up alongside Jacqueline, who was sitting on the porch floor, her back against the wall. He had his favorite too, *When the Roll is Called up Yonder*. He liked the echo effect of repeating a portion of a line, such as, *Oh, when the roll, Oh, when the roll*

"You're not all bad either, Deedle," Harry called over.

Mom went inside and returned with a plastic bag filled with margarine. Margarine had become a replacement for butter, but it didn't look like butter. It looked like lard. Only after the little ball of yellow food coloring was broken and sufficiently blended throughout did the margarine look like butter.

"Someone can be squeezing the coloring into this margarine while we're sittin' here singin," Mom said. I volunteered. I did it most of the time anyway.

Then Herman Coots came over and the singing turned into conversation. "Y'all ought to go over to Mink's and get on the air tomorrow!" he declared. "Mink'd be proud to have you guys sing for him. He'll be on the air tomorrow, twelve sharp."

"Who do you reckon will be singin' or playin', Herman?" Lee asked.

"Lord only knows," Herman answered. "Just whoever shows up. Last week it was Frances and Shirley Moore. They really sounded pretty."

"When *you* gonna sing, Herman?" Lee joked.

"Right about the time you play the banjo!" Herman jostled with his old friend.

Mrs. Coots came onto her porch, followed by her husband, who sat quietly and smoked his pipe. He never had much to say one way or the other. "Don't stop now folks," she called. "Looks like you got the whole neighborhood out listenin'. Might as well make it worth our while."

Dad laughed. He loved it when lots of people gathered round. "Mrs. Coots, come on over here and add your beautiful voice," he called. "We'll have us a regular camp meeting."

"You don't want *my* voice," she said.

"Me neither," Harry shouted from his porch.

"Shut up, Harry." It was Nellie.

Herman laughed. He said he'd best be getting back home to his wife. "I'm just visitin' the folks here a little bit," he said. "Heard you guys singin'. Now, remember, Mink won't be on the air long now. Be sure to tune in right at twelve noon or you might miss him."

Mink Moore was a cousin to the Legg boys, Basil and Billy, who were sons of Bill and Bessie. The brothers had inherited some of their father's electrical know-how and with a little mountaineer ingenuity they had set up a little bandit radio operation in Fred Moore's workshop. How they managed to keep themselves unknown to the FCC was not known, but they went on the air every now and then.

Sometimes Mink would play and sing by himself. He played an electric guitar and a mandolin and had a right nice voice. He invited anyone with talent to join him. We never knew just who it would be. It was fun to listen in though. All part of our coal camp life at Ameagle.

33

On the Road

On what was to be a very important day of his life, in July of 1947, Dad wheeled out onto the porch where he sat calmly, awaiting his *carriage*. David would be along soon to take him to Beckley, the county seat of Raleigh County, where Dad planned to file as a candidate for the office of the Justice of the Peace for the Clear Fork District. He'd done his research and knew what would be required of him. He was ready to start making his moves.

As he waited, Toby's little sister Patsy came calling. "Come on up, Patsy," Dad invited. "Let's take us a little ride." Excited, Patsy climbed onto the wheelchair and placed her hands on Dad's knees and her feet on the footrests. She squealed with delight as Dad rolled the chair back and forth across the porch making childlike noises as he went. Nellie laughed as she called from the fence, "Patsy, you come on home now. Clifford's got to go somewhere!"

David arrived, all smiles and on time. He always was. On time and all smiles. "You sure do look dignified, Cliff," he said, as he carried Dad to the car. "Where'd you get that hat?

"Sears Roebuck special. Fancy enough for a politician?"

"You'll knock 'em dead!"

"All I want is their vote. I don't want to kill them," Dad said with a chuckle.

David grinned as he changed gears to start up Spruce Mountain toward Beckley. "I know we're going to the courthouse, Cliff, but what do we do when we get there?"

"Well, you hustle me inside and get me to the County Clerk's office and I'll take it from there. Shouldn't take too long."

At the courthouse, a young lady greeted them from behind a large desk. "What can I do for you, gentlemen?" she asked.

"I'm here to file for the Justice of the Peace in the Clear Fork District," Dad said.

The young lady looked first at David who stood behind Dad, then at the wheelchair and then at Dad. "Just a minute, Sir," she said. "I'll be right back."

Keeping her voice low but not completely out of earshot she inquired of her superior, "There's a crippled man out here in a wheelchair who says he wants to file to run for the Justice of the Peace in Clear Fork District. Can he do that?"

"Can he do that?" Her superior wasn't sure. "I've never run across this before. We've never had a crippled person run for an elected office that I know of. But I don't see why not. Give me a minute, I'll look into it." With his mouth turned down at the corners, he shook his head from side to side as he scanned the criteria for the office. "Nothin' here says he can't. Give him the papers," he told the waiting clerk.

Her face flushed, the young miss returned and addressed Dad. "Here you are, sir. You'll need to fill out these forms."

As David scowled, Dad wheeled up close to the desk and proceeded to fill out the necessary forms. Handing them back to her, he said cheerfully, "Here you are, young lady."

"That will be $25," she said, not looking at either man.

Dad paid the fee and they left the building. David was miffed. "People act like crippled folks don't have any rights at all," he said as he carried Dad down the stairs and to the car. "You *know* why she went into that back room."

"She doesn't know any better, Dave. Folks aren't used to seeing crippled people out much. Cripples usually stay indoors, out of sight, out of mind. That's why they're called shut-ins. They're supposed to *stay* in. I figure once people start seeing me, they'll get past my crippled legs and see that I'm a thinking, talking, reasonable person just like they are. It will take time, that's all."

"Ain't nothin' wrong with you right now, Cliff. Bein' in a wheel chair don't make you one bit less than the next feller out there. Anybody who can't see that ain't got an ounce of common sense."

"It will happen again and again, Dave," Dad said patiently. He was used to the looks, the pity, the questions in other folk's minds. "Only time will make a difference," he said. "I'll get used to them, and they'll get used to me. This is not the first time I've been slighted. I've been refused service in restaurants and been refused a place to sleep because of no accommodations for handicapped people. No ramps. No restroom facilities. It will be different some day."

"That don't make it right."

"Right's got nothing to do with it. Being out there time and time again is what will take care of it. It just takes getting used to."

"Well, if that's what it takes, you'll be in as many places as *I* can get you to, that's for sure."

Dad smiled. He liked David's spunk. "Well, Dave," he said, "let's do first things first. Before we leave Beckley let's go by the liquor store, then let's go see about getting some cards printed and some flyers made. See how much it's going to cost me. I might have to borrow some money from somebody."

"You've got my paycheck, Cliff. Any time you need it."

Amazed at David's generosity, Dad said he was grateful. "We're going to make a good team, Dave. You and me. We'll get this old crippled man elected to the Justice of the Peace!" He adjusted the new ring-shaped rubber cushion seat he was sitting on. The cushion allowed him to sit taller.

Dad had learned to be a patient man. His years as a shut-in had changed his life forever. He was no longer a *young* common laborer with a limited education. He was now a self-educated mature handicapped man who would use his mind to make a living. He had filed to run for a political office, a first for a handicapped person from his district and maybe from all of West Virginia. He was prepared. He knew he could do it.

*   *   *

On the way back to Ameagle, they met up with Billy who was delivering groceries. Billy screeched to a stop and called out, "How'd it go, guys?"

"Oh, about as well for me as the next guy," Dad said. "David here's agreed to be my campaign manager."

"I thought *I* was going to be your campaign manager!" Billy said, feigning surprise.

"You don't have enough time," Dad said. "Can't hold you down long enough to make any plans. And besides, you don't have a car yet."

"Won't be long," Billy said. "A few more bucks and I'll be totin' you around."

Dad shook his head as Billy drove off in a cloud of dust. "Billy's a little lead-footed at times."

"He's a good driver, though," David said. "He can borrow my car any time he wants to take you out Cliff. In fact, anytime you've got a driver and I'm not usin' the car, it's yours to use."

"I'll have to get me some more drivers, then. Old Jim can't drive yet. Ethel can't. And, Jacqueline can't!

"Don't you worry 'bout Jacqueline. I'll teach her to drive. She's been buggin' me already."

*   *   *

Delivering groceries gave Billy lots of opportunities to campaign for Dad. Billy was fun-loving and gregarious, but dead serious about his work.

Folks liked these traits in a young man. "If your dad is anything like you, son, he has my vote," one lady told him. Billy gave her lots of cards and asked her to help his dad. "He will really appreciate it," he said. "He's a fine person. He won't let you down. He'll be countin' on you, and your friends, too." Billy got many promises for votes from his customers.

Billy sometimes borrowed Dave's car and drove Dad around to meet some of the people to whom he delivered groceries at White Oak, Toney's Fork, and Workman's Creek. Dad, who had not had the opportunity to be known by people in these areas, knew that Billy was the key.

As someone would say "So you're Billy's dad. He's told us about you" Dad would reach to shake hands and say to them: "Glad to meet you. I'm here to put a face with the name. I'd like to be your next Justice of the Peace in this district. Like to have your vote."

Dad made it a point to get out of the car whenever he could. He wanted to know people on a personal level. He wanted them to know him as he was, handicapped physically but very able mentally.

*   *   *

Dad didn't want to be a user. Though he fully appreciated David, he said at times he felt like he was taking advantage. "Dave, you're just too generous," he said once when David was visiting. "Sometimes, I have your car more than you do."

But David was a part of the plan. "My car is here to be used," he said. "Besides, I'm your campaign manager, and I say you'll need to be out every day. I'm teachin' Jackie to drive. She'll be ready soon. I won't be around enough to do you any good all by myself."

Dad said he was truly grateful. "Ethel wants to learn to drive, too," Dad said, giving Mom a *teasing look*. "But, she won't do me much good. She won't take me up Sandlick!"

"She can take you to church. That won't hurt you none." David and Mom exchanged looks of support.

"Maybe not, but I reckon I'll pass on that, David," Dad said. "I had enough going to church in my younger days to do me the rest of my life. But that don't mean I don't have religion. I have a close relationship with the man upstairs. He hasn't failed me yet."

*   *   *

Because Clear Fork District was almost totally Democrat, whichever Democratic candidate won the primary was a shoo-in for the regular election come November. The district supported two JP's, and, in this election, Dad would be running against ten other candidates, two of which were incumbents and unafraid of losing their positions.

Mudslinging was sure to enter the campaign, and Dad knew he had to be prepared to hold his own when the mud slinging started. So, he began to develop his plan.

Sitting down amongst his closest friends and neighbors, he mapped out a strategy he thought would work for him. He figured that first and foremost he must be none other than himself—a physically handicapped man out to win an election. He had no doubt that he could handle the job and that he would be fair and just. But, he also knew there would be many who doubted his ability and he would need a strategy to get them to think otherwise.

He listed his needs. Transportation—lots of it. He had to be out and about. He had to get to know a lot of people on a personal basis. He had to shake a lot of hands and get to some key people in each area. He'd need to build up a cadre of supporters who believed in him, folks who would understand that his handicap was not something that would keep him from doing the job. He had to educate people as to his knowledge and his ability to make decisions in a fair and judicious way. He would need lots of cards and flyers. He would stop and talk to people and would get outside his car where he could be seen in his wheelchair whenever possible.

The family gathered around the kitchen table as each planned to help in whatever way they could. Mom said she would take the churches, her friends, and the Moose Club. She was well liked and respected for her leadership skills among her peers. Mom was also widely admired for staying with her husband and raising her family under the direst of circumstances. Plus, she was attractive and presented herself well. She would get votes for Dad. Her problem: she didn't drive and had no car to drive anyway. She would talk to Bessie. Bessie would help.

Lee would keep things going at home and pass cards whenever he could. Jacqueline saw lots of people at the company store each day and she would speak up for Dad when she could. Also, she would be one of Dad's drivers as soon as she learned to drive. And, she would give over her earnings when money was needed. In that way, Jacqueline and David were alike. Both were totally unselfish.

Billy saw lots of people. He was well liked at school, at work, and in the community. He could drive David's car. And he would drive his own car as soon as he could get it. His problem was time. He had little to spare.

Me, I would pass out cards, hang flyers on telephone poles and put a flyer inside every newspaper I delivered. "And," Mom said, "Jimmy, you are going to have to stay out of scraps and behave yourself in church. And, be respectful to your teachers at school." I had earned a reputation as being on the scrappy side. The family figured I needed some reining in.

*   *   *

Bummy delighted in helping Dad whenever he could. Always in a jovial mood, he stopped by one day to chat. "Cliff, I've been talking it up for you at the mine. Won't take much to get a good number of votes there. Maybe a shot or two of whiskey!"

"That's a start!" Dad knew Bummy was teasing about the whiskey, but he figured whiskey would be a must at some point in his campaign, especially with some people. He remained open. "Just how much whiskey do you think I'll need to carry this out?"

"Oh, a jug or two should do it. It's expected, you know."

"Oh, I know, all right. I've set aside some funds for the whiskey!"

"Now, you know all your votes ain't going to be just the men, Cliff. You're going to have to get out here and hug women and kiss babies, too."

"I'll hug if you won't tell, Bummy!"

Bummy laughed, enjoying his jest. He pulled out his pipe, the one with the big curve in it and took his time to light up. Then, gesturing, he swung the pipe upward and out toward Dad, unable to resist another jab. "Now, Clifford, before I go and give you my vote, tell me, if I get arrested for beatin' up my wife, will you send me to jail or give me a medal?"

Dad laughed as he tried to visualize Bummy beating up his wife. Bummy's wife was a strong portly woman, six inches taller than Bummy and known to keep him in line. "I might expect you to put me to the test, Bummy! How's the wife doing, anyway? Ethel said she's been feeling poorly."

"She's feelin' worse than the weather. The weather's been bad, and she's been "*under the weather*.""

"Well, don't you think you ought to get on home and see about her, then?" Dad said with a sly grin.

"Nah, Cliff, she's liable to beat me up for wakin' her up to ask how she's doin'."

"Well, go get on some clean clothes and come back and take a ride up Sandlick with me. Billy's borrowed David's car and he's going to take me around a bit. You used to live up Sandlick, didn't you."

"Yep, I lived there probably more than a year."

"Well, there must be somebody there you can still talk to, put in a good word for me. Help me get a few votes."

"Shouldn't be too hard to do yourself, seein' as how you're a regular customer. Better tell them to stock up, cause you're gonna need you a mess of whiskey before election time." Bummy gave Dad a knowing smile.

David's car pulled up to the gate with Billy behind the wheel. "Bummy," Dad said, "you had better go with us. Hurry on home and get dressed. We'll pick you up in a little bit. Old Billy's got to have him some vittles before we go, anyway."

"Oh, all right, Cliff," Bummy said, giving in. "The old lady's gonna kill me anyway."

"Well, get on home and get it over with. We'll be there directly."

*   *   *   *

Dad donned his new hat, put several of his campaign cards into his shirt pocket and waited at the door as Billy finished eating. "No need to hurry, Billy. Gotta give Bummy time to change clothes and wash off the coal dust."

Billy grinned and hurried anyway. He put Dad's wheelchair in the trunk of the car. "Just in case you decide to get out," he told Dad. "You're campaigning now. Might need to hug a few women."

"Not you too, Billy," Mom said in good humor as she walked them to the car and waved them off. "Now be careful." She knew where they were most likely headed. And though she worried some, she was delighted to see her son help his father out. She doted on her children.

Bummy was waiting outside his house. As the car pulled up alongside him, Dad thought he saw a curtain open and close. "Did she throw you out so soon?" he asked.

"Nah, Cliff, she didn't even let me in. Just threw me a wet towel and some clean clothes," Bummy said jokingly as he climbed into the back seat and slid forward, giving Dad's hat a light touch.

"How'd you come by such a hat, Cliff?"

"Ethel. She wants me to be a handsome politician."

"I'm sure everybody up Sandlick will fall all over themselves," Bummy said as he leaned forward from the back seat of the car to take a better look at the hat.

*   *   *   *

Pete Tomkins saw them coming. He met them at the bend in the road, prepared to sell a little moonshine, but Dad put up his hand. "Pete," he said, "I'm here to ask a favor of you."

Pete leaned into the window on the passenger side of the car and took a look inside. "Your pleasure, Cliff. What can I do?"

"Well, I'm politickin' Pete. I'm running for the Justice of the Peace and I'd like to have your vote."

"Runnin' for the Justice of the Peace!" Pete stepped back. "Now, Cliff, don't you know the man in that office has already got that race sewed up?"

"I'm not trying to replace him, Pete. There's room for both of us in this race. Clear Fork District has two JP's. I figure he'll get a few votes from up this way, but I'm counting on getting the rest. Now of course, if you don't have a preference you can just vote for me. That way I'll get two votes!"

Pete slapped Dad on the shoulder. "Hey, I like your style, Cliff."

"Cliff's *style* won't mean a hill of beans if you don't get out to vote now Pete," Bummy said from the window of the back seat. "He's gonna need *your* vote and a whole bunch of others up this here holler, you, your wife, and all your kin. I figure Cliff has bought your vote a few times over, now ain't he?"

Pete grimaced and stepped back from the car raising his arms mockingly, saying, "Now, I don't need any arm twistin', Bummy. I figure you'll be lookin' for me down at the polls, and if I don't show up, I'll lose some of my business here, right? I ain't crazy. I didn't just fall off the turnip truck."

"Now, I didn't say that, Pete." Bummy smiled smugly, settling back into his seat.

Pete patted Dad on the back and looked over at Billy whom he recognized from delivering groceries. "Where's old Dave?" he asked.

"Old Dave had to work today," Dad said. "He's loaned us the use of his car. Billy here will be driving me some now. When he can work it in."

"In between all his girls," Bummy butted in.

"Cut it out, you guys," Billy said with a grin, as his face grew hot.

Stepping over to the driver's side of the car, Pete rested his elbows on the window sill and looked Billy over carefully before saying, "Billy, drive your Dad on up the road. Pick you up a few more votes. Stop down by the branch on your way back." Then he disappeared into his house.

Billy drove off. He knew what that meant. The moonshiners didn't hand whiskey directly to the buyer.

"This is good fun, Cliff," Bummy said. "I think I'll make myself a regular on your campaign trail."

"You're welcome to hitch a ride anytime the feeling moves you and the *wife will let you out*," Dad said, giving Bummy a teasing grin.

Remembering that Pete was connected to the many Stovers who lived "up-the-river," Bummy yelled from the window, "Now, don't forget, Pete, Cliff's gonna need the Stover vote, too. One vote for the right man is as good as two!"

Dad grinned broadly. He was having a heck-of-a-good time.

Billy beamed, too. "I just might get out here and run for some office myself someday," he said. "All you gotta do is please everybody!"

34

Campaign Wheels a Rolling

In September of 1947, Uncle Connie's wife Wava died and Dad and Mom invited Connie to come live with us. On the first evening of his stay, Connie sat in the big overstuffed chair that was soon to become his favorite, lit up a cigarette, crossed his legs, and pulled the standing ashtray closer to him, making himself at home as he'd been asked to do. Then he chatted for hours with Mom and Dad.

"Cliff, I want to stay here," Connie said, "but now, I don't want to intrude on your livin' arrangement any more than I have to. If you'll allow me, I'll enclose the front porch so I'll have a place to sleep and I won't be in anyone's way."

"Now Connie, you know good and well you are not an intrusion. We're glad to have you," Dad told him. "But you can close in the front porch if you want to 'cause I'll be needing some office space anyway once I'm elected the Justice of the Peace."

"And you're going to be elected, Cliff. I've heard people speak your name from as far away as Whitesville. That's going pretty far for a *shut-in*. What on earth have you been doin'?"

Dad beamed with pride at the reference to his campaign approach. "People aren't used to seeing a crippled man out politickin'," he said, flipping the ashes from his Chesterfield with a flick of his thumb. "I figure the more of me they see the more of me they will remember. I've been up and down every hollow around here, shaking hands, kissing babies and hugging women."

Connie bellowed at the unlikely scenario. Mom gave Dad a crooked smile. "Clifford, you had better not be out there huggin' women!"

"Well, maybe just shaking hands and kissing babies."

"That's better. Now go ahead and tell Connie what else you've been doin'!"

"Now, Ethel, you tell that part better than I do."

"He's got folks around here takin' him up all these hollers, passin' out whiskey, tryin' to buy votes. If he's not careful, he's gonna be sittin' in jail instead of gettin' himself elected to the Justice of the Peace."

"Sounds to me like Cliff needs some new drivers, Ethel. Why don't you and me start drivin' him around. A pretty woman will get him more votes than a shot of whiskey any day."

"Now, that's a right good idea, Connie," Dad said, ready to go on the spot. "Ethel, all you have to do is sit and look pretty. I'll do all the talking."

"Talkin' is not the problem!" Mom replied.

Connie saw that Mom was still grinning and so he ventured into no man's land. "Cliff, before you go and give away all that good stuff to voters, why don't you see what you can do for a brother who can't even cast a vote for you?"

"Help yourself, Connie. I'll have one with you." Dad never asked Mom to serve beer or whiskey. His brothers knew just where it was kept and helped themselves.

As Connie sprang up to retrieve the beers, he turned to Mom. "Now, Ethel, how about you?" he asked. "You want one, too?"

Mom rolled her eyes and shook her head in resignation. She changed the subject with, "Connie, there'll be plenty for you to do around here. There's always somethin' needin' to be fixed."

"That I can do, Ethel. I take after Pop when it comes to fixin' things. Just point me in the right direction. I'll tackle it 'til I get it done."

Uncle Connie quickly settled into the routines of our house and was soon just another member of the family. Right away he decided he'd teach Mom to drive. "We'll start here in the alley," he said. "That way if you hit something, it will just be a fence or a post."

"I'm not going to hit anything," Mom said. "I've been watchin' good drivers for a long time now. Besides, Bessie and Orphie have been teachin' me, too."

Connie winced. "Women's driving. I'll have my hands full undoin' that!"

"Oh, you men! Just teach me to drive!" Mom was too excited to care about being teased. She got behind the wheel of Connie's big old '46 Roadmaster Buick and said she felt like a queen, except she couldn't see the road. "Get you a cushion," Connie said, amused at her innocence.

Properly situated with a decorative pillow from the living room sofa, Mom was ready to go. She gave herself a minute to get a feel for the car, finding the brake, the clutch, the starter, and handling the steering wheel. "Okay, I'm ready, Connie. Let's get this thing rollin'."

Grinning, Connie handed her the key to the car. "Now, Ethel, I'm going to give you this key and let you drive this car on your own once you get your license. How does that sound?"

Her eyes grew big. "Great!" she said. "It sounds great!" Having a car to drive on her own was an answer to her prayers. Wasting no time, she started the car right up, giving Connie a sweet smile. She changed gears and began to drive the car up and down the lane, dodging children and dogs as she zigzagged from one side of the road to the other to avoid hitting the fences and fence posts.

"Why do you zig and zag, Ethel?"

"I can't help it, Connie, I can't tell how much room I have. It looks like I'm goin' to run smack dab into the fence or the ditch."

"We got to take care of that. I don't want to come crawlin' up out of some ditch," Connie said playfully. "Set your eye on the ornament in the middle of the hood and line it up with the right side of the road. It should look like it's right at the edge of the right hand side of the road."

"Well, now, that makes it a heck-of-a-lot easier. Why didn't you tell me that before?" Mom said as she moved the car ahead with slightly more confidence.

"I was waitin' for you to ask. Don't want to give you too much to think about too soon."

"Connie, I'm a fast learner. You tell me everything I need to know."

Mom kept the car in a straight line after that. A few days later Connie took her out on the highway, where she had a wider area. With all that space, she gave it a bit too much gas, then, going too fast, found she had to brake, which threw Connie forward pretty hard. He let out a squeal as he mockingly braced himself with one hand and covered his eyes with the other.

"You're makin' fun of me," Mom said with a back-to-business look in Connie's direction.

Connie took his cue and decided to behave. "You're tryin' too hard, Ethel," he said. "No need to hurry it. You'll get the hang of it directly. But you do have to learn to go forwards before you go backwards. And right now, I'm so shook up, I can't tell whether we're goin' forwards or backwards."

Mom gave Connie a determined look and said she wanted no more teasing. "I'm **going** to learn to drive, Connie. I've got a lot of catchin' up to do."

Her mind set, Mom sat straight as an arrow and focused on her driving with an intensity Connie said he had never seen. By the end of the afternoon, she was driving forward and backward, parking and turning. "You're the fastest learner I've ever had, Ethel. Tomorrow, we'll hit the big highway. I'll give you your choice, Whitesville or Beckley."

"'Whitesville! I'm not ready to go over Spruce Mountain—yet!"

"Right good choice, Ethel," Connie chided. "I expect it will be easier to pull us out of the river than to pull us back up a mountainside."

Mom gave Connie *the look*, then chuckled. She knew she was mastering the art of driving, and she was as excited as a schoolgirl on her first date.

Her fifth time out on the highway, and a good deal more comfortable as she had planned the drive again and again in her mind, she fixed her eyes on the road and shot off down the highway toward the town of Whitesville, in Boone County. She didn't plan to have any lurches, fast braking or jerky driving of any kind. She was on her way to get her driver's license. She wanted to have this car to drive on her own. A driver's license meant emancipation!

The drive to Whitesville was familiar and she anticipated each curve of the road as it meandered along the river for about eight miles. With not one mishap, she arrived in Whitesville and drove straight to the State Police Headquarters where she passed her test, even the parallel parking, with ease. As a reward, Connie took her for a cup of coffee at Fritz's Dairy Bar. She was forty-one years of age, but said she felt seventeen!

✳   ✳   ✳

"Cliff, I believe you've got yourself another driver," Connie said getting out of the passenger side, after Mom, with confident ease, parked the car in front of the house.

"Won't do me much good. She won't take me the places I want to go to," Dad chided as Mom, all rosy faced from happiness, dangled the keys in front of him.

From then on, Mom had the use of Connie's car at least three days out of each week, which meant she was on the road three days out of each week. She did not need a reason for going. She just went. And before long, Dad was riding along with her. As long as he had someone to put him in the car, he was happy to go. They went out politickin', behaving like children at Christmas time, with each day building in excitement for the big day to come.

One day Mom said, "Clifford, I know you can't go with me, but one day I want to go over to Marfork and see if I can find the place where we buried Lonnie. I always wanted to go back there."

"I wish I could go with you, Ethel," Dad said. "But I doubt you'll find anything. It'll be way overgrown by now." They shared a moment of sadness in silence recognizing that it was probably true. They were left with their memories.

*   *   *

As soon as Jacqueline learned to drive, right away David loaned her the use of his car anytime she wanted it. Mostly, she drove it to work or escorted Dad on one of his trips out politicking. Dad said she did well. And she did. But one day she wheeled in from work just a trifle too fast and, miscalculating her braking distance, was not able to stop in time to avoid driving the car right into the side of the coal bin. Dad and I heard the crunch and looked from the porch to see the car resting partly in the road and partly inside the coal bin. "Oh, mercy," Dad said. "Run see if she's all right, Jim."

I could see right away that it wasn't anything major. Though Jacqueline looked mortified, she'd only dented a fender. All red-faced, she got out of the car, and she wasn't at all pleased to see me standing there with a mocking grin across my face.

"Jimmy, you can just get your silly face out of here," she started.

"But Dad sent me to see if you're all right."

"I'm a heck-of-a-lot better than you're going to be if you don't get that stupid grin off your face."

I continued to laugh as I danced around her.

"You'll see the day you take a ride with me," she said, more upset than before.

"If I'd been ridin' with you today, I'd be sittin' in the bin with a chunk of coal atop my head right about now," I managed to say before she came at me. Dad called from the porch and saved the day.

"Sissie, David will be here directly. He'll just pull her right out of there. Not a problem as I see it."

"I don't know what happened," she said. "I just couldn't stop it in time."

"No matter," Dad said, "so long as you're okay."

"Yeah, so long as you're okay," I said.

She turned to take a slap at me, but Dad spoke up again. "Jim, there's no call for that." I knew he was right. "Sorry," I said.

David came round a little later on. He saw the crease in the right fender and the car lodged against the coal bin. He started to smile, but seeing Jacqueline's demeanor, he took a second look at the car instead. " It looks like somebody moved the coal bin out in front of the car," he said, with not so much as a grin. He then got behind the wheel and moved the car back onto the road.

I helped David repair the coal bin. As he hammered, I held the boards in place, all the while grinning teasingly at Jacqueline. She gave me the evil eye, and I figured that I would pay dearly at another time with a severe tongue-lashing. I ran off to play, wisely steering clear of her for the rest of the evening.

✳   ✳   ✳

With two cars and five drivers at his disposal, Dad planned his itinerary and hit the road as often as he could. He reserved Sandlick for the male drivers allowing Mom to take him to the safer places like Dorothy, Levale, Jarrell's Valley, Colcord, Sycamore, White Oak and Toney's Fork.

Billy didn't end up doing much driving for Dad though by now he had his own car. Between school, delivering groceries and girls, Billy was a busy man. But, he still campaigned. He handed out a lot of cards. "My Dad's running for the Justice of the Peace; he'd appreciate your vote," he'd say with his charming smile and pleasant manner. He probably reached more folks than the rest of us combined because he serviced all the communities around Ameagle.

"Boy works as hard as you most likely has a good dad," one man told Billy on one of his delivery runs to Colored Town.

"Why, that's Clifford White's boy, don't you know?" Joe Lambert said, stepping outside his barbershop in Colored Town. He watched as Billy unloaded groceries for folks nearby. Joe had worked with Dad in the coal mines before the accident.

"Your dad's a good man, son," Joe said. "Why don't you bring him on down here to the barbershop? I might be able to swing him a few votes."

"He'll be here," Billy said, giving Joe one of his widest grins, one that showed all of his perfectly formed teeth and the dimples in his rosy cheeks. He hefted a big hundred pound bag of feed from the back of the truck and pitched it onto the ground near where Cat Gilmore stood.

Cat turned to his friends with a look of pride. "That boy work like colored folk," he said. "He's been workin' since he was knee high to the bottom side of a kitchen chair. Make a daddy proud."

He turned back to Billy. "For sure, you bring old Clifford down here to Joe's barbershop. We'll get Clifford some votes from around here. Colored folk vote, too."

Billy drove off, throwing up his hand with a wave of departure, promising Cat that he'd bring Dad to the shop.

Cat and his wife Leonie liked Dad. Dad always sent for Cat whenever we slaughtered a hog because Cat was really good at hog killing. That's how he'd earned the name Cat. His real name was Nathan, but once he started butchering hogs, folks started saying, "Get old man Gilmore to butcher your hogs; he's quick as a cat." And Nathan would say, "Yeah, just call me Cat, cause I **am** quick as a cat! I'm slick and quick. Ain't nobody quicker than the Cat!"

The first time I watched Cat Gilmore butcher and dress a hog, I was duly impressed. He came about daybreak with two of his sons. Dad went out onto the porch to greet him, and, seeing that Cat had brought only two of his sons, said, "You get that whole family of yours down here, Cat, you'll *really* be fast on the job."

But Cat shook his head no. "Mr. Clifford," he said, "two boys is just fine, but the dressing of the hog slows down with the addition of any one of my other sons." Cat patted his sons on the shoulders and grinned with pride. Rolling their eyes upward, they grinned too and shook their heads in affirmation.

Cat said the cool and nippy day right at the beginning of winter was just right for slaughtering a hog, "You don't want to butcher a hog in warm weather," he said. "For your meat be sure to spoil!"

The killing took place in the back yard. After a blow to the head with an ax, the hog's squeal echoed throughout the whole camp. Spectators came within minutes. A hog killing was a social event of immense proportions.

The hog was strung onto a tripod pole structure, then hoisted upright and split down the middle and left to bleed naturally for an appropriate amount of time. While the hog was bleeding, Cat built a fire under a fifty-five gallon drum of water. While the water heated, he removed all the entrails, the heart, the lungs, liver, everything inside and put it all aside. This would be his take.

With the bleeding done and the entrails removed, the hog was dipped into a fifty-gallon drum of boiling water to get the hair loose so that it could be scraped away before the hog was butchered. Cat was an expert at this. He sang and hummed as he worked, along with his helpers. Dad occasionally passed him a sip of home-brew, which Cat truly appreciated. "Cliff, you is a real gentleman!" he said. "You know just what a man need."

As the meat was butchered, it was passed onto the porch where the whole family, including Dad, became involved. Hams, pork chops, ribs, and bacon were rubbed down with salt and sugar for curing. Mom and Evaline made sausage. I watched in amazement as they put all the left-over meat through a meat-grinder, and then added spices before they shaped it into serving size pieces and put it aside. We'd have sausage for breakfast the next day. I could hardly wait.

We put aside some skins for roasting. These we considered a delicacy, eating them a few at time over a period of several days.

When the butchering job was done, the whole back porch was covered with meat on the curing racks. The entire house smelled like a slaughterhouse.

Cat stood back and smiled with great admiration at his skill. Then he finished off the beer Dad held out to him while his sons packaged up all the chitterlings, pig's fee, and the head and organ meats, which now belonged to them—Cat's pay for butchering the hog. "Cliff, how bout you sell me one of these shoulders?" Cat ventured before leaving. Dad thought about it for a moment and then said he guessed he could do it. He could use the extra money.

Nothing was wasted from the hog. The fat was rendered to make lard which we kept in the cool cellar because left out it would become rancid. We used the extra skins to grease our brogans, which gave them waterproof protection for a while. All the extra grease we saved for another day when Grandma Smars would use it to make lye soap in the same big pot that was used to boil down the lard.

Grandma involved us all when she made the soap. We kids took turns stirring, because it took most of a day to complete the job. Afterwards, Grandma made the soap into bars, and then we wrapped the bars and stored them away. "Lye soap is good for all kinds of skin ailments," Grandma told us. "If you get a rash, or poison ivy or a breakin' out of any kind, wash good with the lye soap and don't rinse it off. It'll heal you right up."

✶   ✶   ✶

Billy couldn't take Dad to Joe Lambert's barbershop the next day, but he made sure he got Dad into the car before he left for work. Mom would be Dad's driver.

Joe came right to the car. "Good to see you, Cliff," he said. "Glad you could come. Don't many of them politicians make it over here to Colored Town. Guess they don't figure we coloreds got a say in these here elections."

"Got every right, Joe," Dad said. "I appreciate the invite."

Two young boys were hanging around and Joe shooed them off to spread the word that Dad was there. The boys ran through the neighborhood calling for people to come on down to the barbershop. First, folks came out on their porches. Then, some came out into the lane. Finally, many, mostly men, made their way down to the barbershop where Dad had an opportunity to shake a few hands and do a little campaigning. Many were men whom Dad had worked with in the mine, long ago. They were as curious to see Dad after so long a time as he was to see them. There appeared a sort of mutual pride in knowing one another.

Dad spoke right up: "I expect you want to know what I can do for you if I'm elected. Well, I intend to be as fair and impartial to you as I would be to the next fellow. Being colored won't have any bearing on doing what is right, and I intend to do what's right—what's right for me, and what's right for you. You'll be treated just like the next man. I can't promise you anything more or anything less than that. But, I need your vote, and I will sure appreciate it if you will take the time to go to the polls and vote for me. I've got to show a few people what this old crippled coalminer can do."

"Amen!" Joe said, moving his head up and down.

Dad shook hands and passed out cards to everyone who had come to see him. "As you know," he'd say again and again, "you can vote for two candidates. But, if you've got no preference then just vote for me. That way I'll get two votes. I can use your vote."

Dad figured many would not go to the polls because they would not have transportation, so as he left, he said, "Now we'll have a car coming through here on Election Day to take people to the polls. I know what it's like not to have a car, not be able to go places."

"Send a car through here, Cliff. We'll send some people to the polls," Cat said. "You can depend on the votes coming your way. You're a good man."

Dad felt good about reconnecting with his old acquaintances in Colored Town. He returned their friendly waves with a smiling wave of his own as he and Mom drove away. He'd also made a few new acquaintances. He felt good about Colored Town.

∗   ∗   ∗

Dad loved it when Billy had the time to campaign with him, but *Cupid* got hold of Billy before his senior year was over and the first thing we knew he was making plans to get married as soon as he graduated from high school. So, as it turned out, Jean Yaden, Billy's girl, saw *more* of Billy, and Dad saw *less* of him.

Mom and Jacqueline and David continued to drive for Dad and to hand out cards for him. The word was spreading through the area that Dad was running for the Justice of the Peace and Dad was getting the recognition he was looking for. He also had campaign workers and friends helping at the mines and in the community at large. But, it wasn't long before he began to get some negative feedback. He'd expected it sooner or later. One of his opponents decided that Dad was perhaps presenting serious competition to him and he had begun to do what he could to counteract it.

Jacqueline, on lunch break from her job, overheard a part of one conversation as she sat at the soda fountain next to the company store. "What does he think he's doing, anyway, running for the Justice of the Peace?" she heard one man say. "He's a crippled man, can't walk. He's not been out of his house for fifteen years. He's read a few law-books, that's all. Folks will do him a favor not to vote for him. I like the man personally, but he'll not be able to do that job."

Jacqueline was livid. She went to the man. "Just what is it you think he won't be able to do?" she asked.

Startled that she had overheard him, the man retorted, "Now, little girlie, don't you go gettin' smart alecky. Your daddy shouldn't be out here runni' for an officer of the law, something he can't handle and you know it. Crippled folks can't do this sort of thing. I hate to see him get hurt, that's all."

Hurt by the remarks, and rattled emotionally, Jacqueline returned to her job at the company store and seethed silently as she went about doing her job.

Dad had chosen to run a clean campaign, and he found it disturbing that one of his opponents, and worse yet, one of the incumbents, was running him down. At the onset, before making his decision to run, Dad had talked with the incumbent and told him plainly that he was not trying to unseat him. Dad truly believed that there was room for the two of them. "We can both get elected," Dad had told him. But now, close to election time, he saw that the communication between the two of them had changed, and he now would be forced to confront the situation and act in his own behalf.

"Sissie," Dad said, "Don't say anything more about the election at the store. I don't want you to lose your job. But keep your ears open. If you hear something like this again, we'll consider the source and plan a way to deal with it."

Jacqueline fumed. "You're way too nice," she said. "That man is out there tearin' you down and you're tellin' me to lay off him. He'll be sorry he ever said a bad word about you."

"Now, Sissie, we've got to play our cards just right. What he's doing is wrong, and we'll do what we have to do to handle it. But, two wrongs don't make a right. You must not do something that might cost you your job."

Jacqueline was never pleased not to be able to speak her mind. But this she understood. She had to keep her job.

Nellie Kinder heard of the rumors, and she told Harry about them. Harry came right to Dad. "Cliff, I'd like to see the sons-a-bitches face to face that would try to imply that you can't do the job. Why you've got more learnin' than the whole kit and caboodle. Don't you worry none, though. I'll handle it."

Dad was worried. He wasn't sure exactly how Harry would handle "it".

Harry spread the word at the mine and throughout the neighborhood that one of Dad's opponents was insinuating that Dad wasn't fit for the job. Harry told them: "Why old Cliff is smart as a tack. He knows just about all there is to know. And one thing's for sure. He'll *always* be at home!"

Miners weren't too keen about cutting on a handicapped man, so the word spread that one of the incumbents was using unfair tactics. The incumbent had been an active union man, and he had counted on the automatic support of the union men. But Dad was also a staunch supporter of the union, even though he had been away from the mines since his accident, and he, too, counted on getting some of the union vote.

Dad told Bummy what was happening, and Bummy also came to his aid. Bummy told it like it was at the local union meeting.

"Men," he said, "I go by and talk to Clifford White about every other day. There's not a mean bone in his body. He's sat there in that house and read and studied for years. He'll talk to anybody that comes around about anything you want to talk about. He's probably the sharpest guy in the district. Now, in my opinion, that's the kind of man we need representin' us as the Justice of the Peace. He was a union man in his younger day. He marched on Blair Mountain. Along with his daddy and brothers. He knows the plight of the miner."

Bummy was ready to go on, but he saw the hands go up. "Okay, Okay, we believe you, Bummy. You shoulda been a preacher. You got no business out here minin' coal!"

Bummy was not deterred. "Now, I'd better see you men at the polls," he said, " or you'll hear my preachin' 'til you're plumb near sick of it." The men backed away from him, stiff-armed and grinning. "We get the picture, Bummy," one said. "We know where you're comin' from."

Bummy knew he was respected among the men, and he also knew he could depend on many votes for Dad. He took pleasure in reporting his successes with, "Cliff, I believe I got you a few votes today."

"You didn't compromise my integrity, now did you?" Dad said with a smile.

Bummy gave Dad a mischievous look that said he could have done worse!

*   *   *

Harry decided he liked campaigning. He told Dad he'd like to be of more help. "Hang, damn, Cliff," he said, "You get me a jug or two of whiskey, and I'll get you all the Kinders and Stovers votes in the valley. There's enough of us to carry any election around."

But Dad was leery. "The way you guys fight amongst yourselves, I'll be lucky to get any votes. You'll cancel each other out at the poles."

"Not a worry, Clifford. Blood is thick. We stick together like flies on a flystick come Election Day. Just get the whiskey. I'll show you. I'll get ever dang one of 'em."

Dad was beginning to wonder if he really was going to have to have whiskey to get votes. "Harry," he said. "I'm going to be honest with you. I can't win this election with whiskey."

"Cliff," Harry said, "I'm going to be honest with you. You got to get these heathens out to the polls. If you ain't prepared to make it worth their while, they ain't gonna show up. That's a damnable fact. The rest of them in the race are gonna be passin' out the booze and doin' all they can to steal a vote! Like they always do. Now the way I see it, you'll have to fight fire with fire!"

"Well, Harry," Dad said, giving in, "let's us plan us a strategy then."

"Now you're a talkin'. I'll make the next run or two with you up these hollers. You'll *have* the votes come Election Day."

Dad drew in his breath. *What was he getting in to?*

✳   ✳   ✳

Never in favor of the whiskey runs, Mom scolded. "Clifford, you're goin' to lose this election by passin' out whiskey."

"Now Ethel," Dad said, "there's all kinds of votes. And I've got to get them all. I want to win this election. I figure after this election I can win as an incumbent because I intend to do the job right. But for right now, I've got to get elected."

"People at church are voters too," Mom said. "A lot of them are supportin' you. What will they think if they hear about you out buyin' whiskey and givin' drinks to people?"

"Old habits are hard to break, Ethel," Dad said. "People are used to it. It's not like you're buying their vote. You're just showing your appreciation *for* their vote. I'm just getting acquainted. That's all. Politickin'. Making myself known."

"Oh, Clifford, I want you to get elected so much. You know I do. It's just that sometimes I get afraid. I didn't know that people could be so mean."

Dad took a sharp turn backward in his wheelchair. "Sometimes meanness backfires, Ethel," he said.

35

Button Holing

Dad planned to make his rounds every day before the primary election; so it was important to keep a cadre of drivers handy. I didn't have my license yet, but when needed I drove too because Dad said it was necessary. He *had* to win this election.

On one of my drives, Dad asked me to stop in Colored Town. He wanted to talk to his friends there, he said. We pulled up in front of Joe's barbershop. Joe came out and Dad spoke right up. "Joe, what's it going to take to get these people to vote, and to vote the right way?"

"Now, Clifford, I've already told you, don't you worry about the colored vote. It will be there. You'll get the vote. You know you're the only white man some of these people talk to, off the job."

Dad nodded, indicating his sincere appreciation. But what counted most to him was the assurance that the colored folks would get to the polls. "I want you to talk it up, Joe, 'cause I'm going to need all the votes I can get. You've got their ear. So, you tell my friends here that the only campaign promise I'm making is that everybody, colored or white, will get a fair deal with me. That's not always happened in times past."

Joe agreed. "Absolutely, Clifford," he said. "And you can be sure I'll talk it up come Election Day. Folk have short minds, you know. But come Election Day, I'll send the vote your way."

Dad gave Joe a handshake before passing him a shot of whiskey. Joe took the drink and gave Dad a smile of approval.

Cat Gilmore saw Dad pull up at the barbershop and as always he came down to say a few words. "Clifford, when you goin' to butcher that hog? I was up the creek fishin' the other day, and I looked in on that hog. He's a big'n, goin' to dress out about 250 to 275 pounds."

"Cat, as soon as the weather is cold enough you get in touch with me and we'll butcher that hog," Dad said. "Right now I've got my mind on the election, and I'm counting on your vote."

"Now, Clifford, you know you've got my vote and all my family's votes."

"And Ottaway's and Hazel's, too. They aim to remember you, too, come Election Day." Dad looked up to see his friends Ottaway and Hazel making their way to the car.

Dad had me pass a bottle off to the side. Ottaway said that was a good idea. "Colored folk like a little drink now and then, too," he said with a sheepish grin, flashing a shiny gold tooth.

The folks in Colored Town had already had a visit from one of the incumbents claiming union ties, but the coloreds had a loyalty to those that treated them with respect and had a human interest in their behalf. They knew Billy. He had delivered groceries and newspapers to them for years and they liked him. They also knew that Dad had been crippled in the mines and that his life had been harder than even they had experienced. They figured he had feeling for them and understood their cause. "Yes, you can be sure Clifford understands the colored folk. He'll get our vote. Mm, humm," Joe said to Ottaway.

Upon leaving, Dad promised to send a car around on Election Day. "As many times as needed," he told those gathered.

✳   ✳   ✳

When Election Day rolled around, we all had our jobs to do. Dad had a few poll workers he paid $10 each to pass out fliers and to collar a few votes if they could. Others, using every car available, went from polling place to polling place. Uncle Connie provided free transportation to the polls for anyone who needed it, and to show his appreciation he shared a bottle or two of whiskey. He said he knew Dad had the colored vote because he personally delivered most of them to the polls.

When the votes were finally counted and all the polling places had reported in, we got the news that Dad had won and won big! New Camp was a jovial place that night. Our house overflowed with people from the community, eager to help us celebrate.

Harry came over to congratulate Dad and said in his teasing way, "Clifford, I might have put myself in a hard spot out here campaignin' for you. I get nervous when I see the law drivin' down the highway; now I got one right in my back door!"

"You don't have to worry yet, Harry. You've got 'til November. We've got the November election yet."

"Oh, you don't need to worry none about that," Harry said. "Ain't enough Republicans in this valley to carry that election." Harry was right about that, but Dad said he would continue to campaign anyway. "I don't want to take any chances," he said.

*   *   *

With the November election soon behind him, Dad had the job he had worked so hard to get. He took a considerable long time studying the dockets from the previous JP because he said he wanted to start off right. He said it felt mighty good after seventeen long, long years to be able to provide for his family again. He was determined to be successful. I was so proud of him.

Harry and Bummy came to celebrate with us, both acting shy and pretending to be ill at ease in the presence of *an elected official!* "Boys, I don't think I could've made it without your help," Dad told them. "But, don't think you're going to get any special treatment now. I've got to live up to my reputation."

"Guess we'll have to start callin' you "Squire" now," Bummy said. After that night, it seemed everyone began calling Dad, "Squire". His new name suited him.

Uncle Connie had donated a lot of his time and certainly a lot of his money to Dad's campaign, and Dad wanted to repay him. But Connie refused, saying he could think of no better way to spend his money than to help his brother. "Besides, Squire," he said, "I'm part of the family now. I live here. I'll just sit back and retire now and let you make the money!"

At first it was not easy; our entire daily schedule changed to accommodate the schedule of the Justice of the Peace. Constables came at all hours of the night to get warrants for arrests. But, we got used to it quickly. Dad had always been an important man to us. Now he was an important man to the community.

36

The Fifties

After Dad became the Justice of the Peace, things really began to look up for him. With a steady income, he soon made enough money to rent office space outside the home. He chose a space on the banks of the river, directly across the road from the Ameagle post office and Mike John Litos's store. At this location he kept regular hours, nine to five—except for the constables, of course, who continued to come to the house at all hours, as they were required to do. But, it was from his office on the highway that Dad became more visible to the people in the area. It was easier for folks to drop in, sit a spell, and chat. He always found time to talk to folks though he diligently recorded all legal transactions and decisions required of him as the Justice of the Peace. The job called for tedious record keeping, and he was glad to do it.

Since Dad was now earning money and able to put some away, he said he felt bad about living in a company house. "I should have my own house now, Connie," he said. And Connie agreed, adding a bit of humor, "*Squire*, you're busy twenty-four hours a day now, but me, now that I've retired, I've got nothin' to do. Let's buy us some land somewhere and build us a house. Between old Dave and Jimmy and me and a few other hired hands here and there, we could build the thing ourselves. One big enough for all of us. I'm tired of sleepin' on the porch! Gettin' woke up at all hours of the night with them constables!"

Smiling at Connie's reference to the nightly interruptions of his sleep, Dad said he regretted the inconvenience, but that it *was,* after all, Connie's idea to sleep on the porch. "I've offered you better accommodations, Connie," Dad said. "There's always the sofa in the living room!"

"Right!" Connie said. "So I get woke up as you pass through the living room on your way to the porch. No difference. Let's build us a house!"

"Ethel would like nothing better," Dad said, noticing that Mom had entered the room. "She's been so good to me all these years. I would like to give her something really nice." Mom stepped into the conversation at this point, saying nothing would delight her more. So, the three of them began having daily talks about building a house.

Dad put feelers out for suitable land on which to build the house and within a few months learned that a double lot overlooking the football field at Clear Fork High School was for sale. The owner of the lot, Donnie Thompson's uncle, was relocating to Florida and was anxious to sell. The land was marshy and needed some fill and the house was in a state of disrepair, so Dad was able to get the parcel at a good price. Dad said the lot was ideal, being as it was at one end of the high school football field. "We'll put a big picture window in the living room, and I'll have a front row seat to all of Jim's football games," he said.

The land had two houses already on it. One house Dad gave to Jacqueline and David since they had finally gotten married and were living a few miles down the road at Lawson, in a house they rented from Joe Asbury, the deputy sheriff. The other house Dad had torn down, saving the good lumber to be used again for the new house.

Dad, Connie and Mom talked about what they wanted in a house, looked at a few pictures, and then Dad and Connie drew up a plan. The house just sort of flowed from there. Though Dad hired an occasional master carpenter for the harder stuff, essentially we built the house ourselves—on a pay-as-you-go-plan. Connie did the electrical and plumbing systems, and much of the carpentry. David and I assisted with the carpentry. Lee did what he could. Within six months, we had a house, and Dad was in the driver's seat again as he had accomplished another of his dreams.

At a time when handicapped access was not required by law, Dad felt that he was a pioneer in the field. He beamed with pride as he viewed the ramps and big doors and bathroom facilities. He could maneuver everywhere he wanted to go—except upstairs. "Dave," he said, "take me to the top floor and let me get a look around. I'll only need one shot at it!" David carried Dad upstairs. He gave all the rooms a once-over, declared he liked what he saw, then said he was satisfied never to go up again.

Mom was ecstatic over her new house. "No visitors will have to sleep on the sofa or on the porch again!" she said with declaration, giving Connie a big smile of appreciation. She had a big kitchen and a separate dining room, big enough to seat all of us at once. She said she couldn't wait for the upcoming holidays. She hoped that Billy would be home soon, but he was smack dab in the middle of the Korean War and instead of coming home, he would earn a Silver Star!

Dad said he was proud of Billy, but he worried about him. "Billy has always put his heart and guts into everything he does," he said. "You might know he'd do the same for his country."

*   *   *

Opie came in the fall of that same year. "I want to see the house I had no hand in buildin'," he said. "Wish I'd been here to help."

"Can't depend on *you*," Connie teased. "You're too busy runnin' all over the country playin' poker."

Opie grinned with pride at the mention of his chosen lifestyle. He made one trip around the outside of the house, stopping to inspect the carpentry work here and there, and commenting as he went along. "You fellers did a decent job," he said. "Couldn't have done it better myself. Didn't know you had it in you, Connie." Then he went inside, stopping to drop his black satchel on the living room sofa.

Mom quickly seized the satchel. "You're not sleeping on the sofa anymore, Pop," she said, motioning Opie to follow her upstairs. "We've got plenty of sleeping room. Come on, I'll show you around."

Opie followed as directed. "Glory be, Ethel, you'll get lost in here," he said, exaggerating his pleasure at the spaciousness of the house. "Cliff you'd better put a bell on Ethel, so you'll know where she is." Dad laughed heartily, visualizing Mom wearing a bell. Mom laughed, too. She loved Opie's humor.

"Well, I like it, and I'd like to spend a night or two if you don't mind," Opie said. "Just show me to my room." So for a few days, Opie, Dad and Connie had some good times playing cards and enjoying each other's company 'til way into the night. Dad and Opie would occasionally have a toddy. Connie didn't drink much anymore.

On the fifth day of Opie's stay, he said his intuition was suddenly telling him to head north, up to Silver Springs, Maryland, to visit his brother John. "You know, John's not gettin' any younger," he said. "The old guy's hittin' ninety. Figure I'd better go see him while I can, and maybe get in a few poker games while I'm there." He planned to leave out on the bus the next day, but Mom stopped him as he packed. "Now Pop," she coaxed, "you've got to stay to see Jimmy play football. We've got good seats!" She pointed through the picture window to the football field beyond. Opie smiled and puffed on his pipe, all the while looking into the faces around him, measuring their interest in his staying. "Well, heck, folks, I guess I could last a few more days if someone would give me a good arm-twistin'—or (he turned to look at Mom) if Ethel would fix me one of her pineapple-upside-down cakes."

*   *   *

On the night of the football game, David carried Dad out to the edge of the football field and situated him comfortably in his wheelchair so that he would have a good view of the game. The rest of the family sat nearby. I was the starting quarterback. Opie said he wanted to see me show my stuff, being as he had foregone a poker game to see me play.

As the game was nearing the end of the first half, Dad turned to David. "Where's old Jim?" he asked. "I don't see Jim in the game." At Dad's inquiry, Mom became alarmed. "David, go see about Jimmy," she said. "He's not on the field." She imagined me injured and unable to play. So David went to inquire and returned with the news.

"Jim's out of the game," he said.

Mom was on her feet. "Oh, mercy, is he hurt bad?"

"No," David said. "He's not hurt at all. He's kicked out for fighting. Out for the rest of the game."

Dad's face dropped as Mom sat down in disgust, but Opie was on his feet. "Might just as well get on in out of the weather then," he said, declaring he wasn't much of a football fan anyway. Dad said he'd stick it out. I represented him, and he was sorely embarrassed.

Afterward, as I came sheepishly through the door, not sure if I would be a hero or a pariah, Dad and I had a heart to heart talk about sportsmanship and self-control. "Jim," he said, "you're not out there to hurt people."

"Well, he hit me a couple of times and I couldn't let him get away with it," I said. I felt it necessary to defend my position. "They were a better team. They were going to beat us anyway. Especially with me wearing this Number 13!"

Dad was disappointed, and my shallow excuse did not play well with him. "Jim," he said, "you know the number had nothing to do with it. You just thought you had to get back at him. You'll get thrown out of every game you play if you think you have to "even" the score with everybody you think is doing you wrong. The team was counting on you. You were the starting quarterback. You let the boy draw you into a fight. Then your team was weakened. You have to think while you're playing the game. You have to use your head for something besides a place to hold your helmet. You let your team down, Jim."

I held my head in my hands as I listened. "I guess I just wanted to win too bad," I said.

"You can't win all the time, Jim" Dad said. "There's something to be gained from losing too. It only matters that you play hard and give it your very best. You don't play at all if you're kicked out of the game."

Opie left the next day, saying, "Now, Jimmy, the next game I come to see my grandson play, I expect to get my money's worth, understand? I don't want to see you sittin' on the bench!" I felt like a failure, but I promised him I would never again get kicked out of a game for fighting or poor sportsmanship. I learned from that experience.

*   *   *

Unfortunately, Opie would never make it back to see me play in another football game. On February 18, 1950, we got the news. Opie had died of a heart attack in Silver Springs, Maryland. And yes, he died with his boots on while playing poker. Dad was told by Coy that the first words out of Rosabelle's mouth were, "How much did he have on him?" I guess their relationship had ended, but she mourned him just as we did. Who could help loving Opie?

*   *   *

Right about this time, Dad received word that Dr. Williams's only son, *James Edward*, had been killed in a single engine airplane crash. It took us all by surprise, and we were deeply saddened at the news. Dr. Williams had years before moved to Alderson, over on the Greenbrier River. Dad had often mentioned that he would like to visit his old friend. Dad wanted a place on the Greenbrier, too.

Mom questioned why such things happen to good people, and Dad said, "Ethel, ours is not to question why? Some things are just for the Good Man upstairs to understand."

· 285 ·

With so much on his mind: the loss of Opie, the news about the doctor's son, and his constant worry over Billy, it was hard to put on a happy face; yet, Dad found a way to keep things going. Fortunately, the work of the Justice of the Peace kept him occupied, as there was never any interruption from the requirements of the job.

His daily contacts with people led him to consider other real estate deals. Finally, one came along too good to pass up. The Flint brothers, Donald and Junior, sons of Roy Flint, whom Billy had worked for, were looking for a buyer for their jointly owned Esso service station and garage. "Squire," they said, "you're a likely person to have this station. You'll have two of the best mechanics in these parts working for you, Les Stover and Donald Estep. Both will do you good. Then you got all those boys, Jimmy, Lee, and David to help you out too. You can have your office right there in the building. Guarantee you'll make money. We'll give it to you for a fair price."

Dad thought about it; it was not something he had considered before, but things were going so well for him that anything seemed possible. "Jim," he said to me, "for some reason, it takes money to make money. When you have none, there's no way to get ahead. But when it starts coming in, there's no way to stop it if you're willing to keep investing it." I liked hearing that. We had been so poor that even having indoor plumbing made me feel rich.

Dad put all the cards on the table, and we had a family discussion. Lee gleamed when he asked, "Dad, do you think I could help you out there?"

Dad smiled with pride, saying, "Lee, it would be a perfect place for you. You can pump gas, clean windshields and put oil in cars. You had that course in auto mechanics. You could give Les a hand now and then. You could mind the counter whenever I have to hold court." I began to think that maybe Dad was getting the service station mostly for Lee. I felt proud that he would do that. Lee's condition had deteriorated. He could do menial things, but the seizures had caused some brain damage, and he was, unfortunately, becoming child-like.

Anyway, Dad suddenly found himself with another source of income—White's Esso Station. The building served a dual purpose for him. He operated a place of business in the front, and he set up his JP office in the back where he had enough space to hold court when necessary.

Les, Dad's main employee, picked Dad up each morning for work. Lee went with them every day that he was able. On days when he'd had seizures the night before he would be too fatigued to go to the garage. On these occasions, Mom would tell him that she needed him to help her at home that day.

*   *   *

White's Esso Station was the only full-service filling station and garage between Whitesville and Beckley, and that, along with being located right beside the baseball field, proved to be a real asset. Business was good when large crowds gathered for baseball during the summer and for shooting matches in the fall and winter. Dad quickly became acquainted with a host of new people. Before long, he knew just about everyone in the valley. His policy was to be fair and give his customers a good deal. "We'll not hold anyone up just because there's no where else to go," he said. "We'll give them a better deal and keep our prices lower than they would be in Whitesville."

Dad loved doing favors for people, and having the service station meant he had many opportunities to be a *do-gooder*. He could now loan money, give credit, give advice without charging for it, give good deals on service and do all the trading his heart desired. His heart was generous, but he was also an astute businessman. He told me more than once, "Jim, it doesn't cost you a thing to do a favor for someone. It pays off big down the road."

Lee handled the routines at the gas pumps quite well. Always friendly, courteous and eager to please, he took great pride that no car left the station without a sparkling clean windshield. Though he became flustered if someone asked him about something mechanical and he wasn't able to give assistance, he learned to be diplomatic and concede the big stuff to Les or Donald. Dad said Lee was a big help.

As a convenience to his customers, Dad sold a few grocery items in the store. For awhile, every time I looked at the candy counter I thought of Aunt Josie and the time she had given me chocolates from her store-case in Lashmeet years before. I thought she'd be proud to see me now.

Dad spent much of his time in the back doing the work of the Squire. He handled civil and criminal cases, garnisheed wages, and collected fines for infractions of the law and other things required of him as the Justice of the Peace. The civil and criminal litigation cases interested me the most.

Some of his court cases were like *Charlie* stories! The jury made the final decisions, and Dad then took the action necessary for restitution or whatever the case dictated.

Dad had a few reliable jurors, one being Quinton Scarbro. Quinton was a big-jowled, heavy-set man, who was known to be highly opinion-ated, but respected for his fairness.

*   *   *

Dad sought Quinton for one of his first cases, which involved a dispute over cows. "Quinton," he said, "I'm going to have a controversial trial on Thursday. Champ Stover's got him a high priced lawyer from over in Beckley and is suing Barney Williams over those two cows they've been squabbling over for two months. I know you're working the nightshift, but this will be during the day, and I'd appreciate it if you could make it as a member of the jury. They're likely to be hostile to each other, and one side or the other is not going to like the decision of the court—whatever the verdict."

"Oh, boy, should be a good one," Quinton said showing his interest. "Squire, I'll be there, and I'll personally assure you there won't be any trouble. None that we can't handle."

"I'll need four or five others on the jury if you can help me out. HoraceThompson and George Southard will serve. I talked to them earlier today."

"Shouldn't be a problem, Squire."

*   *   *

On the day of court, Quinton positioned himself next to Dad, saying he would protect him should there be a problem. Dad banged his gavel and court came to order. Quinton crossed his arms and sat back, ready to do the job. He was big and burly and commanded respect from the puny guys, but when he sat on a jury he was as fair as he could be, listening to both sides and making his decisions based on what he believed to be right as dictated by the law.

Champ's lawyer, Arthur Spirosino, from over in Beckley, was perfectly groomed, dressed in a three pieced suit, brightly polished shoes and sporting well-fitting eyeglasses as he rose to present his client's case. "It appears," he said, "that Barney here is trying to back out of a deal he made in earnest with my client, Champ Stover. Barney bought two cows from Champ, paid half of the money for them, put them out to pasture for a mere two days, and expected them to give milk in abundance. Now, my client has repeatedly told Barney that the cows needed more time than two days to adjust, but Barney has not listened. Instead, he has brought the cows back to my client and left them there, where they are again giving much milk, but Barney has demanded his money back anyway and my client has refused him. Instead, my client will insist that Barney live up to the deal, pay the rest of the money that he owes and pay restitution for the inconvenience my client has been forced to incur from boarding the cows for two months. Furthermore, my client claims that Barney has defamed him, that he has spoken ill of him at church meetings and throughout the valley, claiming that my client has been disreputable. We ask the jury to find Barney responsible for his actions. We ask that Barney pay the remainder owed my client, that he pay my client's legal fees, and that he pay for the expenses incurred during the two months my client has boarded the cows. Furthermore, we ask that Barney give my client the right to keep the cows since he has been forced to board them for so long since the sale."

Barney had no lawyer to represent him, so when it came his turn to speak, he jumped up from his seat and raged about what he considered to be a deal gone bad. He pointed his finger and screamed in the face of Champ. "Champ is dishonorable," he said. "Selling me cows that didn't give enough milk to pay for their board and keep. They was of no use to me, and I did right to take them back to where they belonged and make a demand to get my money back, *for two no-good cows!*"

The jury deliberated a long while, giving each member plenty of time to explore the value judgments made for one side or the other, then decided without question in favor of Champ. Barney, they concluded, had not given the cows a chance to adjust to the new environment, and they knew it to be true that he had openly disparaged Champ's previously unblemished reputation in the community. Barney was in the wrong they said, and therefore Champ was awarded all that he sued for.

As expected, Barney lit into Champ accusing him of being unfair and hiring a "high-falutin'" lawyer to do his dirty work. But, Champ said he felt vindicated. "I was tired of you bad-mouthing me all over town, having people believe the worst about me when you knew it wasn't true. Now, you come pay up and learn your lesson. I want an end to this once and for all!"

Barney raised his fist and went at Champ, and Quinton made his stand. "I wouldn't do that if I were you, Barney," he said calmly. The trial ended. Dad rendered the verdict of the jury and awarded Champ his due. Case closed. Another *Charlie* story for Dad. Quinton asked when the next trial would be.

*　　　　　*　　　　　*

I graduated from high school in 1951, and at Dad's suggestion went off to Morris Harvey College in Charleston. I mostly commuted between Charleston and home because I still liked to be at home. I helped out at the garage and hung around Clear Fork High School during football season, helping with practice. The football coach, Don Gibson, took a liking to me and when he was offered a coaching job at Highlands University in Las Vegas, New Mexico, he offered me a full scholarship to play football there. I took it.

After one year in New Mexico, I came home again, still not sure what I wanted to do with my life. I went to Dayton, Ohio, where many from the area had already gone. I worked at Dayton Pump as an inspector for quality control and later for Dayton Power and Light as a trouble-shooter.

In between jobs I took Dad on some long trips. On one trip, we went to see Uncle Coy in Los Angeles. Dad treated the trip as another one of his big adventures. In St. Louis he splurged on oysters and Budweiser beer and regretted that he couldn't go to a St. Louis Cardinal's baseball game; they were on the road. When we arrived in Amarillo, Texas after having traveled hard all day on Route 66, talking and having a good old time, we stopped at a motel. As I got out of the car I looked over at Dad. Something didn't look right. He had huge rings around his eyes and nostrils from the dust we had driven through. As I chided him about it, he asked, "Jim, have you looked at yourself?"

It had been many years since Dad had seen his brother Coy. They had much to talk about. Coy was prosperous, doing very well at selling real estate in the Los Angeles area. He had a beautiful home, and his wife Edith was the secretary to the then Governor Brown.

Coy took pride in being able to show us a good time. We went to the most exclusive seafood restaurant in Los Angeles, a restaurant which required that we be all decked out in coats and ties. We were a handsome bunch that night. Though the restaurant wasn't handicapped accessible, the establishment was most accommodating. Dad ordered a huge, big lobster and delighted in another one of his adventures.

"Cliff, ain't nothin' like the coal mines, now is it?" Coy said, recalling the days when he and Dad had worked with Opie in the coal mines. Dad smiled and shook his head, saying he reckoned not. "I guess you meant it when you said you were going to get you a clean job, Coy," he said. "It don't get any cleaner than this." Coy shook his head proudly and then began talking about what we would do the next day. He still had a lot to show us.

*   *   *

We'd no sooner returned to West Virginia from our trip to Los Angeles than Dad began planning his next trip. "Jim, if you're not going to go to college, we may as well hit the road again. Let's head down to Florida, down where it's hot, warm up these old bones. We can look at some land there. Maybe make an investment. There's no future here, anymore. The mine's are closing all around. People are leaving the area. We could make the move and open up a filling station down south somewhere."

It didn't take much to talk me into going. At the time my world was small. I would have been content to help Dad in business, anywhere he chose. So, we made the trip, going as far south as Fort Lauderdale.

While in Florida, I carried Dad out to the ocean and put him on an inner tube. "Plop me down in this thing, and I'll just float around," he said with a smile that never left his face. At times like these, I appreciated what adventure meant to Dad. His experiences were few and far between. He relished and savored each one.

Most of the motels and restaurants we patronized had no accommodations for the handicapped though most were accepting and made
Dad feel welcome. Even so, many folks stared as I carried him from
place to place. I wanted to say to them, "Folks, it's not like he has a
choice here."

We had fun in Florida, but we didn't do any investing. I got the feeling it really didn't matter that much to Dad. He said he'd better get back
to work. So we headed north again with more adventure stories for Dad
to tell to his listeners.

*   *   *

Billy came home from the war in 1953, a hero. He had left home, wild
and spontaneous, with a love for fast cars and good times. Upon returning from the war, he was reserved—his spontaneity gone. For a while,
we, as a family, were a captive audience, desiring to get as much out of
Billy as we could about his wartime adventures. But, Billy was not into
telling war stories. Having seen much pain and suffering, he had come
away from the war feeling lucky to be alive. His best friend, Benny
Stover, with whom Billy had enlisted, had been killed during the Korean
conflict. And at one time, seventy percent of Billy's battalion, the
Company "C" 38th Infantry Regiment, Second Infantry Division, was
either killed or captured while attempting retreat at the Yalu River valley
on the border between Korea and Manchuria.

At the time of the retreat, the Chinese had entered the Korean conflict and had successfully infiltrated the American lines. They were
invading and capturing American positions all along the battlefront,
driving the American forces into a massive retreat. It was a time of
chaos and indecision, an overwhelming situation of panic. The
Americans were trying to regroup in the southern part of the Korean
peninsula. They had set up a defensive position at Pusan, but they had
never faced an enemy like this, where life was cheap. It seemed that no

matter how much the armed forces did, it was not enough. Human waves of men just kept coming. American troops were sometimes surrounded, and it was in such a situation that Billy earned his Silver Star. His battalion was in retreat, trying to get back to safe lines when a machine gun emplacement cut them off. Billy took it upon himself to single-handedly attack and open fire on the men behind the machine guns, subsequently killing all four of them. Seeing Billy's bravery, his comrades followed suit, and together they were successful in preventing their company from being wiped out completely.

So it was no wonder that Billy had little interest in talking about the war. He was not the same person who had left Ameagle soon after high school and only a few months of marriage to enter the Korean War. He was no longer the gregarious, fun-loving, thrill-seeking young man who sought after adventure and opportunities for heroism. He was now a subdued, serious-thinking, responsible man who had taken human lives in armed conflict with hostile forces. Life could never be the same.

Dad encouraged Billy to use his GI bill to go to college to further his education. He offered to assist him in any way he could, even offering him a partnership in the garage and service station business. But Billy, long the independent one said: "No, I'm not the college type. I like mechanical and technical things. I think I'll go to Dayton where a lot of my buddies have gone. There's plenty of technical work there. Beside, I'm a married man. Jean's going to have a baby. I want to get a good job, make a decent living." Billy was ever ambitious.

Not long after that, Billy went to Dayton, Ohio where he took a course to become a machinist, and began a career as a tool and die maker. After that, we saw him only when he came to visit, with his wife Jean and sons Billy Jr. and Kenny. Dad said he was mighty proud to have a son like Billy.

*   *   *

Dad was adamant that coal mining for any of his sons was out! Now a self-educated man, he had come to value education and the *doors* his own education had opened for him. He talked about it all the time. "Jim," he persisted, "go back to college. You'll never regret it. Become a lawyer. You'd be a good one. Make us all proud."

But I wasn't ready to listen. I fell for one of the local girls and got married instead. We moved to Dayton, Ohio, where I worked in the factories for about a year before volunteering for the army in 1955. I figured I would be drafted soon anyway, and I wanted to get it over with. I had already decided that working in factories was not going to be my life's work and that as soon as I came out of the army I would do something else.

Just before I left to go overseas, my independent and spicy Grandma Smars died, at seventy-four years of age. In the years before her death, she'd lost much of her eyesight and much of her energy and spunk—debilitating effects of her latent diabetes. She hadn't been coming to stay with us as much. Dad said he would miss Evaline. He was ever grateful for her visits during the difficult years of our lives. He enjoyed her colorful ways and fully appreciated her penchant for hard work. "Evaline was an education in herself," Dad said. "I learned an awful lot from that woman. She'd sit by my bed, chewing that tobacco and tell me stories about her life. She had a hard, hard, life, Evaline did. But she chose to go forward and not look back. Said it would do her no good to look back. I got a lot of inspiration from Evaline. She pretty much kept us alive during the bad years. I'll never forget her." Dad, perhaps more than anyone, saw the good in his mother-in-law.

*   *   *

By the mid-fifties, Billy and I had flown the nest, no longer there for Dad to influence or give direction, but Dad had a life of his own now. He was well known and well respected in the community and financially secure. He had a home, a political position to which he was continually re-elected, and a thriving and profitable business. Except for his handicap, his life was rich and full of adventure. At home, he had his wife and his brother Connie to keep him company. Jacqueline and David lived next door. Lee was yet home, helping out. "Life is good," he'd often say.

While I was overseas, Jacqueline and David had their first child, a baby girl whom they named Denna Rae. Mom was ecstatic, especially when little ringlets began to spring up all over her granddaughter's head. Jacqueline worked at the post office, so Denna was under Mom's care most of the day. Dad sat in his wheelchair and smiled. "Finally, Ethel," he said, "you have your wish!"

In 1957, after a two-year stint in the army, most of which I spent stationed overseas in post-war Korea, I came home. My marriage was over, and I was again at a turning point in my life. A friend, Romeo Williams, who had been two years behind me in school and was now a student at Concord College, in Athens, West Virginia, coaxed me into going to Concord with him. "Come on, Jimmy," he said. "You can play football over there. You can even get a football scholarship." Dad and Mom were happy to see me go as well. They were concerned that I might just hang around home again. But I was different now, more mature and able to make better decisions.

I went with Romeo to Concord College. One evening after football practice Romeo took me to the Sweet Shop, an off-campus hangout for college students, saying he wanted to introduce me to Eleanor Triplett, someone he said he thought a lot of. Eleanor and I hit it off as Romeo had wanted us to and soon thereafter we began to date. Right away, she taught me to play tennis, her favorite sport.

*   *   *

While in college, I was home many weekends and holidays. While at home, I helped out at the garage and helped Dad with his JP work. I served legal papers, did paper work and was his general "gofer" and confidante.

The work of the Justice of the Peace was time consuming, including many late night hours, but the duties never seemed to bore Dad. Each day presented him with more *Charlie* material. Constables and others alike knew where his bedroom was located and took to knocking at his window at night instead of coming to the front door—which Dad came to appreciate. He could conduct his JP business right from his bed, through his bedroom window. Mom came to give him assistance when he needed it. She was a light sleeper, anyway.

*   *   *

"Ethel," Dad said to Mom once after she had been wakened in the night by one of his visitors, "I'm just going to make you my assistant. Put you on the payroll."

"You won't have anything left to pay me after you give it all away!"

"Now, Ethel, old Willie will pay me back. He's just needing a little extra right now to carry him over."

"Clifford, I heard the whole conversation. He came right here to your window in the middle of the night askin' for money because he'd lost all his pay to the numbers racket and he was afraid to go home. He knows you're an old softie."

Dad was an easy touch, but it never bothered him. He helped the truly needy, and he also helped the less deserving. His accounts at the garage were allowed to go uncollected for so long that many times there was little hope of ever being paid. Once I offered to help him get all his accounts in order. I worked for days and then sat down with him to go over what I had learned. "Dad," I said, "did you know that virtually everybody in this valley owes you money? Some as high as a thousand dollars. Some of these people have owed you since you've been in business. You need to collect some of this money. How do you keep track of what you're making?" I was also concerned because I frequently saw folks who owed Dad money making *cash* purchases at other places of business for something they could have gotten from Dad. Dad knew. "They're embarrassed that they owe me so much money, so they don't come around 'til they need credit again. Stores where they pay cash don't give them credit."

"Well, that bothers me," I said. "Maybe you should do the same."

Dad just looked away. I could tell that these things bothered me more than they did him. He didn't seem concerned in the least. But I must've shown my consternation at his lack of caring about something I deemed mighty important in the business world because he began fidgeting in his chair and finally said he'd best explain his method of bookkeeping. "Jim, I use the cracker barrel accounting system. When bills come in, I toss them in the barrel. When somebody pays a bill, I toss that money in the barrel too. When a bill comes due, I reach in the barrel and pay the bill. After all the bills are paid, whatever is left in the barrel is my profit. As long as I've been in business, there's always been something left in the barrel. It's never been empty."

I just sighed, saying, "Well, why did you let me go to all this trouble getting your books straight for you if you don't care who owes you money and you already know anyway."

"I thought you liked doing things like that," he said.

I could tell it was hopeless. But, I felt I must go on. "Well, how do you account for these huge amounts that some of these people owe you? Don't you think they should be paying up? How do you justify that?"

Dad knew he was not off the hook and figured he may as well finish up with me. "Well, Jim," he said, "pull out one of those accounts and let's take a look at it."

I pulled out an account I thought was particularly bad. "Okay," I said. "Here's one. The guy owes you $350, and even though he pays you a little now and then, his bill stays around $300. I handed him the account. He perused it for a moment and then he said, "Let's see. The first entry on here is for a used transmission, $150. Now Jim, see that old car out there. I sold this man the transmission out of that car for $150, and later I sold him a bumper and a door. From that same car, I've also sold a wheel and a windshield to someone else. Now, since I only paid twenty-five dollars for the car in the first place, in my way of thinking, I figure I'm making a profit. So I don't worry about collecting every dime owed me."

I was attempting to understand his logic when a customer came into the garage. "Squire, I want to square up with you," the man said. "At least pay some of what I owe you." He handed Dad a twenty-dollar bill. Dad took out the man's account, marked it accordingly and thanked the man for paying some of his bill. The man had a child with him, and as was Dad's custom if a child was present when a bill was paid, the child was given a piece of candy. Dad handed over a candy bar to the young lad who took it with a smile. The lad's dad frowned at the boy and admonished, "Now, what do you say to the Squire, boy?" The boy looked at Dad, then at *his* dad, then back at Dad before saying, "Charge it?"

I was amused at Dad's way of accounting, but since he seemed to always have money in his barrel I figured it best to leave him be. After all, it was his business, and he was happy with it the way it was. But I knew that I, nor anyone else in the family, would be getting any inheritance! Our inheritance would be shared by virtually everyone in the Clear Fork district. What I did get was a free lesson in philosophy from my dad. I figured I passed with about a C minus.

*　　　　　*　　　　　*

Dad still loved bartering and trading with the locals. Bee Fraley was the one Dad traded with most often. Bee was a horse trader by profession and a part-time truck driver for the coal company on the side. When the two of them got together there was no telling what might come of the trade. But one day Dad went too far when Bee came in with a nanny goat. "Squire," Bee said, "I need some brakeshoes for my truck, and I ain't got a lick of money right now. Wonder if I could trade you this nanny goat for some brake shoes? She's a fine one for milk. Keep your grass cut nice and short, too. Wife says she wouldn't be without a nanny goat now that she's had one around for a spell. But I've got no use for three of them."

"Whew, I don't know, Bee. I don't believe Ethel would want to have a goat around. But David might. Save him having to cut the grass."

"I'll talk to Ethel for you, Squire. She'll like havin' the milk. Goat milk is great to cook with, and I know Ethel is a right good cook."

"Don't know that she's ever considered having a goat though, Bee. A goat might take a little getting used to."

"She'll like the goat, Squire. I can assure you of that."

"Well, if you think you can persuade her, take the goat on up to the house and give it a try."

Bee took the goat to the house, tied it to a tree and got back in his truck. Mom saw him from the window and bolted outside before he got away. "Bee Fraley," she called, "what on earth do you think you're doin' tyin' a goat up to that tree and leavin' it here?"

"Ethel, the goat is yours now," Bee said from the cab of his truck. He had already started the engine. "Squire just traded me some brakeshoes for the nanny goat. It's a good trade, Ethel. That nanny will give you milk for years and all the while keep your grass cut, too. See, she's cuttin' the grass right now. That's a fine deal. You won't have to feed her or anything, just milk her; that's all. If she gets in your way, just tie her to the clothesline. You can even loan her out to your neighbors. She's a good'n all right. Wife said she wouldn't be without a nanny now that's she used to havin' one. You won't either, Ethel."

Mom looked at the nanny goat, who was chewing away at the grass around the tree, then she looked back at Bee. Seeing that he was quite serious, she did not know whether to laugh or cry. She turned to Bee. "Bee Fraley, get that goat out of here," she said. "Clifford has made a mistake. We don't need a goat!" But Bee said, "Ethel, I can't. I traded with Squire, and we shook on the deal. He now owns the goat, and I own the brakeshoes. I can't take the goat back." Bee drove off. The nanny stayed—tied to the tree.

Mom didn't hesitate. Fuming, she marched into the house and got on the phone. "Clifford, you had better have someone come get this goat, or when you come home you're going to find her tied to your bed. And she'll *stay* in your room until you decide what to do with her!" Then she hung up the phone and waited.

Dad looked around for someone to send to get the goat because he knew she'd keep her word. Finally, Horace Thompson came by. Horace, a tall, lanky, older fellow with thinning dark hair, whose spectacles always seemed to hang from the tip of his nose, hung around the garage a lot as Dad did many favors for him. Dad figured it a good time to call in a favor, and Horace was asked to go get the nanny.

"Ethel," Horace said upon arrival, "Squire has sent me to get the goat." Horace stood in the doorway with a sheepish grin on his face, and Mom returned his grin with a knowing smile. She directed him to the goat and waved them on their way.

After Dad saw that he was saddled with the goat at the garage, he wasn't sure whether he himself should laugh or cry. Though he eventually traded the goat to George Southard for some bee stands, Dad thought twice before doing any quick trading after that. During the time he had the goat, it did keep the grass cut around the garage. I'm not sure who did the milking.

Dad and Connie had many laughs over the nanny goat, but Mom never did think that one was too funny. "Clifford," she told him, "you just about pushed your luck too far with that nanny goat."

*   *   *

Dad and I took another of our hunting trips. "Life is good to me now, Jim," he told me, "so long as I have what's left of my health." Health was critical. He had long ago given up "walking" with his crutches and braces, but he continued to wear the braces anyway, putting them on each morning as he arose. They helped to add dimension to his legs. I knew he felt more whole with the braces though they were heavy and uncomfortable. The braces also contributed to the numerous sores he had on his legs, hips and buttocks. The sores almost never healed completely. "Jim, it's a good thing I can't feel them," he said of the sores. "But I can feel in my back, and it's a might sore; see if you can get up on there and crack it a bit, like you used to do for me when you were a kid."

"I can't do that, I might hurt you. I weigh 170 pounds!" I said, remembering how I had walked on his back when I was little, moving up and down his spine as he instructed me to do. I always worried that I might hurt him, but the treatment always seemed to work. Besides, Mom always watched.

"I don't want you to walk on my back," Dad said, "just manipulate the spine. You can do that with your hands." So I massaged his back. He told me it felt great.

*   *   *

It was about this time that an historical event took place in the city of Beckley. All the Raleigh County politicians had been invited to be aboard the first commercial flight out of Beckley, and Dad was among those invited. He told me, "Jim, I can't make this trip, but we don't want not to be represented, so you go take the flight for me." So it was that I myself, got to be a part of a "little history making."

*   *   *

Though not feeling his best, Dad's days and nights were busy with hardly a dull moment. I was happy for him that he remained busy. He stayed centered and occupied.

As for Mom, she now had an income, a house, a car, an active social life and charge accounts at all the major stores in Charleston. She had just been elected President of the Women's Moose Club, and Dad was proud of her.

"Ethel, you're to be congratulated," he told her. "You're becoming an important person in these parts, even heading up responsible positions in the Moose Club. They don't seem to want to elect me to anything big in the Odd Fellows."

"Well," Mom replied, "you should've joined the Moose when I tried to get you to. Now, we go in different directions. That's your fault, Clifford. You're the one that split! If you had joined the Moose, I'd have someone to dance with!" They both smiled remembering the time Dad had promised to dance with her when he got his legs working again. "I tried, Ethel, I really tried," he said.

David, who was listening, said that he too wished that Dad had joined the Moose instead of the Independent Order of Odd Fellows. It was his job to get Dad to his meetings, which meant carrying him up two flights of steep stairs to the IOOF meeting place above Dixie Furniture store in Whitesvillle. David said it was about the hardest work he ever did.

*   *   *

I was summoned home from college in 1957. Uncle Connie, who had endeared himself to all of us and had become such an integral part of our lives, had died. We were all terribly saddened, but Dad and Mom took it the worst. They really missed him. I seemed to notice that Dad's health diminished significantly after Connie's death. Dad went on, as he always did, completing his daily routines, seeking to find the good in whatever came his way. He was like that. It never changed. But I could see the difference whenever I was around.

*　　　　　　*　　　　　　*

In December of 1959, Dad took me to a jeweler he knew in Beckley and helped me select an engagement ring for Eleanor, the girl Romeo had introduced me to in 1957. Dad said the jeweler was quite reputable and would teach me a bit about diamonds so that I could make a good selection. Dad wore his monocle and inspected the diamond with great care himself as he discussed its qualities with the jeweler. Dad said that he had often considered getting another ring for Mom, one with a pretty diamond, but she always refused the offer, saying in her sentimental way that the ring he had given her when they first married carried all the memories of the happy times when they were young lovers, and she could not bring herself to part with it. She never took her ring off, wore it all the time.

Selecting a diamond ring was an unusual thing for me to be doing with Dad. I was intrigued that he knew about such things, but not surprised. Dad had a wide range of interests and a bank of knowledge few knew about.

I gave Eleanor the engagement ring for Christmas and we married in May of 1960, the same month we graduated from college. Mom went with us on our honeymoon to Florida. She never gave up an opportunity to travel! We dropped her off at her sister Ruby's in Tampa. We all had a good time.

Eleanor and I spent the rest of the summer with Mom and Dad at Ameagle. I helped Dad at the garage while Eleanor became acquainted with my family and "*cooking!*" I came home one evening just as Eleanor was lifting the lid on a pot at the same time Mom was saying, "Don't lift the lid!" *Everyone* knows you don't lift the lid on dumplings! At dinner,

Dad said, "What happened to the dumplings? They look a little *sad.*" We all got a lesson in making dumplings!

The three months that we stayed in Ameagle provided many wonderful opportunities for Eleanor to get to know not only my family and extended family, but also our friends and closest neighbors as well. Folks like Herb and Phyllis Honaker, Quinton and June Scarbro, Howard and Reva Thompson and their son Joe Eddie, and Reverend Rasmussen who was now at the Presbyterian Home School Church, Reva and Dixie Byers, many Stovers, and certainly Mom's best friend, Bessie.

Eleanor had a good time learning our ways. She was really impressed at how quickly Mom or Jacqueline gave orders for the nearest male to do their bidding, especially when it came to cooking. If either needed an item to complete a cooking task, they gave orders for it to be fetched on the spot. The cooks were important people at our house, and you better believe they flaunted their importance! It was not uncommon to hear one or the other say, "Lee, go up to Butch's and get us some butter," or whatever. We had a running account at Butch's. Butch Fitzwater had three stores, all creatively named for himself, Butch's #1, Butch's #2 and Butch's #3. We were regular customers at #2.

In late August, Eleanor and I left Ameagle for Dundalk, Maryland, a suburb of Baltimore, where we both had teaching jobs. As we drove away, Mom and Jacqueline lay across my bed and cried. They were like that. Our summer together as a family had been rich in love and growth. I had helped Dad a lot at the garage, and I knew he would miss having me around. Eleanor had grown close to Mom and Jacqueline, as well as David, Lee and Denna Rae.

Our trip began in a most pleasant way, traveling as we were over the Skyline Drive, but we became apprehensive when as we neared Dundalk we went through a depressed area of Baltimore. The area had urban blight with people jammed tightly together in rows and rows of monotonous, dirty and ugly houses with no lawns, just urban filth. As we had not yet visited the city and had no idea of the location where we would be teaching, we both began to worry that we were going to have to live and teach in the midst of what we were presently seeing. Frightened of the big city, Eleanor said, "Jim, let's turn around and go back. We can't live like this." But I'd had some experience with city living and knew that the city would not all be like the part we were in at the moment.

As it was, we found an apartment that same day on Yorkway in the suburb of Dundalk where we would be teaching. Strangely enough, the owner of the apartment building was none other than Manuel Karantonis, a native of Colcord, a good friend of David's and brother to Tony and Fina who owned and operated business establishments just down the road from Dad's garage. Stranger yet, our neighbor across the hall was Nina Cook who was from Eleanor's hometown. Seeing people we both knew made us feel more at ease.

We moved into the second-floor furnished three-room apartment and put our few belongings in place, careful to tread lightly, because the tenant below us had already welcomed us by tapping her broomstick loudly on her ceiling the first time we set a box down too hard.

The temperature the day we moved in was 100 degrees, and with no fan or air conditioning we found it hard to breathe. The first order of business the next morning was to purchase a reverse cycle fan. We placed it in the living room window then barely cracked the other windows throughout the apartment and immediately felt cool air begin to flow around us as the powerful fan did its job.

Fortunately, the weather soon cooled and the town of Dundalk, with its tree-lined streets and small-town atmosphere, began to seem like home. Eleanor and I began our teaching jobs, which we both liked very much. Our annual salary each was $4300, and I was given an extra $200 bonus for my military service. Eager to get ahead, I looked around for a way to make extra money and took a part-time job with the city's recreation department, which meant I did things like supervise sleigh riding on snow days when schools were closed. I'd build a bonfire and make hot chocolate for the kids and wonder why I was being paid to do such a fun thing.

As Dad had often impressed upon me, I suggested to Eleanor that we put some money from our salaries into some form of investment. But even with my part-time job we had little left to invest after bills were paid. I discussed my dilemma with Dad, asking, "How can I save and invest if I have no extra money to do it?" Typical Dad, he said, "Jim, you start with pennies, nickels and dimes and elbow grease!" I thought, "Well, that much I have" and walked away, but the more I thought about it I realized Dad had a good point and filed the idea away for future reference.

Oddly enough, the first investment that Eleanor and I made was in coin collecting. Once a month, as payday rolled around, we converted our entire paychecks into coins and spent many pleasurable hours going through them as we ferreted out the coins that had numismatic value before depositing the remainder in our bank account from which to pay our bills.

When Dad found out what we were doing, he began looking for coins of value too. Whenever we came for a visit, he'd give them to us saying, "Here, I just want to get my two cents in." Though collecting coins was really just a hobby, Dad's advice stuck with me like other advice I had gleaned from him over a lifetime.

∗   ∗   ∗

Election time rolled around every four years, and as always a few months prior to election, Dad would go out "on the campaign trail." It was 1960, and even though he was pretty much a shoo-in for re-election, he still liked to visit his loyal supporters and shake hands and thank them for the help they had given him through the years. Out of economic necessity, many of his original friends, including Harry and Bummy were now gone from the area. The coal mines had shut down. The houses had been removed from the coal camps, leaving empty bottoms of land or land to be used for slate piles. The company store was no more, nor was the company doctor. Dr. Williams had long since moved to Alderson, over on the Greenbrier River. And Dr. Battallion, who had replaced Dr. Williams after the war, had also gone away. The Presbyterian Home School Church, other churches, and the schools remained open though there were far fewer people to be served. The population had dwindled significantly. Many folks had left for good. Some, like David, remained but drove greater distances to work in the mines.

With Billy and me away, and Lee unable to help, Jacqueline and David and Mom were Dad's campaign team now. They handed out flyers and cards and reminded folks of how Dad had represented them as the Justice of the Peace through the years. The card he had chosen for this campaign year was a slogan that said, "I've been cussed and discussed, stepped on and walked on, and the only reason I hang around is to see what will happen next." The card served him well as it nearly always opened conversation, which Dad relished.

In the meantime, Eleanor and I continued to teach. I taught science at Dundalk Junior High School. My teaching supervisors said that my teaching was superb, but that I needed to rid myself of the accent! Eleanor taught fourth grade at Inverness Elementary for *almost* a whole year. Because she was pregnant, she was supposed to stop teaching after five months, but her doctor had said to her, "Work as long as you can. If you feel good, work!" So she worked 'til spring break which was in early April. Then on May 22,1961, our first child, Anna Lynn, was born. Mom came to stay with us for three weeks. She was a huge help, not only with the baby, but also in helping Eleanor learn more about cooking. Mom gave us her Rumford Cook book, saying she no longer needed it. *We did.*

Though Dundalk turned out to be a pleasant suburban area in which to live, Eleanor never did quite get used to the big city itself. The thought of raising a child in a metropolitan area did not seem desirable, so we made plans to move to south Florida, Palm Beach County. Mom was concerned, saying she figured she wouldn't see much of us, but we made her feel better by promising to visit as often as we could. We knew that as teachers we would have winter and summer vacations so we would be able to visit our families twice a year though we lived farther away.

*   *   *

Billy and Jean had another child. Linda Marie was immediately spoiled. There was something special about girls in our family. They seemed distinctly to have an edge! She had curls!

Billy's kids always spent two weeks with Mom and Dad during the summer and with June rolling around, it would soon be time for their visit. Mom and Dad were always eager to see them.

As usual, Mom and Jacqueline planned for lots of picnics while the kids were with them. They took them to all the parks in the area: Little Beaver and Grandview in Beckley; Coonskin, in Charleston; and Walhonde in Montcoal, on the Coal River. It was at one of the picnics that Mom noticed that Billy Jr.'s legs seemed different. "Jacqueline," she said, "look at Billy Jr.'s legs, how tight his muscles are. It looks like he's walking on his toes all the time, like he can't bring his heels down." Jacqueline said she had noticed it too. And when Mom asked Billy about it later, he told her. "Mom, Billy Jr. has muscular dystrophy."

Mom was devastated. Another dreaded disease that she did not understand was in the family. Dad said little, but he, too, was deeply affected. He didn't have Dr. Williams, or Dr. Battalion, his "good doctors," to go to now for help in understanding. But he said he would read about it, and he did. What he learned did not make him happy. His grandson would not live beyond his teens.

37

Alone

It was May, 1964; Jacqueline had just given birth to a baby boy, Michael, and the house was again filled with baby sounds. Dad looked forward to having a little boy around to share his conversations with. Mom, who still had the fascination for babies and hair, resigned herself to the fact that Michael was bald and wasn't likely to have much hair for awhile. She said that she adored him just the same. Neighbors, Phyllis and Herb Honaker, having no children of their own, decided to become Michael's surrogate parents, declaring to spoil him rotten. So it was that the new grandson, Michael, fell into a community of love.

*   *   *

A few weeks later, a day in mid-June, the house bustled with energy as Mom and Jacqueline made preparations for company. Eleanor (whom we all now called Ellie) and I were coming home with the kids for our summer visit.

Mom happily set out to go to Whitesville, where she planned to have her hair done and do some last minute shopping. "Now, is there anything else I'll need to get?" she asked of Jacqueline as she prepared to leave the house.

"A new dress, I need a new dress!" Jacqueline joked as she wrapped her one-size-fits-all housecoat around her and struck a cheesecake pose with one hand behind her head and the other behind her hip. "Look at me!" she said, "Ain't I pretty."

"You're pretty all right," Mom snickered. "If we don't get you some decent clothes, Jim and Ellie won't recognize you. You can't hide behind that tent forever!" It had become a topic of conversation around the house that Jacqueline had not been able to fit into her clothes since having the baby.

"I might get you six dresses," Mom said as she backed the car out into the driveway. "All the same color and size. Make my shopping easy."

"Get blue. I like blue," Jacqueline said in her nonsensical way. "Or polka-dot, how about polka-dot?"

Jacqueline started back into the house, then turned back and called after Mom, "And, go by Dixie Furniture. See if they have a swing set for the kids."

"That's enough, Jacqueline!" Mom called back, smiling as she dismissed Jacqueline with a flip of her hand. Mom wondered if she'd have time to do all that she had planned as it was; she needed no extra duties.

As she drove down the lane toward the highway, she caught sight of her neighbor, Phyllis Honaker. The two exchanged waves as Phyllis made her way across the back yard. Phyllis was on her way to see Michael, as she'd done every day since he'd come home from the hospital. She was like the good fairy, showing up just about the time he needed to be fed or to have his diaper changed.

Once in Whitesville, Mom went straight to see her hairdresser, Mary Bragg. "Fix me up real nice, Mary," she said. "Jimmy and Ellie are coming home today."

"Oh, that's great," Mary said. Then she called to her daughter Kay, who was home for lunch from her summer job at the bank. "Kay," she said, "did you hear that? Jim and Ellie are coming up from Florida today." Kay, who had gone to Concord College at the same time as Ellie and I, came bouncing in to see Mom. "Oh, goodie," she said. "Tell them they had better come by and see me. No excuses. We've got a lot to talk about."

"Kay's thinking about going to Florida to teach, too," Mary said.

"If there are any jobs left!" Kay added, laughing. "I think half the state of West Virginia has gone to Florida."

"I know there's not many people left here!" Mom said. "There's hardly anybody left up our way. Anyway, Jimmy and Ellie will be real glad to hear that you're coming to Florida, Kay. Remember now, you'll have to call Eleanor, Ellie now. She's changed her name!"

"That shouldn't be too hard. I like that better anyway," Kay said.

*   *   *

Returning to visit our families in West Virginia was something Ellie and I relished being able to do. This time we were going to my home first. The trip up from Florida normally took two days of travel, which meant an overnight stay somewhere along the way. This time we had stayed in Sumter, South Carolina, where Ellie's sister Sue and her dentist husband Michael Towery lived. Michael had done some dental work for Ellie, which required us to stay an extra night in South Carolina.

We left Sumter around 11 a.m., beginning our third day of traveling north. As we traveled, we made stops along the way at Hornes' or Stuckeys' (fast food restaurants with service stations) for food, gas, rest and reprieve from the heat. Our Volkswagen bug had no air conditioning.

At a Stuckeys near Charlotte, North Carolina, five hours from the time Mom expected us, I stopped to make a call. "Mom," I said, "we're going to be a little later than we planned. Ellie left her purse at a Horne's back in South Carolina, and we're going back for it." I could tell Mom was disappointed. But, she took it in stride, saying that it was more important to be careful, and that she would have lots of goodies ready for us when we arrived. I visualized all the good food. Mom had me addicted to her food by now. She no longer used a bread drawer in which to store her goodies; she used a whole countertop. I knew it would be laden.

I wasn't pleased about driving back for the purse, but I did. We made it to West Virginia about an hour before dark—all of us tired, rumpled, and hungry. We gathered the girls, Anna and Mary, and made our way into the house. Ellie carried Mary, who was nine months old and not yet walking. We stopped in the kitchen where true to my thinking the countertop was filled with pies, cakes, cookies, and candy. At one end of the counter was a huge ham. We lingered near the counter, waiting for our usual greeting party.

Reasoning that perhaps they were out of the house for some reason we proceeded to make ourselves at home. Anna rushed to the bathroom; Ellie looked around for a place to put Mary down. I held a knife in my hand and was preparing to slice the ham when neighbor Phyllis Honaker came toward me from the living room. Red-eyed and face drawn, she carried a whimpering month-old Michael in her arms.

"Jimmy," she said, "you'd better sit down."

I knew right away that something dreadful had happened and I took the nearest seat. I looked at Phyllis anxiously, weakened and shocked when I heard, "Jimmy, your mom's dead. She had a heart attack a few hours ago, soon after you called. We called for an ambulance, but it was too late. We laid her on the bed, and she wasn't breathing. I put a mirror over her mouth and I knew. Oh, Jimmy, I'm just so sorry."

I was stunned, shocked beyond belief. Mom was only fifty-seven years old. Struck dead in the prime of her life, just when everything was coming together for her. She had a home, a car of her own, a social life, grandchildren, and charge accounts at all the finest stores in Charleston. She was as happy as she'd ever been, with much to look forward to. *It couldn't be. I had come home to see my mother. She was always here to greet me.* For a moment, I could only look at Phyllis with my mouth open. I was unable to grasp what she was saying.

After some time, I found my voice and murmured. "Where is everyone?"

"Clifford's in his room. He's in shock, Jimmy. Everyone is. Jacqueline and David are at the funeral home. Denna is down at Bonnie Stover's. Lee's in the living room. I'm worried to death he's going to have a seizure. He's just sitting there." She carried Michael Ray in her arms, shaking him up and down and feeding him from a bottle, though he seemed to sense the anxiety around him and squirmed and whimpered. "Oh, Jimmy, it's just awful. Jacqueline's completely gone to pieces. I don't know how David got her down to the funeral home. She was screaming for Ethel to wake up. I knew she wasn't going to wake up. She died immediately. Reva and Dixie Byers were here. They'd come by to see Michael. They went with Jacqueline and David.

"Reva and Dixie were the last to see your Mom alive. They were visiting along with Colleen Morris and Bonnie Asbury. Ethel and Jacqueline had gone out to see them off. She was standing at the window on the driver's side talking to Dixie when it happened. Dixie said Ethel just fell backward and fell to the ground. Jacqueline came running for David. I just happened to be here. I called for an ambulance, and then David carried her inside. Clifford swung his whole body over to the bed, trying to give her mouth to mouth. But it was too late. She was dead."

Not knowing what to say, I said nothing. I went to Dad's room. He was sitting in his chair with his head lowered. He couldn't talk. I put my hand on his wheelchair, and both of us just sat for a moment. It was too much to take in. I didn't want to believe it.

I reached over and took Dad's hand. "Would you like me to help you into bed, Dad?" I finally murmured.

"No, Jim," he said as he choked back his tears, "I'll just sit here a little longer." Michael had begun to cry. Dad looked up, his heart going out to his grandson as he characteristically said, "Mike will be all right when Sissie and Dave get back. He likes to have all of his people around."

The next hour was like walking around in a fog as we all moved from room to room, doing little things that had to be done like feeding and caring for the little ones who had no understanding of what had transpired.

Lee talked to Ellie a bit. "Mother was too young to die," he told her. "I don't know what made her die. They talk like it was a heart attack."

I sat in the kitchen amid all the warm welcoming signs of home, and I was suddenly overcome with a terrible sadness. I went upstairs to my old room and lay across the bed and cried. "She didn't even get to see our new house," I said to Ellie when she came to comfort me.

Jacqueline and David returned from the funeral home. Reva and Dixie were still with them. Jacqueline had no words for anyone; she kept fainting, coming to, and fainting again. At that time, I realized that she was not going to accept Mom's death.

Jacqueline had made it her mission early in life to always be near her parents where she could care for them. And, here she was, with no warning, no preparation for this trauma.

Reva and Dixie came to speak to me. "Your mom was so happy, Jimmy," Reva said. "She was really looking forward to seeing you and Eleanor and the girls. She said she'd just talked to you on the phone and that you were going to be late getting in. We're just so sorry, Jimmy, but if you'd gotten here on time she might have died in your arms. Maybe it was meant to be this way." I thought she might be right.

Jacqueline was wearing a new dress. "Your mom bought that dress for Jacqueline today," Phyllis informed me as she bounced Michael on her lap. She wanted to look nice for you. They both did. Your mom had Mary do her hair while she was in Whitesville. She was looking her best. Jimmy, I just don't understand it." I looked at Phyllis and decided she was a really good person. I truly felt grateful to have her as a neighbor.

Dad, too weak to deal with the shock, had finally gone to bed. I went to see about him, seeing as to how I could offer little comfort to Jacqueline. She kept calling for Mom. "Take me with you, Mom. Take me with you." Then, she'd faint again. Dad's heart was broken. "It hurts, Jim. It hurts real bad," he said. "I never thought I'd ever be without her." But he said we'd all have to be strong for Sissie. "Sissie's gone to pieces. I don't know what she'll do without her mom."

I understood. Jacqueline had always clung to Mom. They had become like sisters, together many hours of each and every day, finding joy and companionship in each other's company. For Jacqueline, it would be like someone had taken a pole ax and split them apart. Her other half would be forever missing.

Dad and I talked. I was worried about him. But, I could see that he was thinking of others before himself and that he wanted me to do the same. I laid my hand on Dad's hand. We both cried.

"Your Mom was taking digitalis, Jim, for her heart," Dad told me. "But she never acted like she was sick. She was always busy—always cooking, cleaning, or washing clothes. She never ever seemed to tire. She didn't act like there was anything wrong with her. The only time she ever stopped was to take time out to watch her TV soaps."

Mom timed everything so that she could watch her soaps. She lived a part of her life in those soap operas, when every weekday around 3:30 p.m., she'd go into the living room, close the drapes, turn on the television and sit down. Her eyes would intently focus on *Young Doctor Malone*, followed by *As the World Turns*. Everyone knew better than to interrupt her during this time. "Ethel's soaps are on," Dad would say. "Watch them and cry with her or stay out of the room. There's no in-between."

Only once did Jacqueline remember a time that Mom's soaps did not take precedence over something else. Jacqueline, who has a habit of making nonsensical comments upon entering a room recalls the day she burst into the living room where Mom and Dad sat gazing intently at the television set and blurted out in her usual fashion, "I'm home! Would anyone like something to drink? We have…." Most of the time when Jacqueline spoke like this she was ignored, but this time Mom shushed her, saying, "Not now, Jacqueline."

"Oh, what has Claire done now?" Jacqueline asked, referring to the evil nature of Claire, a character whom Mom loathed on *Young Doctor Malone*. Mom, who sat on the sofa holding a bowl of apples she had been paring, did not look up, but put up her hand and Dad, who usually paid no attention to Jacqueline's prattle, put up his hand too, and said in a quiet voice, "Jacqueline, this is serious. President Kennedy has been shot." A cold chill ran over Jacqueline as she took a seat on the sofa beside Mom and watched the television set with the same intensity as the rest of America.

*　　　　　*　　　　　*

Billy arrived from Ohio, wearing a long sleeved white shirt. He had left directly from work. He strode into the house, looking neither left nor right, but marching straight ahead, offering no sympathy nor allowing any sympathy for himself. Ellie placed her hand on his shoulder and said how sorry she was. He shrugged her away. I could tell he was still in shock and wondered how he had managed to make the six-hour drive. I knew how he and his family felt. They were tired and weary and deeply affected.

Eventually, after carrying Billy Jr. in and placing him in his wheelchair, Billy took a seat in the living room where he pondered the situation in his closed-off way. Finally, he rose and strode out of the room, saying, "I could believe it if it had been Jacqueline. She's always been sickly, but not Mom." It was true, though, what he said about Jacqueline. In the past ten years, Jacqueline had suffered two miscarriages. She was prone to be a bleeder and she also fainted a lot. We were never sure of her state of health. But Mom seemed invincible. Moms aren't supposed to die!

The house was overflowing the day of the funeral. Countless relatives I hadn't seen in years were there. Aunt Orphie and all of Mom's family were there. Rosabelle and all of Dad's sisters and brothers and their spouses were there too. Aunt Cova commanded the kitchen, slicing the ham that Mom had baked and feeding people from the numerous food items brought in by neighbors and friends. We were glad to have Cova take over the duty. She behaved as always, a no-frills person. If you said you wanted one biscuit, you got one biscuit.

Then it was time to go to the Presbyterian Church at the Home School, the same building where Mom had washed windows in the early forties. Reverend Pindar was long gone. Reverend Rasmussen would officiate. He kept the service brief and as upbeat as possible, seeing as to how Jacqueline was carrying on. It was the first time for Dad to be in the Home School Church, and it was a sad, sad time for him, but he held himself together courageously. Phyllis Honaker sang in the choir. The choir sang a special song for Mom, a song that she had liked a lot, *How Great Thou Art.*

As the undertakers rolled the casket out of the church, Jacqueline rose and raced after it, calling to Mom to please take her with her, and then she fainted. There seemed to be no consolation for Jacqueline.

Then came the long ride to Charleston and on to Cunningham Cemetery in St. Albans where Mom was buried alongside her mother Evaline as she had planned it to be. It was a beautiful day; the birds chirped and the breezes blew softly through the trees. A day Mom would have liked, I thought.

Afterward, the rest of us went home to a house now filled with memories of a dear, dear mother whose life had been whisked from us leaving us no time to prepare. It would be difficult.

*   *   *

Jacqueline became the matriarch in the family. She quit work; she and David moved into the home place, and though she still grieved, she picked up the pieces and began assuming full responsibility for her family. She and David would now care for Denna and Michael as well as for Dad and also for Lee. Poor Lee. He had become totally dependent on Mom for direction. Now he would depend upon Jacqueline and David.

Dad seemed lost, but he didn't talk about how he felt. Instead, each day, he attempted to be a little more upbeat as he struggled to somehow turn this adversity into something he could live with. But he wasn't well. He had terrible bedsores which seemed to take longer and longer to heal. He also knew that renal poisoning was slowly overtaking him and that it would eventually cause his death. Hardest for him would be his dependency on someone else. It had been hard for him to rely on Mom for all of his necessary care. Now, he would rely on Jacqueline.

Caring for Dad gave Jacqueline something to focus on instead of her unrelenting grief. She lovingly took her mother's place at his side, soaking compresses in salt water and placing them on his sores as she had seen Mom do. It shamed Dad for her to see him like he was. "Sissie, I should have been the one to go," he'd tell her. "You shouldn't have to be doing this." But Jacqueline only shushed him. Dad knew he had a jewel in his daughter. He always understood Jacqueline.

As the year progressed after Mom's death, Dad grew weaker. The renal poisoning worsened, leaving his skin yellow and his energy level significantly diminished. But he still got up each morning, strapped the braces to his harness, dressed himself, shaved and wheeled himself out to the kitchen for breakfast. Les still came to pick him up for work. Going to the garage each day kept him alive, gave him a reason to get up each morning. He had been re-elected as Justice of the Peace for the fifth time and had won handily. He would do the work, he said, as long as he could do it.

But, by July of 1965, after he had just turned 62, Dad began to have days when he could not get up. He could no longer handle both the full responsibility of the garage and the work of the JP. Though the garage had been his independence for more than a decade, his refuge away from home and a place of importance in the community, he said it was time to sell. It was a simple transaction. Les Stover, who had been Dad's chief mechanic for the entire time he had owned the garage, wanted to buy it. It would be an easy takeover.

With the garage sold, Dad had nowhere to go each day. Though he continued the business of the Justice of the Peace, his life was slowly trickling away. He no longer had the sparkle, the drive for living. Billy and I visited him as often as we could. I brought him to Florida for a short vacation, and he said he enjoyed it, but I sensed that he really wanted to be at home. Not long afterwards, at the end of the summer of 1966, he was hospitalized. He did not want to stay at the hospital. He wanted to be at home. But he needed the kind of care the hospital offered.

Jacqueline remained at Dad's side, bringing to him what comfort she could. She ushered in his visitors, the very last one being Hibert Burgess, a constable who had become Dad's good friend as they had worked together through the years. Taking Dad's hand, Hibert said, "Squire, old buddy, won't you take a sip of water?" Dad opened his eyes and attempted a smile but was unable to sip from the straw, so Hibert took a spoon and placed a drop at a time on Dad's parched lips as tears streamed down both of their faces.

Knowing how Mom's death had devastated Jacqueline, Dad had kept his own feelings of grief hidden deep inside. But, in his final hours, he could no longer bear his pent-up sadness, and he allowed his pain release. His body began to shake uncontrollably, and he looked at Jacqueline with a tenderness that seemed to ask her forgiveness as between pitiful sobs he said, "Sissie, I miss her so. I loved her so much."

A few hours later, on September 17, 1966, Squire went to be with his loving wife, in heaven.

Epilogue

Quinton Scarbro served out the rest of Clifford's term as the Justice of the Peace for the Clear Fork District.

Jacqueline never left the homeplace, though she eventually earned a master's degree in education and taught First Grade at Clear Fork Elementary School for twenty years before retiring in 1990.

David, at age 48, suffered a heart attack while running a bulldozer on the hoot-owl shift at his cousin Horace's coal mine at Montcoal. Four years later he had a quadruple by-pass. He never worked in the mines or anywhere else again.

As of this writing, David and Jacqueline, now in their seventies, still reside in the home place at Ameagle. They have two children, Denna and Michael, a son-in-law, Randall Persinger, daughter-in-law, Barbara Stover, and five granddaughters, April, Jada, Sheila, Sarah and Mikala.

Lee died July 12, 1978, at age 55, of complications resulting from his epilepsy.

Billy died on New Year's Eve, December 31, 1980 at the age of 49, of a heart attack. His wife Jean still lives in Dayton, Ohio. Billy Jr. died in January of 1982, at age sixteen, four years away from the age boys with muscular dystrophy aspire to reach. Kenneth and Linda both married and have families of their own.

The authors, James and Eleanor are now retired educators from the Palm Beach County School system in the state of Florida. In the summer of the year 2000, they opened a bed and breakfast, Nostalgia Inn, at Pipestem, West Virginia, near Concord College where first they met. They have three children, Anna, Mary, and Brandon, a son-in-law, Gregory Sell and three grandchildren, Angela, James, and Sarah.

As of this writing, Clifford's only sibling still living is his sister Cora, who was a significant contributor to the telling of this story. She resides in St. Albans, West Virginia.

Some of the persons written about in this book are still living and often gather at the Clear Fork High School reunion, which now meets bi-annually the first weekend in August in Beckley, West Virginia.

Odie Opie White, 1898

White Family: Rosabelle and Opie holding Clarence and Cora, surrounded by Clifford, Corbitt, Connie and Coy, 1916

Coy (11), Clifford (13)

Clifford (age 14), 1917

Clifford playing marbles

Clifford joins USMC, 1918

Clifford and Ethel, 1920's

Clifford with Lee, 1925 at Marfork

Evaline

Lee, Billy, Jacqueline, 1931

Ethel with Jacqueline and Lee, at Crites, 1927

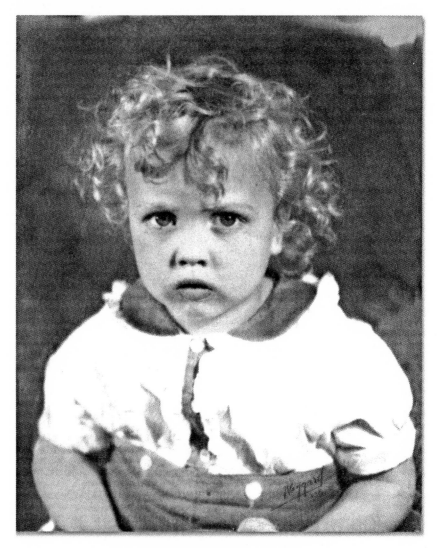

Jim, "Blue Ribbon Baby"

Wills hollow house, 1920

Fourth of July at Wills Hollow, 1942

Card game on the Fourth of July

"Picture man" captures Jim with Ethel

Jim, Ethel, Lee, Jacqueline and Billy

Sisters: Ethel and Orphie

Odie with Sons
Front: Coy, Clarence, Charles
Back: Corbitt, Connie, Clifford and Opie

Jacqueline (center right) begins work at Peabody Company Store in Ameagle

David joins the Navy during WWII, 1943

Toby Kinder (age 9)

*Jacqueline and Opie go to Washington D.C. for President
Franklin Roosevelt's funeral, 1945*

*Jim at New Camp, preparing for state championship
baseball game, 1949*

Clifford walks along the fence atNew Camp, using braces and crutches, 1940's

Bessie and Bill Legg congratulate Ethel as President of Women's Moose Club in Whitesville, WV, 1949

New house, built in 1950 across from Clear Fork High School football field, at Ameagle

Ethel with Connie's car, 1948

Connie White, 1950's

*David carries Clifford to a new term in office as the Justice of the Peace,
Clear Fork District, Raleigh County*

Lee begins work at White's Esso Station at Colcord

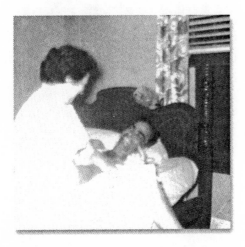

Happy in our new home! 1950's

Dressed for dinner on a visit to see Coy in Califorina, 1950's

Sgt. Billie White Gets Silver Star

AMEAGLE, April 23—Sgt. Billie E. White, who is serving with the U. S. Army as a member of Company C, 28th Infantry Regiment, Second Infantry Division was awarded the silver star for displaying gallantry in action against an armed enemy on Feb. 12 in the vicinity of Sarmal, Korea.

Sgt. White's regiment, which was attempting to penetrate an enemy road block, was subjected to intense hostile machine gun fire delivered from commanding ground overlooking the escape route. Company C was committed in an effort to dislodge the enemy.

Sgt. White was assisting in laying down a strong base of fire when he realized that fire power alone would not neutralize the enemy because of heavy machine gun fire delivered from a cleverly concealed emplacement. Displaying complete disregard for his safety, Sgt. White, left his position and dashed forward in a singlehanded assault of the enemy emplacement and succeeded in killing the hostile crew of four with his rifle fire.

White's outstanding courage so inspired his comrades that they immediately followed him in the attack and quickly gained their objective.

Sgt. White is the husband of Mrs. Billy White of Ameagle and the son of Mr. and Mrs. C. W. White of Ameagle.

Politicking in 1950's

David, Jacqueline and Denna

Clifford's family grows in 1960's
First row: Denna, Linda, Kenny
Second: Ethel, Anna, Clifford, Billy Jr.
Third: Jacqueline, Jean, and Ellie
Fourth: Lee, David, Billy, Jim

Rosabelle celebrates 90th Birthday

Presbyterian Home School

About the Athor

Retired educators, the authors are graduates of Concord College, Florida Atlantic University, and the University of Mississippi. They are now innkeepers/owners of Nostalgia Inn, Pipestem, WV.